PENGUIN BOOKS

The Badness of King George

By the same author

NON-FICTION

Soho: A History of London's Most Colourful
Neighbourhood

The Empress of Pleasure:
The Life and Loves of Teresa Cornelys, Queen of
Masquerades and Casanova's Lover

Casanova's Women: The Great Seducer and
The Women He Loved

My Life with George:
Surviving Life with the King of the Canines

FICTION

Dear Sister

I, Gloria Gold

Crime and Ravishment

Frogs and Lovers

Who Gets Fluffy?

The Badness of
King George

JUDITH SUMMERS

PENGUIN BOOKS

PENGUIN BOOKS

Published by the Penguin Group
Penguin Books Ltd, 80 Strand, London WC2R ORL, England
Penguin Group (USA) Inc., 375 Hudson Street, New York, New York 10014, USA
Penguin Group (Canada), 90 Eglinton Avenue East, Suite 700, Toronto, Ontario, Canada M4P 2Y3
(a division of Pearson Penguin Canada Inc.)
Penguin Ireland, 25 St Stephen's Green, Dublin 2, Ireland (a division of Penguin Books Ltd)
Penguin Group (Australia), 250 Camberwell Road, Camberwell, Victoria 3124, Australia
(a division of Pearson Australia Group Pty Ltd)
Penguin Books India Pvt Ltd, 11 Community Centre, Panchsheel Park, New Delhi – 110 017, India
Penguin Group (NZ), 67 Apollo Drive, Rosedale, North Shore 0632, New Zealand
(a division of Pearson New Zealand Ltd)
Penguin Books (South Africa) (Pty) Ltd, 24 Sturdee Avenue, Rosebank,
Johannesburg 2196, South Africa

Penguin Books Ltd, Registered Offices: 80 Strand, London WC2R ORL, England

www.penguin.com

First published 2010
1

Set in 12.5/14.75 pt Monotype Garamond
Typeset by Ellipsis Books Limited, Glasgow
Printed in England by Clays Ltd, St Ives plc

A CIP catalogue record for this book is available from the British Library

ISBN: 978-0-141-04647-1

www.greenpenguin.co.uk

For Paul

Prologue

It was what I'd dreaded for years – coming home to find that the place had been burgled.

Worse than that, well and truly trashed. From what I could see when I opened the front door, the perpetrator, or maybe perpetrators, had made as much gratuitous mess as possible. For all I knew they were still in the flat.

I stood on the threshold, listening for noises that might indicate as much. Then, when I heard nothing, I tiptoed into my ransacked kitchen. A ceramic vase that had stood on the mantelpiece until I'd gone out an hour earlier lay in pieces on the hearthstone, along with the water and tulips it had contained. The fortnight's accumulation of newspapers that I'd been meaning to remove from the top of the radiator was scattered across the floor, and the fridge door was wide open. Spilled milk and ketchup formed bloody pools in front of it, speckled with cheese, Crunchy Corner cartons and some withered broccoli stems I'd bought a week ago in a bid to be healthier but had never got around to eating.

I glanced through the archway into the living room. The cushions had been pulled off the sofas, presumably in search of hidden cash, and a single book lay on the fireside rug, its spine broken and some of the pages ripped out. As I bent down to pick it up I saw that it was a copy of my first published novel, and that someone had urinated on it. How revolting was that?

All this chaos, and the bastards hadn't even bothered to steal my seventeen-inch pre-digital TV set, I noted. They'd probably been after a fifty-inch HD-ready plasma model, or else cash and small items that were easy to dispose of. Mobile phones, for instance. Credit cards. Electronic gadgets. Jewellery. Computers.

I drew a sharp breath. My laptop was downstairs in my study, with several chapters of the new novel I'd been writing on it – in my habitually sloppy fashion, I hadn't backed up the files for weeks. And although I didn't exactly keep the Crown Jewels in my bedroom, I did own a few pairs of lovely silver earrings and a special necklace that my late husband had given me, items of priceless sentimental value that could never be replaced.

I was about to dash down to see if they'd been taken when I realized how stupid that would be. Someone might well be lying in wait for me. How to find out? I crept cautiously to the top of the stairs and shouted, 'Is anyone there?' at the top of my voice. There was no reply. What was I expecting? For them to shout back up, 'Just a couple of us, love, armed with crowbars and machetes – so come on down'?

I knew I ought to get out of the house, call 999 and wait for the police to arrive before I explored any further. At the very least, I should get someone else to come with me.

But there *was* no one else. Dealing with burglars single-handed was one of the drawbacks of living alone. As was dealing with wasps and spiders.

Well, I'd learned to dispose of those by myself since my son Joshua had left home. And, that being the case, I wasn't going to let a few bloody intruders scare me. I ran back into the kitchen and grabbed the wooden rolling pin (cliché that it was, it was the only appropriate self-defence weapon to hand except for a rather blunt bread knife, and other than asking the intruders to keep still while I cut them into neat, thin slices I wasn't sure what use it would be). Thus armed, I marched downstairs wielding my weapon like a rounders bat and shouting, 'Okay, you bastards, I've called the police and they're on their way, so you'd better run for it while you can!' The furious tone of my voice was belied by the pneumatic thumping of my heart. I was terrified.

Towels and books were strewn all over the downstairs hall floor and a foul stench was coming from somewhere. I peeped through the half-open study door. My desk chair had been overturned, there were papers all over the floor, the cover on the day-bed had been torn off but – a wave of relief washed over me – my laptop was still on my desk. And . . . Oh, God, that was where the stench was coming from: a big pile of excrement on the carpet. What sort of people would do such a thing?

Retching, I slammed the door on it, then put my ear to Joshua's bedroom door, which was firmly closed. The fact that I could hear no sound from inside told me nothing: the burglars might well be hiding in there. There was only one way to find out. I took a deep breath, slowly turned the knob, then kicked the door open in true *Avengers* style. This room had looked perpetually ransacked until my son had moved out the previous September, but now it was as pristine as it had been for ages: the bed crisply made, the books lined up neatly on the shelves, and not so much as a single abandoned sock on the floor.

Even more curious, the french windows, which led out

to the garden, were still firmly shuttered. Since the front door had been undamaged when I'd come home, I'd assumed that the intruders must have broken in through here. The only alternative point of entry was my bedroom window.

I took another deep breath, then crept into my room. The windows hadn't been smashed, but the wardrobe doors were open, and my favourite little black dress – a vintage Jean Muir number I'd bought way back in the eighties – lay in shreds on the floor, along with a single black leather L. K. Bennett boot.

Its pair, well chewed, was on my bed.

And so was the culprit.

He was stretched out, all six foot of him, snoring gently, with a blissful smile on his pointed face. Had the ruined boot not been tucked between his front paws he'd have looked the picture of innocence.

Perched on the window-ledge, well out of harm's way, sat George, my ten-year-old Cavalier King Charles Spaniel. His tail thumped against the pane when he saw me, and the black headlamps of his eyes glittered with excitement. Slowly but surely, they rolled towards the sleeping dog on the bed, then settled for a moment on my ruined dress before swivelling back to me. Drawing himself up to his full, rotund eighteen inches, George sniffed loudly, as if to say, 'This has nothing to do with me!'

He was right. I alone was responsible for the chaos.

Why had I ever thought that fostering rescue dogs was something I'd be good at?

I

It was a Sunday morning in September 2008, and George and I were standing in the doorway of Joshua's room, watching him pack his things.

I'd always known that my son would leave home one day because he'd told me so when he was five years old. After spending half an hour bent over a sheet of paper at the kitchen table, a pencil gripped between his little fingers and his brows knotted in concentration, the diminutive apple of my eye had finally handed me a note he'd been labouring over. His face had been one big beaming smile.

On reflection, perhaps it was a smirk.

'Is this for me, darling?' I'd cooed, ever the doting mother; he was, after all, my only child and this was the first thing he'd written for me.

'Yes, Mummy.'

'Thank you, my angel! And you wrote it all by yourself?' He'd nodded solemnly. 'How completely brilliant of you!'

My heart bursting with love and pride, I'd read the note. This was what it said:

> *To mum I which*
> *I kud lev my Famley!!*
> *from Joshua.*
> *the same to you*
> *dad.*
> *And I will.*
> *YES!!!*

Appalled that our adored son couldn't wait to cram his Pokémon card collection into his Bart Simpson rucksack and put some distance between us, I'd rushed downstairs and shown the note to his father. Udi had burst out laughing. As a psychotherapist, he was used to dealing with people who suppressed their negative feelings towards their families, often with disastrous consequences for their own emotional well-being. Now his son was expressing in the plainest language possible the natural, healthy, love-hate feelings that all children have for their parents. When it came to speaking his mind freely, Joshua was clearly a chip off the old block – his, not mine. And Udi couldn't have been more delighted.

However, always the pedant when it came to spelling, as people for whom English is a second language often are, my Austrian-born partner did feel the need to add a few corrections to the message – a pencilled-in *wish* above Joshua's *which*, a *could* above his *kud*, and the word *family* spelled properly at the bottom of the page.

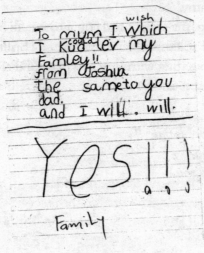

When I'd got over the initial shock of being rejected by my five-year-old I, too, found Joshua's note so amusing, if in a bitter-sweet way, that I framed it and gave it pride of place in my bedroom, where it has remained ever since. As well as making Udi and me laugh it served as a constant reminder that, however much our life revolved around him then, one day our feisty chick would spread his wings and fly the coop. He wasn't ours for keeps, only on borrowed time, so we'd better make the most of him while he was still around.

As it turned out it was Udi who was on borrowed time. Unknown to any of us, he was already suffering from a rare and extremely hard to detect form of stomach cancer, which was diagnosed in July 1997, when Joshua was seven years old. His only chance was to have a life-threatening operation, and even if he were to survive it, the prognosis was terrible. It was shattering news.

In dire need of something to light up the bleak horizon in front of us, we decided on the spur of the moment that we'd get married at long last; though we'd been together for twelve years, had a child and owned a home, we hadn't yet got around to tying the knot. Doing so now was the most positive gesture we could think of. I rushed down to Camden register office to book an appointment, only to be told that the earliest available slot was in nine weeks' time. I burst into tears and told the official that my partner had just been diagnosed with cancer. He reopened the appointments book, ran his finger down a few pages, then said, 'How about next Monday?'

With only three days to organize the event, there was no time to fret about details – or even the essentials. I borrowed a cream trouser suit from my sister and, to add a touch of glitz to the occasion, hired a white stretch limo to ferry us and our seven guests – Tabby and Hannah, Udi's grown-up daughters from his first marriage, Tabby's four-year-old son, Nathaniel, and his father, Carlton, my sister and brother-in-law, Sue and Philip, and their six-year-old daughter, Jessica – to the wedding. The limo made the day. The driver couldn't have been more accommodating, or the car a bigger hit with the children who, on the drive down to Euston Road, drank Cokes from the built-in fridge and watched cartoons on the in-car television while we grown-ups larked around and sipped Champagne.

In the register office, Udi experimented with the music on the PA system while the rest of us, including the female registrar, giggled and laughed. During the ceremony (if you can use such a word for the short formalities) he gave me one of my own rings as a wedding band, while I produced a plastic prisoner's ball-and-chain that I'd stolen from Joshua's toy box and proceeded to shackle him with it.

Catering the wedding breakfast couldn't have been easier: on the way back to Hampstead our driver stopped outside a local deli, and Udi and I went inside and bought whatever we felt like. Back home, we ate in the kitchen, while the children picnicked in the limo, which, to their delight, remained parked outside for several hours. Then some good friends arrived with a Sacher-Torte to serve as our wedding cake. I think everyone must have made the same wish when Udi and I cut it together: that he would survive.

Despite the dire circumstances under which all this was taking place, it was an unforgettable day, which we followed with a brief trip to France. My parents, who lived there, hadn't been able to attend our last-minute wedding because my father also had cancer. I was in danger of losing the two most important men in my life.

At the beginning of August we returned to London and reality. After surviving a radical gastrectomy, Udi embarked on a gruelling six months of chemotherapy in the vain hope that it might save his life. But it wasn't possible. His cancer was at a very advanced stage when it was discovered – the main tumour was literally the size of a brick – and despite his heroic attempts to defy Fate by embarking on a frenetic round of socializing, he couldn't escape his prognosis, which shrank from an over-optimistic couple of years to a more realistic six months, then three weeks.

Only three weeks until Udi died? Though we'd known it was going to happen at some point, his approaching death had remained remote until the moment this news was broken to us, partly because Udi still seemed such a live wire. As always, his presence filled our lives. Now the reality finally sank in. The full-frontal honesty with which he'd faced cancer didn't desert him during those last weeks: if death was coming for him, he'd meet it head on. 'So damn much not yet lived,' he wrote, days later, to Professor Mark Winslett, his surgeon at London's Royal Free Hospital. 'Even though I have packed at least two lives into my time, it just hasn't been enough!'

Unique, brilliant, larger-than-life, Udi had achieved a huge amount in his fifty-six years, including two successful careers, the first as the producer of serious TV documentaries and discussion programmes, the second, more recently, as a psychotherapist, a profession for which he had a rare talent.

Highly respected for his razor-sharp intellect, often alarming honesty, and provocative line of questioning, beloved for his kindness, generosity and stimulating company by hundreds of friends, acquaintances and clients, in recent years he'd been relishing life as never before. Now all this was to end in a brutal and, as he put it, ignominious way as, one by one, his organs stopped functioning.

Most painful of all for him was having to come to terms with the fact that he'd no longer be there for Tabby and Hannah, his adult daughters, and would not see his four-year-old grandson, Nathaniel, or his beloved Joshua grow up.

Joshua was his greatest concern. Having himself had an absent father, Udi doted on our son. He indulged him to the hilt, took delight in joining him in childish pranks, and rarely said no to him – that side of parenting was left to me. 'Don't smother him,' he instructed me, from his bed in the local Marie Curie hospice less than twenty-four hours before he died. This went against the grain – I was nothing if not an over-anxious mother, the kind who hovers beneath the climbing frame in the playground in case her precious child should take a tumble. Still, I promised him I'd do my utmost to bring Joshua up in a manner of which he would have approved.

That evening, Udi suddenly got out of bed as if nothing was wrong and asked Hannah, who was with him at the time, for his black fedora hat. Then he said, 'Come on, let's go!' She persuaded him back to bed, and a few hours later he fell into a coma. He died in the early hours of the following morning, with Hannah, Tabby and me at his bedside.

It was just past dawn when I left the hospice. The sky

was a clear light blue, the June air unusually balmy, and birdsong floated down from the plane trees in the street. The perfect day seemed an affront: I couldn't connect with it; I felt completely numb inside. The worst thing in the world had just happened. Or had it? I now had to go home and break the news to Joshua. He'd known for some weeks that his father was dying but, at eight years old, he had little concept of what death actually meant. How was I going to explain it to him? How was I going to cope with his grief, not to mention my own?

And there was more grief to come. Just eleven days later, my father died. The whole family was shattered.

Slowly, painfully, we began picking up the broken pieces and rebuilding our lives as best we could – not because we felt like doing so, but because, when someone dies, the living are left with no alternative. I was now effectively a single mother. And, in common with most single mums, bringing up my child became the over-whelming focus of my existence. However, every night I'd see that framed note from Joshua on my bedside table. Though it could have been spelled a little more accurately, my son couldn't have spelled out his meaning more clearly. And now that it was just the two of us the message seemed more relevant than ever. However much time I was investing in him at the moment, and however close our bond, one day he'd be off to live his own life. And so he should.

Of course, when faced with a young child, particularly one who's grieving for his father, it's pretty hard to imagine the day he'll leave home. He's too small, too vulnerable and far too needy. You know that ten years hence he'll have shot up two and a half feet, communicate with you only in monosyllables and be wearing his trousers well below the point of decency, but all that seems an unimaginably long time away. For the moment all that counts is getting him fed, clothed and through the next day or week, and trying to make sure he grows up into a happy, healthy, well-adjusted adult. Accomplishing all that seems pretty impossible much of the time.

But, by some miracle, the years pass and it happens.

Suddenly Joshua was nineteen years old. The tyranny of years of SATS, GCSEs, AS and A levels was over and he was off to university. Not next month, not next week, but that very afternoon.

George and I watched him unplug his TV set, his Freeview box, his computer, his monitor, his external hard drive and his PlayStation, then untangle the squid-ink spaghetti that had linked them all together and throw it all into a big cardboard box, along with his iPod and phone chargers. Next he scooped his clothes out of the cupboards and drawers into which they'd been haphazardly crammed for years and crammed them haphazardly into plastic bin-liners, the better to be transported from the tip his room had lately become to the tip he was no doubt about to create in a university hall of residence.

I have to admit that, during the long post-A-level summer, there had been times when I'd looked forward to the day he'd move out. No more abandoned shoes in the hall to trip over in the mornings! No more noisy teenagers marauding around the house until dawn! Even better, after all the years of having to behave like a responsible adult, I was at last going to be as carefree as I'd been before I'd become a parent. And I intended to make the most of it.

However, watching my son pack his belongings was strangely disturbing. This was it: Joshua was finally doing what he'd been threatening to since he'd written me that note when he was five years old. He was leaving his family. Nowadays that meant me. And although I'd had nearly fifteen years to get used to the idea, that didn't stop me feeling upset now that it was actually happening.

'Want any help, darling?'

'No thanks, I'm good.'

I frowned as he pushed an accumulation of socks into a plastic carrier bag. 'You don't have to take *everything* with you today. You can always come back and get things, you know.'

'Oh, I might as well take it all with me now.'

Later on that day we crammed the boxes and bin-bags into our car. I'd planned to leave George at home, but when he realized we were going out without him he barked so ferociously that both his front legs lifted right off the ground. This was a momentous occasion, he seemed to be telling us, and as a member of the family he deserved to be in on it, too. So I clipped on his lead and took him out to the car, where he jumped into the back and squeezed himself into a tiny niche between Joshua's computer monitor and a rolled-up duvet.

Joshua had passed his driving test a few weeks before. However, without either of us saying anything, we both knew this was a symbolic occasion that demanded I, as his parent, take the wheel.

We eventually arrived, found the right street and joined

a long line of double-parked cars and vans that were off-loading their precious cargos of eighteen-, nineteen- and twenty-year-olds outside a university hall of residence. There were students walking down the road pulling small suitcases behind them, and students hanging out of the windows, and students weighed down by huge rucksacks, and yet more students heaving their belongings out of their parents' cars.

As our offspring transported bag after bag, box after box, through the sliding doors and into the parent-free inner sanctum, we adults regarded one another with tight smiles. Not everyone managed to control their emotions. 'My son's the first of our four children to leave home,' one red-eyed father admitted to me, in a choked voice, as he waited for his son to come out for the rest of his things. 'I'm ashamed to say I wept all day yesterday.' Having not shed a single tear myself, I felt most superior.

At last our car was empty. Joshua slammed the boot shut, then ruffled the top of George's head through the back window. "Bye, George!'

Then it was our turn to say goodbye. I opened my mouth intending to come out with something suitably light and encouraging, only to find that an apple-sized lump was blocking my throat. I attempted to swallow it as we hugged briefly on the pavement.

"Bye, Mum.'

"Bye, darling.'

'Love you.'

'Love you, too.'

'Speak soon.' He turned and walked jauntily away, striking up a conversation with a fellow student as they entered the building. As I watched the sliding doors close on them, I was seized with panic. There went my son! From now on he was going to live here, not at home with me. Surely that couldn't be right.

Then I remembered the promise I'd made on Udi's deathbed: to raise Joshua without smothering him. Well, I'd just about managed it, and he'd grown up into an independent, strong-minded, original young man of whom his father would have been as proud as I was.

Now my job was to let go of him.

How simple.

Resisting the urge to run into the building after him, throw my arms around him and plead with him to come home with me (which would probably have provoked him into disowning me for ever), I stumbled into the car, where George was squeezing through the handbrake gap to take up residence in Joshua's empty place on the front seat. By now, the apple in my throat had swollen to the size of a grapefruit. I fumbled the key into the ignition, roared around the corner, pulled up on the nearest double yellow line and collapsed over the steering-wheel, sobbing uncontrollably. I felt like Celia Johnson after she'd bade a final farewell to Trevor Howard in *Brief Encounter* – only Johnson's character, Laura, was in love with Howard's character, Dr Alec Harvey, and he was going off to live in Africa for ever and ever and she knew their paths would never cross again. Whereas Joshua was my *son*, for God's sake, and he was only going to university!

Feeling drained of emotion, I blew my nose, helped George out of the footwell where he'd landed when I'd slammed on the brakes, then drove home.

When I let myself in, the flat echoed with silence. Not the blessed silence of finding that Joshua was out and had left a trail of open cupboard doors, dirty plates and abandoned shoes behind him, all the lights blazing and his computer on – evidence not only of what he'd been doing before he'd gone out but proof that he'd soon be back to create even more havoc. No, this silence rang as cold and hollow as a deserted church crypt, and the tap-tap of George's claws as he dogged my footsteps across the floor accentuated it.

Determined not to brood, I put on one of the Sinatra LPs I'd inherited from my father (there'd be no more tuneless rock or expletive-rich hip-hop in this house for the time being!), made myself a cup of tea, raided the biscuit tin and put my feet up to read the Sunday papers. George dozed in his basket nearby, the tip of his tongue protruding from his muzzle, like a little pink postage stamp, and one eye half open, as always, to keep track of my whereabouts. 'Come Fly With Me', Frank crooned, and 'It's So Nice To Go Travelling'. Then 'Let's Get Away From It All'. All songs about the delights of leaving home. I turned the hifi off. After half an hour of supposedly concentrating on articles about mayhem in the financial markets and Cheryl Cole's latest appearance on *The X-Factor*, I realized I hadn't taken in a word, perhaps because the newsprint kept blurring – probably something to do with my contact lenses.

Abandoning the papers, I shared the last remaining shortbread with my canine companion who, though he was growing deaf to my commands in his old age, still had the ability to hear a biscuit snap while seemingly fast asleep.

Then I went downstairs, which is where the bedrooms are situated in our upside-down maisonette.

Instead of going into my study to check my e-mail, as I'd intended, I found myself standing in the doorway of Joshua's room. I went inside. After picking my way across the odd socks, loose poker chips and torn T-shirts that were the debris of his packing, I threw myself down on his stripped-bare bed and stared blankly at the black marks on the shelves where his TV and electrical equipment had stood until a few hours before.

I reminded myself of how lucky I was to have time to myself after more than ten years of single-motherhood, the responsibilities and enforced selflessness that went with it – selflessness that hadn't always come naturally to me. At long last I could put myself first! No more school terms to bind me. No more twice-weekly supermarket runs. No more brewing endless pots of Bolognese sauce to divide into single portions and shove in the freezer so there was always something to defrost for a short-order meal. No more heaving a reluctant teenager out of bed in the mornings. No more feeling that I shouldn't go out too often at night because . . . well, simply because I wanted my son to know that someone was keeping the home fires burning, whether he was around to warm himself at them or not. From now on it was me-time! I was free!

But – and this was the big question – free to do what?

Without Joshua in it on a day-to-day basis, my life suddenly felt as empty as those dusty spaces on his shelves.

'Whoever thought that children leaving home was a good idea?' I wailed aloud.

In reply, a small furry head appeared around the door, followed by a stocky chestnut-and-white body. Shining darkly, a pair of huge Spaniel eyes flitted around the room before alighting on my horizontal body. Not one to spend precious energy on too much activity, George raised his tail and swished it once. Then he picked his way fastidiously across the obstacle course on the carpet, put his big hairy front paws up on the edge of the mattress and, inching them towards me one at a time, gave a delicate little stretch. Muzzle open in a smile, tongue flicking the air in its usual compulsive fashion, he crouched back on his haunches and sprang – or, rather, scrambled – up beside me, looking as clumsy as a turtle out of water. At ten and a bit years old, George wasn't nearly as nimble as he used to be.

Once on my level, he trundled across the mattress, stepped onto my heaving chest and sat down facing me. He weighed a ton. Five years on a diet of low-cal dog food had failed to slim him down, probably because he always refused to touch it unless it was sprinkled with chopped left-over chicken, or flakes of tinned tuna. If I refused to add these extras – after all, he had to lose weight, and I was in charge of him, at least nominally – he'd bark and bark and bark and bark until I caved in.

He stared down at me, his face looming large because of its proximity.

'Oh, George! Joshua's left home.' I wept. 'Now it's just the two of us.'

I swear that George's smile grew into a grin.

A few months before, and after a long campaign, he'd finally seen off Zach, my partner of the past five years. Now he'd got rid of Joshua, too. After a lifetime of having to share me, my Cavalier had me all to himself at last. And I had an uneasy feeling that he meant to take full advantage of it.

2

A fortnight later the house still felt horribly quiet without Joshua around. After having him at home all day long, on and off, since he'd finished taking his A levels in June, I'd grown used to him popping into my study every half-hour or so to disturb my concentration and, more often than not, make me laugh. I missed him terribly.

This was how my own parents must have felt after my sister and I had left home, I suddenly realized, with a rush of empathy – a very belated one, since this had happened well over thirty years before. Infuriating as living with two emotional, rebellious teenage daughters, their paraphernalia and their friends had probably been, life must have felt distinctly flat without us around creating havoc, particularly for my mother. And after she and my father had moved to France (from which Mum had returned a couple of years after Dad's death), they'd seen even less of us. Now I understood how much they must have missed us. No wonder they'd been on the phone every day!

Determined not to come across as the over-anxious mother I was, I'd been resisting the temptation to call Joshua every day on the slightest pretext, just to check that he was still alive. But I had sent him several wordy texts, telling him my news and asking him how he was. In return I'd received such enlightening replies as *Good*, or *Great* or even *TTYL LOL*, which I'd had to ask eleven-year-old

Chloë, who lived next door, to translate into 'Talk to you later. Lots of Love.'

Living alone was made worse because I worked alone, too. Before I'd turned to writing in my mid-thirties, I'd had a rather chequered career: among other things I'd been a shop assistant (who'd never sold much); a secretary (who couldn't touch-type, spell accurately, or do shorthand); the administrator of a fringe theatre company (hopeless at admin); a Blue Badge London tourist guide, who took Americans around Westminster Abbey (great fun); and a BBC-trained assistant film editor (in reality, a glorified name for a gofer and floor-sweeper). Latterly I'd attempted to live on my earnings as a freelance writer, but although I'd published eight books, as well as countless newspaper and magazine articles, it was a constant struggle to make ends meet. I certainly needed to get on and finish the novel I was now writing – and not just to take my mind off Joshua having left home. With the car insurance and the house insurance and the pet insurance and the mortgage to pay – not to mention Dobromierz, the middle-aged, stocky Polish builder I'd hired to do some essential work around the house – I was in danger of following in the financial footsteps of Lehman Brothers, the American bank that had recently gone belly-up.

As well as working, I'd also spent time catching up with old friends. 'How are you doing now that Joshua's left home?' they'd ask, in the concerned tones they hadn't used since Udi had died.

'Fine,' I enthused. 'It's great – I've got so much time to myself. And the place has never been so tidy!'

I'm not sure I convinced them.

I kept reminding myself that the last thing I'd ever wanted was a son who was so umbilically attached to me that he'd never want to leave home. Shades of Hitchcock's *Psycho* and all that.

Chance would be a fine thing! Joshua was like a racehorse in the traps: the gates had clicked open and he was galloping off into the future without a backwards glance. I, by contrast, felt like an old nag left behind in the stables: redundant, unloved and thoroughly sorry for myself.

Perhaps I wouldn't have felt quite so much at a loss if Zach and I hadn't broken up. My ex-partner and I had met when Joshua was thirteen and, give or take a few major hiccups along the way, we'd been together ever since. But what had started out as a wonderful love affair had eventually hit the rocks, in part because we'd wanted very different things. I loved family life, but to Zach, an American university lecturer resident in London, it was anathema. He was looking for a partner who was free to enjoy the unencumbered life with him, but I was a single mother, with all the responsibilities that came with it. Until my teenage son grew up he and our home would have to be the centre of my universe – and I wouldn't have had it any other way.

The fact that I had to look after a Cavalier as well as a teenager didn't exactly help the inevitable tensions. Zach didn't like dogs, and he certainly didn't appreciate the amount of time and attention they needed. In retaliation, George went head to head with him in a series of battles. He chewed up Zach's work papers, tipped over the bin in his kitchen and slept on his clothes, leaving a fine coating of hair. Worst of all, furious at being excluded from my bedroom whenever Zach stayed over, he'd yelp for hours, driving us all mad. When it came to persistent barking, George could have won Olympic gold for Britain.

We tried everything the experts recommended to make him stop, including ignoring him, leaving the radio on all night for him, and placing a furry hot-water bottle and ticking clock in his basket to emulate my warmth and heartbeat (George wasn't fooled for a minute). I even hired a pet psychologist, who recommended that I spray George's sleeping quarters with an expensive doggy pheromone perfume, which was supposed to calm him down – but the whiff of Canine No. 5 stimulated George to bark louder than ever. Naturally we resorted to telling him off, too, but that didn't make the slightest difference either. George wouldn't give up. He wanted to sleep with me, and that was that. The trouble was, so did Zach.

Then, one night, Zach finally lost his temper and yelled at poor George so loudly that even I was petrified. No matter that it went against all the canine rule books, it was the right thing to do: from that moment on the little devil behaved like an angel.

With Joshua grown-up, and George at long last trained to sleep by himself, the future should have been rosy for Zach and me. But, ironically, our relationship finally bit the dust on a Portuguese holiday *à deux*. We quarrelled in the departure lounge at Gatwick, were bitten by bed bugs in a *pousada*, backed our hired car into a stone wall in a remote village, then broke up on day four – and those were the *good* times.

When we returned to England, there seemed little to say but farewell. If we couldn't enjoy being together in the beautiful Douro valley, eating delicious *bacalhau* washed down with the local white port, and with the impossible pooch nowhere on the scene, what hope was there for us?

Maybe all failed relationships took the same trajectory: you fell in love with a romantic Casanova, but ended up enmeshed with Dorothea's Mr Casaubon, feeling that you could do nothing right. I was terrified of cutting loose after investing five years in our relationship, but it was high time to face facts: it wasn't making either of us happy any more, and it was destroying my self-confidence. If I wanted to move on and, hopefully, find myself again, I had to make the break.

When Zach and I had met I'd been forty-nine years old. By the time we finally split up I was fifty-five. Before I knew it I'd be fifty-six, the same age as Udi had been when he'd died, and my own mortality seemed horribly close. It was time to come to terms with reality: there was no cosy future awaiting me. After Udi's death I'd hoped I'd eventually meet a man who'd become a stepfather to Joshua, someone with whom I could spend the rest of my life. Though I'd made some wonderful friendships along the way, I hadn't succeeded in finding this paragon. Loving, supportive and such stimulating company, Udi was a hard act to follow, so maybe I'd been asking for too much.

And now that Joshua had left home, and I was entering a new phase of my life, maybe it was time, too, to hang up those stilettos, ditch the flirting and accept that I was destined to be alone for the rest of my life. I'd always dreaded growing old on my own. In fact, I was almost phobic about it.

But I wasn't entirely alone, was I? I still had George,

who'd stood by me loyally over the past ten years while male companions came and went. During the past few weeks he'd even crept back into the bedroom to sleep. As if he knew I was in need of extra comfort now that Joshua had moved out, he'd sidle in when he thought I wasn't looking and curl up in the small space between the bedside chest and the wardrobe, just out of sight. I hadn't the heart to send him back into exile in the study, and to tell the truth I rather liked to hear his heavy breathing. Okay, snoring. The sound was very reassuring in the otherwise silent flat.

I decided to stick to relationships with dogs in future. They were certainly a much safer bet than men. Tolerant and accepting. Loyal and faithful. Always cheerful and good-natured and happy to fit in with your plans. They were there when you needed them, and there when you didn't. Like Bridget Jones's Mark Darcy, dogs loved you just as you were: you didn't have to knock yourself out to please them. Dogs knew what it was to give, and they gave willingly. They were happy simply to be near you whatever you were doing. And there was no need to slave over a hot stove for them because a can of Pedigree Chum and the odd biscuit earned you three stars in the canine *Michelin Guide*.

On the minus side, conversation with dogs was limited. And sex was completely out.

We'd acquired George back in November 1998. I hadn't wanted a dog at the time. In the aftermath of Udi's and my father's deaths, life had seemed so bleak – not just to me, but to all the family – and I didn't want any more responsibility than I already had. I pasted on a brave face in front of everyone, particularly when Joshua was around, but I wasn't fooling him or anyone else that things were back to normal. One look at his wan expression and you could see that my son knew as well as I did that 'normal' no longer existed for us.

That September he turned nine years old. It was his first birthday without his father, and although I'd dreaded the day, the whole family rallied round and it didn't turn out to be as miserable an occasion as I'd feared. We got through the celebrations somehow, though more than a few tears were shed.

Now there were the short days of winter to 'look forward' to. After months of trying to escape Udi's absence by being out of the house as much as possible, the nights closed in. I'd walk Joshua home from school in the afternoons, but after that he and I would be stuck in the flat for the evening with only each other for company. Oh, yes, and the bullish, spiteful tabby cat we owned at the time, who was aptly named Monster Mog. We were back to facing real life. Or, rather, real life as it now was: a shell of its former, action-packed self. Udi's absence now dominated us as surely as his vivacious presence once had.

As Joshua and I sat opposite each other at supper one evening in early October, the carver chair at the head of the kitchen table gaped at us. This had always been Udi's chair. Here he'd sit for hours on end, surveying the length of our open-plan room, a packet of Gauloise loose tobacco, some Rizlas and a cold double espresso in front of him, with books, newspapers, letters and electronic organizers to hand. Inevitably there'd be a house phone tucked under his chin, a mobile phone at his elbow, and a thin, damp roll-up gripped between the nicotine-stained thumb and first finger of his right hand. Though I'd nagged him to stop since the day in 1985 when he'd first steamrollered into my life – a larger-than-life presence somewhat eccentrically dressed in a floral Liberty shirt teamed with black leather motorbike trousers – my libertarian husband had remained an unreconstructed, unrepentant chain-smoker.

Dripping ash everywhere except into the ashtray in front of him, Udi had continued to hold court from his chair until a week before he'd died. He'd make business calls, advise friends on their marital or professional problems, play with and talk to Joshua, or engage in the heated political and philosophical arguments he loved so much with whomsoever happened to be there. Some days it might be a well-known philosopher or writer, or a family member, on others it was Mark, a retired businessman who now delivered dry cleaning for a living, or Jacob, an Eritrean minicab driver Udi had taken under his wing. Udi would debate with anyone who was willing to engage with him.

Now, instead of his voice – animated, mellifluous, or occasionally raised in anger as he wrangled with Camden's Parking Enforcement Department on the phone over some disputed parking ticket (by the time he was dying he'd accumulated some £2000 worth, all unpaid, as he boasted to his visitors with great pride) – the only sounds in the room were the scraping of two sets of cutlery and the thin echo of my voice as I made a stab at keeping up a bright, superficial conversation with Joshua. That particular night I wasn't doing too well.

We were halfway through the meal when Joshua looked across at me and said, 'Mum, I think we should get a dog.'

When I asked him why, he started to talk about his school friend Tom, with whom he'd spent the previous Saturday afternoon. Apparently Tom's home was overflowing with pets, including cats, guinea pigs and an adorable rescued Jack Russell called Molly. 'There's always something going on there,' Joshua told me.

'It sounds like fun.'

'If you and me had a dog, well, we'd have someone to talk to when we came home.' And when I protested that we already had each other to talk to, he continued pointedly, 'Someone else to talk to. Now that Dad's not here.'

Although I was completely thrown by this perceptive comment, I tried to be noncommittal. But, like his father before him, Joshua wasn't one to give up when he really wanted something.

'Mum, remember what Dad used to say?'

'What?'

'He said, "Always say *yes* when someone asks you if they can do something, unless there's a really, really good reason to say *no*."'

This was true. Udi had always been an enabler, and the 'yes' man in our joint parenting, while my role had been as his fall guy, a.k.a. the depressing 'no' woman.

'Well, Mum,' Joshua continued, giving me a steady look that should have warned me I was about to be emotionally manipulated, 'now that Dad's not here to say yes to things, don't you think *you* should instead?'

I gritted my teeth and, playing for time, said I'd think about it.

A week later, Joshua persuaded me to take him to Discover Dogs, the Kennel Club's annual try-before-you-buy dog exhibition, where we both fell in love with the prettiest, friendliest, waggiest-tailed dog on show – the Cavalier King Charles Spaniel. The breed had been developed from the old King Charles spaniel by a New Yorker named Roswell Eldridge, who was attempting to re-create the original English Toy Spaniel, once so beloved by the Stuart monarchs. In 1926 Elridge had placed an advertisement in the catalogue of Crufts Dog Show offering a financial prize of £25 for long-nosed 'Blenheim Spaniels of the Old Type, as shown in the pictures of Charles II's time'. Within a few years, and after some careful interbreeding, he'd succeeded in re-creating this dog, and the new old-style King Charles was given the extra name Cavalier.

When we came back from Earl's Court, where Discover Dogs was held, Joshua made me phone up the Kennel Club and find out about Cavalier breeders. Just days later, and with the proviso that we were only going to *look* at the puppies, and definitely not buy one, I agreed to take him to visit a Cavalier breeder who lived near Henley-on-Thames.

I'd already spoken to Mrs Coleman on the phone, and her puppies were far too young to leave their mother yet, I explained, as we drove down. Besides, I hadn't yet made up my mind if I was going to buy one, so Joshua mustn't be disappointed when we returned home empty-handed.

'Don't worry, Mum, I won't be,' was his assured response.

He wasn't. When we drove back to London that afternoon a five-month-old chestnut-and-white Cavalier was lying asleep across his knees.

George, as she'd named him, was one of Mrs Coleman's favourite dogs. She'd planned to keep him as a pet but his head was slightly too big for the standard so he couldn't be used as a stud dog and her husband wanted her to sell him (this was understandable: they had twenty-five other Cavaliers). In two minds about parting with him, she'd clung on to him for ages, and it was easy to see why: he was utterly beautiful.

Big head or not – and, to my inexpert eye, his head looked no different from those of her other dogs – George was the prettiest Cavalier King Charles I'd ever seen. There are four different types of Cavalier: the Black-and-tan, the Tricolour (white, black and chestnut), the Ruby (chestnut brown all over) and the Blenheim (a mixture of chestnut and white) – and each is lovely in its own way. But George was a Blenheim, to my mind the most fetching Cavalier of all. He had a mainly chestnut coat with a few big white splodges, silky chestnut ears with ringlets that might have graced a Restoration wig, two slightly asymmetrical chestnut eye patches in an otherwise all-white face, and a very soft, fluffy patch of white on the top of his head – a marking known in the trade as a lozenge or, alternatively, the 'Kiss of Buddha'.

A round black nose at the end of a delicate ski-jump muzzle and two huge, round black eyes were arranged in an equilateral triangle in the centre of George's face, giving him the heart-melting look of a seal pup. When his mouth opened, and his pink tongue flicked out, he appeared to smile at you, and his long, flagged tail never stopped wagging. To top it all, a tiny round chestnut beauty spot just above his nostrils lent him the flirtatious air of an eighteenth-century rake, and hinted that, underneath his obvious sweetness, George was probably a bit of a lad.

Joshua fell in love with him at first sight. As did I. And when Mrs Coleman showed me his pedigree, and I noticed that he'd been born on 16 June, just days after Udi and my father had both died, I realized he was meant for us. It was destiny.

Driving him back to London was a new beginning for Joshua and me.

George brought humour back into our house, and re-awoke joy in our hearts.

He also turned my life upside-down.

On the way back from Henley I resolved to be top dog in our house, and I told Joshua as much. There were to be rules about George's upbringing, I said, rules that were to be kept, not bent or broken. Top of the list was a rule that our new acquisition was not going to be allowed to jump up onto the furniture. I'd been to enough homes where the sofas and chairs were covered with dog hair and where the dribbling pets climbed on people's laps whether they wanted them there or not to know that I didn't want to live like that. Moreover, I wanted a dog I could take to other people's houses knowing that he'd behave himself.

But George, however, had other ideas. He trampled all over our sofas on day one (minute one, actually) and he looked so regal sitting on the red velvet cushions that I didn't have the audacity to turf him off.

My second firm rule was that George wasn't to be allowed to sleep in our bedrooms at night.

'Why not?' Joshua asked, in the annoying way that children of his age do. It was now around midnight, and George was yelping in the upstairs bathroom, where I'd shut him in an hour before, with a makeshift cardboard-box dog-bed lined with blankets, and a Winnie-the-Pooh hot-water bottle tucked among them to keep him warm. George, who obviously didn't like being alone, kept barking to be let out. We'd popped in countless times to try to calm him down, and were now standing outside the door, arguing about what to do next. Joshua wanted to let our new puppy sleep in his bedroom that night, but I was sticking to my guns.

'I told you, it's a Rule that he's not to sleep in the bedrooms. It's unhealthy.'

'Why?'

I tried to think of a genuine reason, other than that I had a hunch it wasn't good for you to breathe in exhaled doggy breath all night long, but I only managed another lame 'Because.'

'That's not a reason,' Joshua replied, proving that, when it came to persistence during an argument, he was as much a chip off his father's old block as when he'd written that note about wanting to leave home. Though I knew he had a point I stood my ground and we returned to our beds. Neither of us could sleep because of the constant yelps and barks, and when they eventually stopped we were both so worried by the sudden silence that we went upstairs again, this time to see if he was all right. Coughing and choking noises floated to us through the bathroom door so we rushed in to find that George had demolished an entire roll of lavatory paper and made himself sick. Not sick enough, however, to prevent him pushing out past us and running downstairs.

We eventually found him in my bedroom, curled up on the duvet. He opened one eye for a split second as we approached him, shut it, then tucked his little black button nose firmly under his paws and pretended to go back to sleep. Not for nothing are Cavaliers nicknamed the kings of the canine world – and a super king-size mattress was a far more appropriate bed for him than a pile of blankets in a cardboard box, or so his body-language said.

Too tired to engage in another battle, I crawled into bed on one side of George, while Josh crawled in on the other. The pattern for George's future behaviour was set. It had taken him a matter of hours to suss out that, though I was a relatively strict mother, dog discipline wasn't my forte. With a little cunning, a pathetic expression and some sustained barking, our Cavalier could manipulate me to do whatsoever he wished.

By day two, George wasn't just trampling all over the furniture, he was walking all over me. And so it continued. Over the years he perfected the art of making me feel guilty if I didn't give in to his slightest whim. So I usually did. No matter how hard I tried to be assertive, George remained the ruler of our house.

The fact that I eventually wrote a book about him – *My Life with George* – didn't help matters. George lapped up his fifteen minutes of fame. Having his photograph taken by professional photographers (a process that demanded a great deal of bribery in the form of dog treats – how else to make a dog sit still in front of the camera?); making public appearances and being fussed over at book signings; constantly being told by total strangers how handsome, how sweet, how simply *adorable* he was – it was enough to turn the head of any ordinary pooch, let alone one that was already spoiled rotten.

The high point came on Hampstead Heath one Sunday afternoon, when some Italian tourists asked me for directions to Parliament Hill. No sooner had I explained the way in my broken Italian than one man pointed at George, and gasped in an incredulous voice, '*Ma è Giorgio, si?*' It turned out that the entire family group – uncles, aunts, parents and teenage children – had read 'Giorgio's' book in its Italian translation and had actually come to Hampstead Heath in search of him. Now there he was, in the mud-caked, dog-breathy flesh, ready to pose for photographs and bestow licks in return for some extra adoration.

From then on, George flounced about the house like some fluffed-up D-list diva on *Celebrity Big Brother*, throwing his substantial weight around and acting as if the world owed him a living.

Poor George! In the end those fifteen minutes of fame were all too brief, and celebrity didn't bring him the long-lasting rewards he'd come to expect; I guess it rarely does. The public appearances dried up, strangers stopped recognizing him, and the hoped-for dog-food endorsement contracts did not come rolling in. Failing to make the shortlist in the Most Handsome Dog contest at the Kennel Club's Discover Dogs exhibition in 2007 struck the killer blow. From then on it was back to normal life as a normal dog, and I wasn't sure that George had adapted to it very well.

He still had one adoring fan, of course. Me.

And now that Joshua had left home, he had my undivided attention.

But not for long.

3

As I walked down the garden path one night in October to go to the cinema, George climbed onto the back of the sofa and glared at me reproachfully through the bay window.

Three hours later I came home to see his small, ghostly face peering out from the now dark room, now looking as worried as a toddler lost in a supermarket.

Had he been sitting there for the entire time I was out? Or had he had a sixth sense that I was approaching the house? I had a suspicion it was the former because the moment I walked in George threw himself at me, whining as if we'd been parted for months. And when I clipped on his lead and took him out to his lamppost (*his*, because the local council had very kindly installed it right outside our house three years before, since when George had left his calling card there every day) he let loose such a flood that I realized he'd been saving himself for my return, rather than go downstairs, exit via the cat flap and relieve himself in the back garden, which he'd always done quite happily in the past. He must have been afraid that he'd miss me coming home if he left his observation post.

This wasn't the first time since Joshua had moved out that something like this had happened. I'd left George alone for a couple of hours a few days before, and he'd been equally frantic when I got back, even though I'd left Radio 4 on while

I was out so that he shouldn't feel lonely. Andrew Marr and his guests on *Start the Week* were obviously no substitute for my company.

Why was George suddenly so clingy? He'd never been quite as bad as this before.

The day after the sofa incident I drove him over to Highgate Woods, where I was meeting some friends, Elizabeth and Clare, and their respective dogs: Elizabeth's Jack Russell Molly, collie Flynn, and Archie, Clare's young and gloriously macho Cavalier. Halfway through our walk we stopped at the café in the woods for a cup of coffee and to compare notes on how we were feeling: all three of us had sons of the same age who'd just started at university. Since dogs weren't allowed inside the café, or even in the open-air section, we left our mini-pack tied up together just beyond the café's railings.

Minutes later, armed with our cappuccinos, we sat down at one of the outdoor tables just yards from where the dogs were, but hidden from them by a hedge.

'No children to distract us!' Elizabeth sighed. 'Isn't this civilized?'

'Wonderful,' Clare said. 'And it's so gloriously peaceful here!'

Just then a distraught yelp came from behind the hedge. Like a mother who recognizes her own baby's cry, I immediately knew whose dog was complaining, but I ignored him and lazily spooned up the froth from my coffee. As if he was determined I wasn't going to enjoy a single chocolaty bubble, George yelped again, then again and again, at increasingly short intervals, until the yelps became staccato yaps, then trills, followed by embarrassing

arpeggios. Up and down the scales he went, like a stran-
gulated castrato practising his vocal exercises. Just like he
used to do whenever Zach had stayed the night.

I smiled apologetically at the others and, in an ironic
tone, called, 'Do be quiet, George!' over the hedge. The
three of us tried chatting through the continuing barrage,
but George's behaviour soon dominated our conversation
as thoroughly as it did the airwaves.

'Perhaps he's tangled up in his leash? Or maybe he's
being dog-napped?' Clare suggested – not without a touch
of hope, I suspected. I jumped up and peered over the
hedge to see if this was indeed the case. Archie, Flynn and
Molly were all sitting quietly patiently in a line, wagging
their tails, while George was pulling on his leash and looking distraught. The moment he saw me, his face lit up and
he lunged towards me with such force that he almost
garrotted himself with his collar.

'There's nothing wrong – he's fine,' I said, resuming my
seat and leaving him to it. 'He just wants attention.'

'What? More than he already gets? Perhaps he's suffering
from separation anxiety,' said Elizabeth, who's a psychotherapist. 'Joshua's left home and abandoned him, and he's
afraid you will, too.'

All three of us sniggered.

However, soon after I came home George went down
to Joshua's empty room and stood in the middle of it for
a while. Then he sniffed around beside the bed in search
of the biscuit crumbs, popcorn and shards of old pizza
that were once to be found there. In vain: the floor had
never been so clean.

Looking distinctly confused, he pottered out into the hall.

Maybe Elizabeth was right. Maybe he *was* suffering from separation anxiety.

I knew exactly how he felt.

Early the next morning, the robins that had built a late nest in the back garden started kicking up a terrible racket. I peered down from the kitchen window to see them twittering furiously around the ivy-clad wall in which their young were tucked away. Standing on two legs on the patio beneath it was a big mangy fox, reaching up to grab one of the two fledglings the parent birds had been nurturing for weeks.

It looked up as I banged loudly on the window. Then, closely followed by an excited George, I rushed downstairs, unlocked the french windows and burst out onto the patio. But it was too late. Feathers just visible in the corner of his mouth, the fox was making off with its prey.

George's ears pricked and he was after it, barking madly, tail wagging like a windscreen wiper on top speed. Though he froze every time he saw a dog on the Heath, even at a distance, the faintest whiff of fox sent him into a hunting-dog frenzy; underneath the pampered-pooch persona lurked a bona-fide hound. I don't know what he would have done if he'd caught up with it, but mercifully the fox was far too quick for him and, in a flash, it slunk over the side fence into my neighbour's garden. Gleeful at having seen off the intruder – or so he presumed – George turned tail and, eyes glittering and nose to the ground, rushed around our patchy excuse for a lawn, tracing its trail.

It led him back to the patio, where the second fledgling was lying on the ground underneath the nest; the fox must have knocked it out when it grabbed its sibling. George sniffed at the feathery body curiously while the distraught parents fluttered around crying in distress. I rushed over and picked the baby robin up, but the poor little thing was already dead. Its little neck was broken, and its tiny head lolled in my hand, weightless as a fragment of eggshell.

Over the past weeks I'd watched the adult robins tirelessly bringing their chirping offspring an endless supply of food. Now their hard work had been rendered futile. Of course, a fox killing baby birds was perfectly natural: the law of the jungle or, rather, the back garden, *Nature red in tooth and claw*, and all that. What a tragedy for the parents, though. Stunned by what had happened, they spent the rest of the day darting in and out of the ivy searching for their lost babies, and when they failed to find them they fluttered around the garden looking dreadfully distressed.

I recognized the symptoms. It was empty-nest syndrome. The parents didn't know what to do with themselves now that their young had disappeared.

Feeling excessively upset, I threw on some clothes and dragged George out for a walk, partly because we both needed the exercise and partly to cheer myself up. The 791 acres of Hampstead Heath are almost literally on our doorstep, which I'd always counted an incredible privilege. Over the last nineteen years I'd grown to love its muddy paths, mossy woods and open fields with a passion. Not so King George. You'd think a city dog would appreciate a lifetime of instant access to quasi-countryside where he could hunt squirrels, feast on rabbit droppings and romp with his mates. But apart from the rabbit droppings, of which George had become inordinately fond over the years, the opposite was true. The only mate he'd ever deigned to romp with was Snizz, the Miniature Schnauzer bitch who'd once lived next door. Since she'd moved out he'd preferred snoozing on his red-velvet throne – the sofa – to the great outdoors, unless he was going for a chauffeur-driven ride into town (me being the chauffeur, naturally). Consequently he'd got into the habit of making our daily promenades on the Heath as joyless as possible.

Since Joshua had left home, George seemed more reluctant than ever to step outside the house; perhaps he was afraid he wouldn't be allowed back in. So when I fixed on his extendable leash that morning he backed off, jumped onto the sofa and sat down facing me with a defiant expression. A gentle tug did nothing to encourage him, so I ended up lifting him off the sofa, setting him down on the floorboards, then dragging him slowly towards the front door on his bottom, his outstretched front paws, which he'd hoped would act as brakes, sliding inexorably across the slippery wood.

Once we exited the garden gate George limped up to his lamppost, autographed it, then pulled to return home. I coaxed him on with another tug, but instead of co-operating he dug his claws into the paving stones. I tugged again. He plodded after me, but only up to the nearest car, a swanky Volvo four-by-four, beside which he stopped again, head cocked to one side, staring intently at its doors as if willing them to spring open.

'Sorry, old boy,' I explained. 'But (a) that car's not ours and (b) we're doing our bit for global warming and walking to the Heath. *On foot.* As you know it's all of fifty yards away.'

As I strode resolutely on, I heard the leash whirr out of its plastic sheath behind me, like a builder's tape measure. When it reached its full length it jerked me to a halt. I glanced over my shoulder to find George still standing by the four-by-four glaring at me down five metres of bright red tape.

'Come on,' I coaxed. 'Be a good boy.'

Eyes wide with defiance, George backed off. As the leash grew ever tauter his collar slipped over one long, curly ear and he began to choke. A woman walking past on the opposite side of the road looked on aghast as I stood watching my beautiful dog splutter and tremble in a manner guaranteed to spark her sympathy. Perhaps I should have explained that the choking and leg-shaking were but theatrical ploys he used every single day to try to get out of walking, and that in reality George wasn't as elderly or as pathetic as he sometimes liked to make out. On the occasions when I did give in and head home he'd execute an abrupt, youthful about-turn and instantly break into a sprightly canter, tossing his head in a cocky manner that shouted, 'Yah, boo, sucks! I won!'

Once the woman had gone I gave his leash a much firmer yank. With obvious reluctance, George placed one big hairy paw in front of the other and limped after me towards the end of the road. Ten painfully slow paces later he stopped again, this time to poop in full view of a neighbour who, as luck would have it, happened to be looking out of his ground-floor window.

Carefully avoiding the man's outraged gaze, I stared dreamily into space while, back arched, George took his time. Then, also watched by the man, I got out the scrunched-up plastic bag that was distending my jeans' pocket, shoved my hand inside it, took a deep breath and scooped. With the warm, pungent sack dangling from my fingers like a designer handbag, I finally succeeded in getting George across the road and onto Hampstead Heath.

Just after I'd deposited his lordship's doings in the dedicated bin at the top of Elm Walk – over the years I'd worked out that the most bearable method was to pull the end of my jumper sleeve over my hand, flick open the hatch with a covered fingertip, hurl the bag in, snap the hatch shut, then run, all the while holding my breath – George arched his back again, this time bang in the middle of the main path. I gritted my teeth. Defecating twice in close succession had recently become a habit of his, one I suspected he'd developed to punish me for his daily frog-march. I rifled my jeans pockets for a second plastic bag only to find I didn't have one. I contemplated walking on as if the steaming rosette on the ground was nothing to do with me – after all, short of running a genetic test on it there was no way anyone could prove that it was George's, could they? But my conscience wouldn't allow me to leave it. Besides, one of the green-shirted Heath keepers was somewhere nearby, and I suspected that he was watching me.

Holding my breath again, I resorted to the tricky practice of using a handful of tissues to clear up, then disposed of the bundle and made my way into Pryors Field, the meadow that undulated downhill to the large ponds at South End Green. This was perhaps my favourite spot of all on the Heath, with views down to the towering office blocks of the City of London and the dome of St Paul's Cathedral.

Although there was a steep, busy road hidden at one side of it, I could easily imagine myself deep in the middle of the countryside as I strode through the long grass and wild flowers, stumbling over the occasional molehill and setting butterflies dancing. Early in the morning and again at dusk, the occasional fox slunk by, and rabbits ventured out of the bushes in search of food, the tips of their soft, pink-lined ears barely visible among the vegetation. Scraggy crows hopped along the well-trodden paths, sparrow hawks wheeled overhead in search of field mice, woodpeckers hammered in the distance, and the large flock of rose-ringed parakeets that had made its home there flitted between the oak trees, their exotic neon-green plumage, long tails and loud squeals completely out of place in this most quintessentially English setting.

The meadow was also the location of the two small, low-branched oaks where Udi used to take Joshua tree climbing, and opposite them was the bench that the family and I had dedicated to his memory a year after his death. The phrase 'In loving memory of the one and only Udi Eichler' was carved on the back – 'one and only' not just because he was a unique person, but because it was a point of pride with him that he was the only person ever to bear that name. During the past ten years the bench had been the focus of many family gatherings, as well as a place I would escape to whenever I wanted headspace.

When I was near the bench I let George off the lead, and while I walked on he remained frozen to the spot, staring after me as if willing me to turn back. When I didn't, he threw a calculating glance at me, then started to sniff the ground.

'No, George!' I called.

As he nosed the grass with renewed interest, I began walking back towards him as fast as I could. 'I said no, George! Don't!' I broke into a run, but it was too late to stop him: his front paws were already down on the ground, his hindquarters now followed, and a second later he was writhing around joyously on his back, all four legs kicking the air in orgasmic abandon. Once he'd thoroughly anointed himself in whatever muck he'd found, George jumped up, shook himself violently, then raced towards me, eyes glittering with triumph and long ears flapping up and down. Like a snake shedding its skin, George had left his pampered-pooch persona on the grass and, as when he'd scented the fox in the garden earlier that morning, become a real dog again.

The protest was over for the time being, and as I strode off down the slope, annoyed that I'd now have to bath him when I got home, he followed at a distance, deviating every now and then to scare off a basking woodpecker or to have another roll in the grass. However, when I headed down the narrow causeway between the ponds, George came to a halt yet again. He knew as well as I did that this route led to the long, steep walk up Parliament Hill, whereas if we were to double back at this point we'd be home in five minutes. In case I'd forgotten this salient fact he gave a reminding yap-yap and waited for me to turn around.

When I didn't, he barked again, this time with the outraged amazement of a monarch used to ruling by divine right, who suddenly finds that his servants are disobeying his commands. Since he usually trailed after me once I was out of sight – he didn't want to risk losing his meal ticket – I carried on in my original direction and, halfway along the path, stopped to wait for him to catch me up.

And waited. When, after a good five minutes, George still didn't appear over the crest of the hill, I began to worry that something had happened to him. Had he trapped his foot? Broken his leg? Maybe even been dog-napped? My will cracked, and I ran back up the short stony slope to search for him.

There he was, still standing exactly where I'd left him, still staring after me. The moment he spotted me his tail started wagging and he did a smart 180-degree turn, then skipped off towards home. I attempted to catch up with him so that I could clip on his leash and drag him back where I wanted to go, but it was futile. Whatever ruses I used – cooing, a strident command, even bending down with my arm outstretched and offering him imaginary treats – George kept several paces ahead. It was the story of our relationship.

Suddenly he stopped. Coming across the field towards him now was a very thin, very tall Weimaraner. Though its ribs and hip bones were clearly visible through its skin, even at a distance, the huge dog carried itself with the noble air of an aristocrat who had seen better days. No matter that it didn't look aggressive from where I was standing, George didn't want to approach it without me. He'd been frightened of strange dogs ever since he was attacked by a Staffordshire Bull Terrier in 2005.

'Don't worry, he's not going to attack,' said his female owner, as we both caught up with our dogs. 'In fact, he's really nervous. And he's very obedient. Stop, Jupiter!' she ordered, as the giant creature, who was as tall as a Great

Dane, bent down to sniff my now cowering Cavalier. Jupiter raised his vast head. 'Come here!' his owner commanded. And Jupiter immediately trotted over to her.

I knew the woman by sight: she was a natural beauty in her late thirties with light brown hair and very pale skin. We'd passed each other in the street numerous times, and always smiled at each other without speaking. As I'd never seen her with a dog before, we now struck up one of those canine-themed conversations that dog owners so easily fall into: fascinating to us, dead boring to non-pooch owners. It turned out that her name was Kathryn, she was an actress, and she'd recently adopted Jupiter from an animal rescue centre called Many Tears in South Wales. His early history wasn't clear, but someone had found him, half starved, wandering around on a road somewhere in the Midlands, and had taken him to a local dog pound. Since no one had claimed him, and no one had come forward to adopt him, this magnificent creature had been destined for the knacker's yard until Many Tears had stepped in and saved him.

Kathryn had fallen for Jupiter after seeing his photograph on the Many Tears website, and she'd applied to adopt him. They'd sent someone round to her home to see if she was a suitable owner, and now Jupiter was hers. Though he'd been terribly nervous when she'd picked him up three weeks before, she'd already managed to housetrain him, taught him to walk to heel both on and off the leash *and* to obey a whole array of commands, including 'Come!', 'Stop!' and 'Sit!'

'How wonderful,' I said, not without a tinge of envy. I shot George a black look. I hoped he was listening.

'He follows me everywhere and we all love him to bits,' she enthused. 'He really has the most adorable easy-going nature. But I suppose everyone thinks that about their own dog, don't they?'

'Of course!'

Just then George wandered off in the direction of a small, rain-filled hollow. 'Come back, George!' George took no notice. 'George! Sweetie!' I cooed. 'Come back! He's quite old now, and rather hard of hearing,' I apologized, as I ran after him. But it was too late: he was already wallowing in the puddle as if it were a Dead Sea mud bath in some expensive spa.

As I grabbed hold of his collar and yanked him out, his fur dripping with brown slime, I wondered how Kathryn had succeeded in training her stray over a matter of weeks when in ten years I'd taught George precisely nothing.

4

The next day I woke up to find George lying across my chest licking one of his left paws with such relish you'd have thought it was a Cornetto. When I examined it I saw that one of the pads was swollen and red, with a big, gaping wound.

No wonder the poor thing hadn't wanted to go for a walk the day before – every step must have been agony for him. And I'd assumed he'd been faking that limp on the way to the Heath!

'Ah, yes, there's definitely something in there,' said Howard, the vet, squinting at George's paw, after I'd driven him to the surgery in a guilty panic. 'It's probably a grass seed.'

I groaned. 'Not again!' This was the fourth time in two years that George had been plagued by grass seeds. In July 2006 one had got lodged in his ear. In order to fish it out before it navigated its way right down the narrow canal, punctured his eardrum and, no doubt, headed for his brain, the vet had had to operate, which meant a general anaesthetic and a bill for four hundred pounds. Not long afterwards another grass seed had embedded itself between George's paw pads, and his whole foot had swollen. No sooner had he got over *that* operation (£569.27) than the same thing had happened again. The vet had suggested, laughing, that I buy him a set of all-terrain dog-boots, a cinch at £45 for four, with the matching socks at only £8.99.

It wasn't the price of the boots that had put me off buying them so much as the thought of how some of the other dogs on the Heath would react to them. The aggressive, macho brutes already picked on George, and when it came to standing up for himself against them, George was a complete wuss: he didn't have an ounce of aggression in him. I could only imagine what they'd do to him if he turned up in a set of high-heeled Poochi sandals, Dogverse trainers or miniature flower-bedecked Cath Kidston wellies.

'I'm afraid I'll need to investigate,' Howard said now, peering into the wound with a magnifying glass.

'Right.' I swallowed. 'I suppose that means another general anaesthetic, does it?'

'There's no other way, my dear.'

Somewhere at the back of my brain I heard the chink of a cash register. How much was all this going to cost? During his ten-plus years George had been in and out of veterinary surgeries almost as often as he'd had hot roast-chicken dinners. He'd had periodontal problems; sore throats and infected ears; skin allergies and auto-immune disorders; suspected anorexia and its opposite, confirmed obesity; possible mange and actual mitral-valve disease, a life-shortening condition shared by practically every other member of his breed (50 per cent of Cavaliers over the age of five years have it, and almost 100 per cent of those over ten).

Then there was the time George stepped on broken glass and cut his pad badly. And the time he slipped a disc while scrambling up the back of the sofa. And the time he found a baited fish-hook on a huge, otherwise pristine Cornish beach. The bacon on the end of it proved irresistible, with the result that George ended up looking like a drug-crazed, body-pierced punk out clubbing, dancing in circles on the sand with a sharp silver barb through his upper lip.

Most serious of all was the occasion when George was almost killed by that Staffordshire Bull Terrier. In a completely unprovoked attack, the vicious brute pounced on him, bit him savagely and shook him like a rag doll, gouging great lumps out of his side as he did so. Had he grabbed George by the neck, he would have killed him, but the fact that he attacked from the rear, not the front, saved George's life. Even so, we nearly lost him. Through the brilliance of the emergency vet we took him to, he eventually made a miraculous recovery – much faster than my finances did. The veterinary bills for that, as for all his previous ailments, were enough to set me reeling – plus there was the added cost of a pet psychologist brought in to help George deal with his post-traumatic stress disorder (a session with Sigmund Freud would have been cheaper – and George could have snoozed comfortably throughout on the professor's famous couch).

As anyone who owned one was well aware, keeping a pet nowadays was an expensive business. Add to George's huge vet bills the dosh I'd doled out over the years for worm pills, antibiotics, anti-flea products, anti-fungal shampoos, prescription-only foods that he, unlike other dogs, seemed to need, dog vitamin pills, dog leads, dog collars, dog-beds, dog coats, dog blankets, dog haircuts, plus the occasional holiday at the luxurious Paw Seasons Dog Hotel near Bristol (the handful of select residents got hugs galore, walks on the local beach and their own spa pool to splash around in, as well as chicken for supper and designer beds to curl up in at night) and my Cavalier had probably cost me, and the pet-insurance company, nearly twenty thousand quid. It would probably have been cheaper to run a Lamborghini, even at current petrol prices.

Amazingly, even though 'Stuff happens to George', as one vet put it, and despite his worsening heart-valve problems (which in recent years had risen to four on a scale of one to six), my Cavalier had so far survived to the ripe old age of ten and a half. Not just survived, but flourished. I was the one who was worn out. As was my credit card.

But, as I often said, what was money for if not for spending on the people and things you loved most in the world? Oh, yes, it was for paying Dobromierz the builder. And the tax man.

Howard slipped on his stethoscope, and pressed it against George's well-padded ribs. After listening for a while, he shook his head. 'Hmm. Before we anaesthetize him, I really should give him an ultrasound cardiac scan to see how that ticker's doing. We don't want George to go into heart failure during the op, do we?'

'Of course not!' The cash register in my brain chinked again.

'Do you know? I think we may have reached the point where we start him on cardiac medication.'

'Really?' *Chink, chink.*

'I'd also like to run a routine urine analysis. And, of course, some blood tests. Just to make sure his liver's functioning properly.'

Chink, chink, chink.

Howard eased a thumb between George's lips, and gently prised his mouth open, an indignity George bore with growing impatience. 'What a dismal sight! Mummy hasn't been cleaning those teeth very well, has she? Tooth decay won't do his heart any favours, so why don't we use this opportunity to give them a quick scale and polish? It'll save him having to have another general anaesthetic in a few months' time – and save you money in the long run.'

Chink, chink, chink, chink.

I'm sure George understood every word of what Howard was saying because by then he was practically hurling himself off the examination table and into my arms. Knowing it was for his own good, I tore myself away and ran out into the reception area where I brushed his hairs off my jacket, signed the operation consent form, without reading it through thoroughly, and went home, leaving him there for the afternoon.

I collected him later. His liver function and blood had been double-checked and found to be perfect, his heart had been scanned, his few remaining teeth scoured so thoroughly they looked like they'd been professionally whitened by a cosmetic dentist (less one decayed stump that had needed to be extracted) and George was looking very perky, sporting a golf club of a bandage on his paw.

Including VAT, the bill for his treatment came to £1006.93.

'*How* much?' I gasped.

The receptionist repeated the sum as casually as if she'd been saying ten pounds fifty. 'The insurance will cover two-thirds of it, won't it?' she soothed, as I fumbled for my credit card.

One thousand and six pounds and ninety-three pence worth of ops, tests, dentistry and scans? I'd only taken him in because he had a grass seed stuck in his toe! Perhaps the vet had hired a specialist army bomb-disposal unit to search for it.

The irony was that they couldn't even find the damn thing. Apparently it must already have worked its way out of George's paw.

5

Hannah telephoned me a few days later.

When Udi had first introduced me to his daughters back in 1985, Tabby was a twenty-one-year-old sociology student and Hannah was eighteen, working in rock music, an exciting job involving egoistic megastars, late nights and excessive partying. After helping to care for her dying father, she had courageously decided to leave this beguiling but ultimately superficial world and retrain for what she felt was a much more meaningful career. Ten years on, she had a first-class degree in paediatric nursing and had helped to save the lives of countless acutely sick children. During the same period she'd also turned a decrepit house in West London into a home fit for *Grand Designs* and had recently moved in. The family was incredibly proud of her achievements. However, this hadn't stopped Hannah feeling that something was missing from her life.

'I need your advice about something,' she said, when she phoned. 'Look, I really want to get a dog.'

This wasn't the first time she'd brought up the subject, and on previous occasions I'd done my best to put her off. As I'd learned over the years, owning a dog was a huge commitment by any stretch of the imagination. It was a wonderful thing for those already tied down by domesticity and small children, but for the fancy-free like Hannah it could turn out to be a huge burden, particularly when they had the opportunity to make the most of being unencumbered.

'Really, darling?' I murmured, in a doubtful tone.

'Why do you say it like that?'

'Oh, you know what I think. Much as I love George, a dog is a rather a big responsibility for one person to take on. Your life won't be your own any more. You'll have no time to yourself. Are you sure you've thought the whole thing through properly?' I asked – pointlessly, as it happened, because if Hannah had decided to do something, you could bet anything you liked that she'd already weighed up the pros and cons. She was one of the most efficient, organized people I knew. 'Having a dog's a huge tie – much more so than a cat. I mean, what will you do with it while you're at work?'

'Well, as you know, I work from home part of the time, and when I'm not around Mum's volunteered to help walk it.' Hannah's mother, Diana, lived immediately next door to her. 'And when she can't, I'll use a dog walker.'

'Right. Very good. What about the cost, though? Don't forget that dogs aren't cheap to run.'

'I've budgeted for that.'

I glanced at George, who'd just limped into my study on his bandaged paw, looking like an old man with gout, and I told Hannah about his recent hole-in-the-foot surgery and what the bill had come to. An appropriately horrified gasp blasted down the telephone. 'And what about your new house and that lovely white carpet of yours?' I pressed on, sensing a slit in her armour.

'Well, there isn't any carpet on the ground floor, it's all wood. And my dog won't be allowed upstairs.'

'Really?' I said, in a shocked voice. 'What – never?'

'No, never. I'm going to put a baby gate at the bottom to stop it going up there.'

I laughed. 'You mean you're not going to allow this future dog of yours to sleep in your bedroom with you?'

'Absolutely not!'

After my experiences with George, this was a subject on which I felt qualified – I'd almost say over-qualified – to give good advice. 'That's what you think now, darling, but this dog, when you get it, well, let me tell you, it may have other ideas.'

'That's too bad. My dog's going to learn to sleep in the kitchen, in a puppy crate at first,' she said firmly. 'It's going to be very well trained . . .' The words *unlike George* hung in the air, unsaid because Hannah's far too nice a person to say them. So I said them myself and we both laughed. 'I've decided that I'm going to take my dog to proper puppy-training classes right from the start. Because, well, I don't want to run into trouble when I next have a man in my life. I mean,' Hannah added, after a short pause, 'like you did with Zach.'

'No, of course not. Very sensible of you. Still, I'm not sure this is a good idea.'

'Honestly, Judith,' she said, clearly surprised, 'you're always trying to talk me out of getting a dog yet you and Joshua have both got so much pleasure from George. I have given this a lot of thought, you know.'

Of course she had. And who was I to tell her she was making a mistake? I reminded myself that Hannah was now a responsible adult more than capable of making her own decisions. Come to think of it, she was probably more capable than I was of making *mine*. 'Oh, don't listen to me – I'm just playing devil's advocate. Well, what can I say but wonderful, darling? Another dog in the family!'

'Yes. A playmate for George!'

'As a matter of fact I think he needs one now that your brother's left home. It's very quiet in the house, and I suspect he's rather lonely.'

'What about you?'

'Me?'

'Yes. You must miss Joshua, too,' she said thoughtfully.

'Oh, you know, a bit. But I'm fine!' I changed the subject before my voice faltered. 'So, what kind of dog are you planning to get? A Cavalier like George, perhaps?'

'No. Not that George isn't gorgeous. But I definitely want to get a dog from a rescue centre. And I'd like a young puppy if at all possible, one that needs a nice, loving home and lots of cuddles. Which is why I'm calling you, actually. You're the family expert on all things canine so I thought you might know where I can get a good rescue dog from.'

I told Hannah about Jupiter, the magnificent Weimaraner I'd met on Hampstead Heath, then racked my brain for the name of the place in Wales his owner Kathryn had told me he'd come from. As far as I could recall it was something like No More Tears.

6

Two days later Hannah called again. This time she sounded elated.

'I Googled the name of that rescue centre you told me about,' she said. 'No More Tears turns out to be the name of a baby shampoo – oh, yes, and an Ozzy Osbourne song. But I managed to trace the place. It's called Many Tears Animal Rescue. It has to be the one because it's in South Wales, near Llanelli. And guess what?'

'What?'

If a voice could beam with happiness, hers did now: 'I've found the perfect puppy on their website!'

'*Already?*' The moment the word was out of my mouth, I castigated myself for sounding so horrified.

Hannah didn't seem to notice. 'Yes. His name's Billy, he's nearly three months old, and he's absolutely gorgeous! I've just contacted Many Tears and reserved him.'

'*Already?*' I repeated. 'That's . . . wonderful, darling!' I tried to sound enthusiastic. 'But . . . isn't this a teensy bit, well, impulsive of you? I mean, you haven't actually seen this dog yet. You don't know anything about him. What sort of dog is he?'

'He's a crossbreed. Apparently his mother's a Parson Jack Russell.'

'And his father?'

'Well, no one knows because his mother ran away from

her owners for a week or so and she'd been knocked up by the time she came back. And when the poor thing had her puppies – four of them – they couldn't cope, so the whole lot, mother and all, were taken in by one of their friends. And when the puppies became too much for *him*, he passed them all on to the animal rescue centre.'

'Great. Marvellous.' Suddenly my self-control left me and I blurted out, 'I don't know . . . A runaway teenager for a mother . . . father unknown . . . three homes in less than three months . . . That's not a good start in life, Hannah. Are you sure about this?'

'Oh, yes. I've fallen in love with Billy and, as I said, I've asked the people at Many Tears to reserve him for me. I don't want anyone else to snap him up. I can't have him for a few days yet, though, because apparently he's being looked after by someone in Swindon and I've got to go and collect him from there. And, of course, the rescue centre wants to vet me first.'

'Vet you?' I glanced at George's paw, which was only just out of bandages. 'I hope they don't charge you a thousand pounds for the privilege.'

'Home-vet me. You know, send someone round to make sure I'm not Cruella de Vil. That I'm a suitable dog owner who lives in a dog-friendly place, and that I can afford to look after Billy. You don't pay for that, only for the puppy – that is, if everything's okay and they allow you to have it.'

'How much?' I asked.

'A hundred and sixty pounds.'

'That seems rather a lot to pay for a mutt.'

'He's not a mutt, he's a crossbreed! And he's beautiful!

And they've had to look after him – they've castrated him and microchipped him and given him his shots. Many Tears is a small family-run refuge, Judith, not a famous place like Battersea Dogs Home. They've got to keep going somehow. Look, do go online when you have time and check out Billy's photo. I'd love to know what you think of him.'

I did feel anxious for Hannah. On the strength of seeing a snapshot on the Internet she was about to enter into what might be a fifteen-year relationship with a crossbreed puppy of dubious origin that she'd never even seen in the flesh. What was she *thinking*?

I hoped she wasn't destined to be as disappointed by the reality of Billy as I'd been by a couple of online dates I'd gone on some years before. At least on Internet dating sites, like match.com, you could arrange to meet the supposed new love of your life before you made a long-term commitment to him. You could flinch at his bad breath, if he had it, measure the extra inches his Cuban heels added to his diminutive stature, and see the true extent of his thinning hair. You could even ask him a few pertinent questions. How long is your criminal record? Do you prefer sleeping on the left-hand side of the bed or, God forbid, the right, which is *my* side? Which of these alternatives appeals to you most: a night of S&M or – my preference – a day in M&S? Whereas on the equivalent canine website – mutt.com, I suppose you could call it – you arranged to adopt a rescue dog sight unseen, with no idea whether it was housetrained or enjoyed playing ball, or what it was going to look like when it grew up. You didn't even know what its ears felt like to stroke, and you'd never once heard it bark.

If Billy turned out to be Hannah's dream dog, well and good. If, on the other hand, he was an unhealthy little specimen who got sick and died after a few weeks, or he grew up to be an aggressive monster, I'd feel terrible for having played a part in helping her find him.

I immediately Googled Many Tears to check its credentials. I had to admit that the website was pretty impressive. The home page explained that Many Tears Animal Rescue was a small organization based in Carmarthenshire, run by a married couple named Sylvia and Bill VanAtta. Apparently they took in dogs from various different sources, including strays from dog pounds that were on Death Row because no one had claimed them, dogs whose owners were no longer able to keep them and, for the most part, ex-breeding dogs.

Ex-breeding dogs? Until recently I'd naïvely thought that all dog breeders were reputable people who cared deeply about their animals, people like Mrs Coleman, from whom I'd bought George. Cavaliers weren't Mrs Coleman's livelihood, they were her passion. The village house near Henley where she and her husband lived was decorated with a plethora of Cavalieriana – everything, from the cushions to the door handles, had pictures of Cavaliers on it, and there were paintings of them on every wall. A twenty-five strong pack of glossy Cavaliers lived in the house with the Colemans, and had free romp of a spotless living room, an equally spotless kitchen and a pretty, well-kept cottage garden. As dogs' lives went, theirs were just about perfect.

When Mrs Coleman's bitches gave birth they were temporarily separated from the glorious, gregarious, gleaming pack and taken upstairs to a quiet bedroom, where they were treated like princesses in a luxurious private maternity hospital. Stretched out on extra-soft bedding, they were given extra food while they were feeding their pups, kept extra warm, given lashings of extra love and encouragement, and made an extra-special fuss of (mind you, the Colemans made so much fuss of all their dogs at all times that this was scarcely possible).

To me, the Colemans represented all that was best about pedigree-dog breeders. However, I'd recently watched a couple of television documentaries that had opened my eyes to a different side of the dog-breeding industry. It consisted of so-called 'puppy farms', or 'puppy mills', as they're called in the United States, run by people who bred dogs for one reason alone: to make as much money as possible out of them. In their view dogs weren't pets, they were commercial commodities, cash-cows that they'd milk for all they were worth.

Actually, these people weren't so much dog *breeders* as irresponsible factory farmers who didn't give a stuff about the welfare of their animals. Their breeding bitches and stud dogs were treated with less respect than machines on a production line. Sometimes they spent their entire lives locked up in small, concrete-floored kennels or even in cages or crates where they were unable to exercise at all. Overcrowding was rife: in Ireland, where the laws governing dog breeding had always been extremely lax, one puppy farm was suspected of producing *five thousand* puppies in a year, another of having *seven hundred* breeding bitches on the premises. Seven hundred bitches, all having puppies? The mind boggled. How could anyone look after all those animals, even with the best will in the world?

In these substandard, often cruel conditions, breeding bitches were forced to mate and then give birth to litter after litter with no thought as to their health. Filthy drinking water, contaminated food, fetid, cramped accommodation, little or no bedding, solitary confinement in crates, violence and neglect, lice, fleas and diseases, no regular veterinary care, no contact with any humans other than the ones who doled out their food pellets once a day, often throwing them straight on the filthy ground among the dogs' faeces ... The list of the appalling conditions some of these factory-farmed creatures had to endure went on and on. Yet despite the paucity of care they received, their puppies were often sold on for hundreds of pounds each, either in small pet shops, through free newspapers or via the internet (according to recent Kennel Club figures, a third of puppies bought in the UK change hands this way).

The unsuspecting members of the public who bought them – sometimes collecting them from their breeders in back-streets or anonymous car parks – thought that they were getting a bargain, because these so-called pedigree puppies were often a little cheaper than those from reputable breeders. They had no idea what horrific conditions their puppies had been reared in, or that the pedigree and vaccination certificates that came with them weren't worth the paper they were written on. Neither did they suspect that the cute little balls of fluff they took home with them might be severely malnourished and/or suffering from, among other infections, mange, pneumonia, eye disease and serious or even life-threatening gastrointestinal viruses, such as parvovirus or campylobacter, which are communicable to humans.

As for the sires and dams of these puppies, when, after years of abuse and exploitation, they could no longer mate or produce litters, they were discarded like useless dish-rags. Often they were shot or drowned. If they were extremely lucky they'd be handed over to an animal refuge, who'd find them a proper home.

I'm not an animal-rights activist, but watching those documentaries had left me shocked and sickened that, in this day and age and in our supposedly dog-loving country, such dreadful puppy farms were allowed to exist at all. Yet there were hundreds and hundreds of these places, some licensed by local authorities, others unlicensed but still tacitly allowed to operate. It was disgraceful. You wouldn't be allowed to keep battery chickens in such awful conditions so why dogs?

Did the ex-breeding dogs that ended up at Many Tears originate from puppy farms, from reputable breeders, or from both? I couldn't tell. Any dog in distress, from whatever background, was obviously worth saving in their eyes. Their website simply went on to explain that, 'With the help of our staff and volunteers we provide a special and loving environment to help all our animals adapt and find permanent, loving new homes. All our dogs and cats are spayed/neutered, microchipped, inoculated and wormed and our dogs are also kennel-cough vaccinated. All potential adopters are interviewed and homes vetted.' It sounded very efficient and well organized.

In search of Billy, I clicked on a link to 'Dogs Looking for Homes' and scrolled down past a few notices, one announcing a fund-raising raffle, another appealing for donations to keep the rescue centre on its feet – or should

I say paws? Then I came to the photographs of dogs. The first was an overweight, elderly black Labrador that was slumped on the ground. A pair of wide-spaced dark eyes, sad and dejected, stared out at me from its grizzled face. The description underneath read:

Katy is a simply beautiful, faithful twelve-year-old Lab. Her mistress has gone into a care home, and Katy is lost without her. No one in the family could have her so she was sent to the local pound. When her time was up she was due to be put down. Then an angel rescued her and brought her to us. Katy doesn't understand why she's here and she's feeling frightened and very confused at the moment. We think she's housetrained, and she walks well on a lead. She's sharing a kennel with a couple of Chows without any difficulty, though she hasn't shown much interest in playing with them so far. She's good with children and just wants a quiet, loving home where she can see out her days.

Poor old Katy. I really felt for her. To my surprise I even found myself wondering if I should take her in. But hang on! Another dog was the last thing I needed!

The next photograph was of a West Highland White Terrier, with a thin, patchy coat and small, sore-looking eyes:

Bobbie is a very sweet five-year-old ex-stud Westie. He came in with infected ears and ingrown eyelashes, which have since been operated on. Now he can see and hear again. His skin is still very sore and he's lost a lot of hair.

He's had little contact with people during his life, and at the moment he's so scared that he won't give eye contact. He's never learned to walk on a lead and he's not lived in a home before so he will need another dog to help him learn the ropes. Please only apply to adopt him if you already have a kind and gentle dog living in the house.

A kind and gentle dog? George certainly had both those qualities, I mused – when he wasn't being wilful or prancing around Hampstead as if he was expecting to be recognized by adoring fans . . . I scrolled further down the page to a photograph of a petite cream-coloured mutt with a pointed face and sticking-up ears somewhat like a Corgi. It had a short stubby tail, even shorter bandy legs and large paws that pointed outwards, like a little girl taking second position in ballet class. 'Shelley is a five-year-old crossbreed. She's very emaciated and extremely scared of people. She's spent most of her life chained to a pole in a dark, unheated shed and because of this she has a bad neck injury which we're treating . . .'

Suddenly I felt outraged. I tried to imagine what kind of person would acquire a dog only to keep it chained to a pole in a shed. How could anyone do such a thing? And why would they want to? It was beyond me. Dogs are by nature pack animals, so what had it been like for poor Shelley, imprisoned alone in the dark, in constant pain from something cutting into her neck? What torture for her!

Holding back tears, I glanced at my own pooch, now snoozing contentedly on a fleecy throw on the day-bed in my study, his head nestled comfortably against an old cushion with the words *Dog Lover* embroidered on it.

George had never known a moment's pain or unkindness, thank goodness. The gulf between his existence and poor Shelley's was as vast as that between a pampered eighteenth-century monarch – King George I, for example – and some condemned prisoner shackled to a wall in the depths of Newgate gaol.

Feeling sick, I skimmed down the rest of the page in search of Billy, trying not to look at the other rescue dogs' faces or to take in their details – they were too awful. But I kept catching snippets of their histories. *Found soaking wet and starving, wandering on a mountain pass . . . unwanted by her breeder because she can no longer get into pup . . . lost all his hair through mange . . . burned repeatedly with acid . . . rescued with a horrific open wound on his front leg . . . saved on his last day at an Irish pound . . . used as a football . . . thrown away in a plastic bag . . . has never lived in a home or had any contact with people . . . scared . . . terrified . . . malnourished . . .*

On and on went the list of dogs and the awful wrongs that had been done to them by my fellow humans. No wonder they called the rescue centre Many Tears: by now I couldn't stop mine rolling down my cheeks. There must have been around sixty of the poor dogs, and I could only wonder at what it cost the rescue centre in money, time and effort to feed and care for them – and at their optimism in believing they'd be able to find homes for all of them.

At last I came to Billy's photograph. The cheerful foxy face of a Jack Russell peered out at me, and I wiped my tears away. Unlike many of the other dogs, who appeared somewhat shell-shocked by the bad experiences they'd been through, Billy looked happy, well cared-for and bright as a button. Here was a young pup who obviously *hadn't* been mistreated in his short life. No wonder Hannah had fallen for him. He was lovely.

I immediately texted her.

Billy gets Wicked Stepmother Seal of Approval.
Good luck with the home vetting!

Much as I prized my pedigree Cavalier, I had to admit that Hannah was doing a wonderful thing by adopting a rescue crossbreed. I was almost tempted to take one on myself.

After that, I closed down the Internet page, and attempted to get back to writing my novel. But I couldn't put my mind to it. Instead I kept finding myself clicking back on to the Many Tears website and scrolling up and down it, soaking up as I did so the histories of exhausted Cocker Spaniel bitches, bouncy Fox Terriers, bewildered mutts and sad-faced Chows.

Then, at the very bottom of the webpage, I suddenly spotted a face that transfixed me. Not only was it grinning out at me inanely, it was stuck onto the oddest-looking creature imaginable. And suddenly I couldn't stop smiling.

She had the head of a Retriever and the big floppy ears of a Bull Mastiff – only they were curly, like a Spaniel's. She was the height of a giant French Poodle, her muscular middle section was speckled black and brown, like a Staffordshire Bull Terrier's, and her hindquarters were pure Boxer, except that she had a hairy tail like an Afghan Hound's. All four of her legs, which were longer than a Greyhound's, ended in big white paws with uneven mark-ings, which made her look like an unruly four-legged schoolgirl wearing odd tennis socks, three of which were falling down.

Her name was Vera. As for her breed . . . I suppose you could have called her a Retroxer or a Bullstaffie. A Spanafghan or a Boxhound. There was actually a touch of sheepdog in her face, too, so maybe she was a Border Coxterrier, or even a Mastiffoodle. To put it another way, Vera was a veritable Heinz 57 of breeds, and the nearest thing imaginable to a pedigree mutt. I'd never seen a dog like her before. And whoever had written her description on the website had come to the same conclusion:

Do you want a dog that no one else has one like? A unique-looking, friendly dog that everyone will want to know her breed? Do you want to have a friend who will look up to you, forgive your bad moods, worship and adore you? Then look no further – here is Vera. Vera is 3 years old and has a boxer's love disguised in an intriguing wrapper! Just a wonderful dog!

I sighed. This unique, wonderful dog deserved a unique and wonderful home, one in which she'd be loved and appreciated and well looked after. Ideally by someone with a lot of time on their hands and a lot of love to give.

Someone, for example, with an empty nest to fill.

In return, Vera would undoubtedly flourish and become a loyal, loving and well-behaved pet, just like Jupiter, that Weimaraner I'd met on Hampstead Heath.

No, I told myself. What was I thinking? I couldn't possible afford another set of vet's bills and pet insurance. I could scarcely pay George's.

Just then George woke up from his long siesta on the

day-bed, gave himself a small shake and inched to the edge of the mattress where he hung his front paws over the edge and set about reminding me that it was time for his supper. No matter that it was only half past four in the afternoon, King George was hungry. He wanted his supper, and he wanted it straight away. I did my best to ignore him, but he kept up the noisy volley of barking until it was hammering through my head, just as it had during the bad old Zach nights.

Suddenly something snapped inside me. I scooped him up and plonked him on my lap. 'George, don't you realize how spoiled and privileged you are?' I said to him as I pointed his head at the monitor. 'Look at these pictures! Dogs like Vera, here, and all these others, they have no one to love them. No one to wait on them hand and foot! No one! Some of them have been kept in terrible conditions all their lives and others are strays who've had to fend for themselves. If and when they're lucky enough to find a home and someone to love them, they're not demanding and spoiled and yappy like you are, they're incredibly grateful for everything they receive. Grateful!' In case he hadn't understood, I spelled the word out for him.

Totally uninterested in my rant, George slid down from my lap, sat on the floor, fixed me with his headlamp eyes and started barking again.

Still thinking of Vera, I gave in, went upstairs and fed him. It was true what they said – you couldn't teach an old dog new tricks.

However, you might just be able to teach a *new* dog that not everyone in the world was evil.

I simply couldn't get Vera out of my mind.

7

'Hi. What are you doing here so early?'

When my sister Sue opened her front door the following morning, George hurled himself over the threshold and dived for the stairs down to the kitchen. Since he associated her house with human food, which she always fed him in generous amounts, he was ecstatic at being taken there so soon after finishing his breakfast.

'Sue . . .' I began.

'Is something wrong?'

'No. But. . .'

'It's not even seven thirty!' My sister tossed back her glossy black hair and gathered the folds of her long red dressing-gown around her; how she managed to look so well groomed and glam when she'd just got out of bed I'd never know. 'What do you want?'

'Nothing. Well, just for you to look after George today,' I said, as casually as I could. But I knew very well that, a journalist by training, Sue wasn't going to be content with this minimal amount of information.

'Why?' she prodded.

'I'm going out for a bit.'

'Obviously. But where to?'

'Um, South Wales, actually.'

Her mouth fell open. 'No one goes "out for a bit" to South Wales. It's miles away! What are you going to *do* there?'

'Well . . . The thing is, I've found this animal rescue centre outside Swansea and . . . You see, the idea came to me last night . . . I'm going to visit it. Um, there's this funny-looking rescue dog there that I just might want to adopt.'

Predictably, she was horrified. 'Have you gone *mad*? *Another* dog? You can only just cope with the one you've got!' Before I could protest at how easy George had become lately, the sound of manic barking issued from the basement where he'd no doubt taken up his usual position, which was next to her oven and in front of her fridge. 'And what about George?' Sue went on protectively. 'He's used to being an only dog. He won't like having a rival in the house!'

'Actually, it's partly for him that I'm thinking of getting another dog. Now that Joshua's not there I think he'd really appreciate having a companion at home. Preferably one who's less spoiled than he is.'

Sue sighed in the disapproving way she'd perfected at the age of ten for dealing with me, her younger sibling. 'If George is spoiled who's to blame for that? And you know what'll happen – you'll just end up with two spoiled dogs! Anyway, if you must rescue a dog why go all the way to South Wales to get it? Couldn't you find one at Battersea Dogs Home? Surely there must be some that need rescuing in London.'

It was a reasonable question, but I had no time to explain about the Many Tears website and how I'd fallen in love with Vera's photograph on it, and how I hadn't been able to sleep all night for worrying about her, and I didn't think that Sue would have understood if I had. So I merely said I'd be back later – or, at the latest, the following morning

– and thanks for volunteering to have George ('I didn't,' she retorted). And before she could dissuade me from my impetuous mission I jumped back into my car and sped off.

According to the Internet route planner I'd consulted before I'd left home, the village where Many Tears was situated was 202 miles down the M4, and the journey would take me precisely three hours and fifty-six minutes. But given the rain and the terrible traffic, not to mention a pit stop at a service station outside Bristol to sip a cup of indeterminate warm brown liquid and gnaw on what I can only describe as a Scone of Stone, it took me nearer five hours to get there. I didn't need sat nav to tell me that I'd arrived at the right place: I only had to open the car window and listen to the barking.

I parked beside a paddock containing three small ponies, walked past a pretty white cottage that bore a sign saying 'Cawdor Kennels', went through a wrought-iron gate and entered a labyrinth of small buildings and dog kennels. As I passed, dogs of all sizes and shapes jumped up at the wire-mesh walls of their runs, barking at me as if they were desperate to be noticed. 'Choose me!' they seemed to be saying. Each one wore a winning expression, and I wanted to take them all home with me.

At last I came to a reception office. Organized chaos reigned within. Phones rang, kettles boiled, and half a dozen people seemed to be talking at once. In addition, mutts in all shapes and sizes were milling around behind the counter, curled up on table-tops, under desks or in the dog-beds that were squeezed into every free corner. It turned out that most of the staff at Many Tears had adopted rescue dogs, and they were allowed to bring them in to work.

I don't think I've ever seen such a busy office, or met such good-natured people. Mounds of paperwork were piled up on the desks and tables, the telephone didn't stop ringing with people enquiring about dogs they'd seen on the website, volunteering to help or reporting strays they'd found, and a slow but steady stream of visitors trickled in behind me. Most, like me, were wanting to adopt dogs, but others were distraught because they could no longer cope with their own pet's behaviour or simply didn't have the time or money to look after it and they needed to hand it in to be rehomed. Where there was a spare inch on a table-top it was being used as a perch by a member of staff trying to snatch a sandwich or a bag of crisps on the hoof.

Yet, despite the pressure they were obviously working under, and the cramped conditions (there was a kitchenette on one side, bunk beds for visitors in the back office, and animals underfoot everywhere), everyone seemed incredibly cheerful and happy. If they'd had tails I swear they'd have been wagging them.

The office work was just the start because the main business of the day was rescuing and caring for the dogs, along with a handful of cats and horses.

'About four or five days a week, Sylvia, who's the owner here, or I go out in our van and do the rounds of the local dog pounds and breeders,' James, the enthusiastic thirty-year-old kennel manager, explained to me, as he tossed his dark brown hair out of his eyes and flashed me a grin. 'We collect all kinds of dogs, strays that are destined to be put down because no one's claimed them and breeding dogs that, for some reason or other, are no longer considered fit for purpose and are given to us to rehome. Occasionally we get handed a puppy that's either not healthy enough to sell through the usual channels, or too old for that.' Once every three weeks or so, he or Sylvia even did an exhausting thirty-six-hour round-trip to the Irish Republic, where the dog pounds were only obliged to keep strays for five days before euthanizing them, with the result that around ten thousand dogs were put down there every year.

That morning Sylvia had driven around Carmarthenshire collecting dogs, and as she was due to return any minute, I followed James back up to the road to take a look at the new arrivals.

A big white Transit van had just pulled up outside. Dressed in old black trousers and a sweatshirt covered with dog hair, Sylvia still managed to look pretty, but she seemed exhausted and preoccupied as she climbed down from behind the wheel. She greeted me, then handed James the keys to the van and disappeared into the small cottage at the front of the property where she and her husband lived.

James slid open the side door of the van. Inside there were pet crates, three tiers high, bolted securely together to form a wall of cages. One look at the occupants made me realize why Sylvia had seemed so stressed.

Nearly all of the dogs in the crates were in a terrible condition. They bore as much resemblance to the beloved pets I was used to seeing on Hampstead Heath as a sick old battery hen would to a prize free-range organically reared cockerel. Not a tail wagged. Not a single bark or whimper issued from any muzzle. It was heartbreaking.

On the lower tier, a fully grown Dalmatian with scars

all over his muzzle trembled with fear. Next to him, an emaciated bearded collie cowered at the back of her cage. In the tier above I saw a couple of West Highland White Terriers, their dingy cream coats so matted that you couldn't see their faces. From another crate an old Cocker Spaniel stared at me blankly through infected eyes, while beside him a tiny Yorkshire Terrier slumped silently in its cage, its head between paws that were pink and raw. There were some skinny crossbreeds, too, that looked as if they hadn't eaten for weeks, and a mangy Chow that was shaking with fright.

James undid the catch on one of the crates and carefully lifted out the Westie inside it. She had a sagging belly, from which hung huge sore teats – a sign that, young as she was, she was an ex-breeding bitch that had given birth to and suckled countless litters.

'Are the dogs you get always in such a bad state as this one?' I asked.

'No, not always, but quite often.' James put her gently over his shoulder and climbed down from the van. 'Some have been so neglected that their claws are growing into their footpads, or their eyelashes into their eyes.' Many were infested with fleas, he said, and others were suffering from advanced tumours or had such sore skin that their coats had fallen out. And quite a few of the dogs had had so little contact with people during their lives that they were terrified of them.

No matter what state a dog arrived in, though, if it was humanly possible the Many Tears team would nurse it back to health and find it a home. Blind dogs, deaf dogs, three-legged dogs, dogs with digestive problems, dogs with malignant tumours or congenital problems – there was always some kind soul who'd take them in. Very few were deemed too sick, too traumatized or too disabled to be rehabilitated.

Leaving the other new arrivals on the van – for safety reasons the dogs were always unloaded one at a time – James carried the Westie to the office where she was given a name, Nona, and booked in. Then, like all new arrivals, she was taken straight to a cramped bathroom at the back of the building for a quick makeover. Gently but firmly, Rebecca, a volunteer, put Nona into a bath and shampooed and rinsed her. After wrapping Nona in a towel, she stood her on a small table and slowly combed her patchy coat, carefully and patiently cutting out the worst of the tangles with a pair of scissors. To my amazement, Nona submitted to the whole process – then to being inoculated and microchipped – without a single growl, snarl or yelp of protest, even though she was quivering with terror because of the unaccustomed things that were happening to her. Some of the dogs the rescue centre took in would only rarely have been handled by a human before. Still, Rebecca insisted, they rarely bit the kennel staff: 'If you're gentle with them, they're gentle with you. Actually, they're more scared of people than aggressive towards them.'

After Nona had been dried with a hairdryer, Rebecca let me carry the little bitch outside, where James took her photograph as I held her rigid body in my arms. Within an hour or two, her portrait and description would be placed on the website alongside those of the other dogs at the centre, and she, too, would be up for adoption. It was mostly through the website that Sylvia succeeded in finding homes for all her rescue animals. If a dog or a bitch was hard to place, the centre would keep it for as long as it took, whether that was months or years.

I asked James why Nona was being carried everywhere. Couldn't he put a leash on her and let her walk? 'The trouble is, many ex-breeding dogs have no idea *how* to walk on a leash,' he told me.

'What do you mean?'

'They've never been leash-trained, or even taken for a walk. But let's see what happens with her.'

I put Nona on the ground, and she stood exactly where she was while he looped a collar around her neck and attached a leash. The moment he tried to walk her, though, she immediately changed from a mild little dog into a furious bucking bronco, kicking her hindquarters in the air, arching her back and twisting her neck. When James removed the collar and picked her up, she immediately calmed down.

After her photo-call it was time for Nona to be checked over by Chris, the vet who worked part-time in the rescue centre's well-equipped but simple Portakabin surgery. If she was ill, she'd be prescribed medicines, and if she needed spaying she'd be booked in for an op. Then Nona would be taken through to one of the centre's roomy kennels, where she'd live with two or three other dogs until she was adopted – or found a 'for-ever home', as the staff liked to call it. 'You might as well come with me again,' James said. 'Then I can show you Vera. She's the one you're interested in adopting, isn't she?'

We dropped Nona at the surgery, then went through so many bolted gates, fenced-in courtyards and grey wire runs that the place began to look rather like Guantánamo. However, there the resemblance to the notorious detention camp ended. For the dogs at Many Tears, the rescue centre was anything but a prison: a little bewildering, and even scary to nervous newcomers, perhaps, but after the appalling conditions that many had endured before they'd arrived, it was the nearest thing to heaven they'd ever known. They had plenty to eat, exercise yards to run around in, warm, comfortable sleeping quarters and friends to play with. The staff treated them with more love and respect than many had experienced before.

As far as I could see, there was only one other thing that these dogs needed in order to be perfectly content: a human of their own to love, who'd love them back and take care of them. Although the odd frightened dog shrank into the shadows as we passed, most bounded towards us and scrabbled at the wire-mesh walls of their kennels, clamouring for our attention. Collies, crossbreeds, Chows, Border Terriers, a Yorkie, a huge German Shepherd and, of course, Staffordshire Bull Terriers – nowadays the sixth most popular breed in Britain, as well as the one most likely to be abandoned and turn up in rescue centres.

Some dogs I recognized from their photographs on the website, including Katy, the elderly black Labrador, no longer sad but wagging her tail as she played with a couple of Jack Russells in her kennel, one of which was Shelley, who'd been chained to a pole in a shed. Though many must have been on the receiving end of cruelty in the past, so strong was their age-old bond with humans that they still craved the attention of the very species that had once mistreated them. It was the triumph of instinct over experience.

As we passed along the blocks, the dogs in the runs grew ever more excitable and their barking fiercer. I began to feel somewhat apprehensive.

'Here she is!'

James stopped beside a covered outdoor run in which there were three dogs: a black-and-white Staffie cross built like a wrestling champion, a Foxhound the size of a Great Dane, with the thick woolly coat of a stuffed toy, and – exactly like her photograph on the website, only an awful lot bigger than I'd imagined – Vera, the most comical-looking dog I'd ever seen. My mind boggled when I thought of the chains of genetic couplings that must have taken place to produce a specimen with her long legs, stocky body, hairy tail, curly ears and erratic coat markings; by the look of her, she was an A–Z of breeds, part everything from the Affenpinscher to the Zuchon, the fancy new name for a Bichon/Shih Tzu cross.

Vera and the Staffie, whose name was Blossom, had both come from a pound, James told me, while the giant Foxhound had been picked up as a stray in the Welsh mountains, which might have accounted for his wild temperament: imagine an ancient Celtic warrior crossed with a celebrity footballer out clubbing on a Saturday night and you just about have it. Muddle, as he'd been aptly named by the rescue staff, was beautiful to look at and glorious fun, but he was also anarchic and totally undisciplined. Everyone adored him, but he was proving extremely difficult to rehome. Taken away by one potential owner, who'd obviously relished a challenge, he'd been returned after only two days because he wouldn't settle; he'd been at Many Tears ever since. He and Blossom were the longest-standing residents. Both dogs had been with them for months and months, and unless the staff managed to instil a few manners in them, they might be there for ever.

James tried to open the gate so that I could meet Vera, but by now she, Muddle and Blossom were all battering at it, barking for attention and trying to embrace us through the wire mesh. On his hind legs, the big furry giant towered over us, but Vera bounced up and pushed him aside. A moment later Blossom shouldered her way forward and did the same to Vera. In the end James decided to let the three of them out into a large, walled-in exercise yard, where Muddle and Blossom chased each other in big circles, while Vera leaped up at me boisterously, nearly sending me flying.

Clearly none of these dogs was for the faint-hearted, and my heart was growing fainter by the second. Vera was adorable – desperate for love, and as irrepressibly energetic as an overgrown puppy – but when I tried to imagine sharing my home with her I could only succeed in summoning up visions of chaos in the house, not to mention a squashed-flat Cavalier. My heart sank. It had taken me five hours to drive to Wales to see her, and less than five minutes to realize that, endearing and needy through she was – the over-exuberant mutt to beat all mutts – Vera was not the right dog for me. Neither I nor George would be able to handle her.

So much for falling in love on an Internet website. Why had I been so impulsive? Still, now that I was actually in the frame of mind to get a companion for George, there were scores of other contenders on the premises to choose from. Dogs such as the stunningly handsome Muddle, who now came lolloping towards me and, without so much as a how-do-you-do, shoved his outsize nose into my crotch. When I eventually managed to push him away he galloped off and flung himself at Blossom in what looked like a vicious attack but was in reality a game. As the two snarled happily at each other, I quickly changed my mind about him, too. Magnificent he might be, but neither George nor I would be able to cope with him either. I couldn't imagine who would, other than a professional dog trainer.

James had already got my measure. 'Perhaps you'd like to have a look at some of our smaller dogs?' he suggested as, arms raised in surrender, I backed away from the over-enthusiastic trio who were all circling me at once. 'A little one might suit you better.'

While he got on with mucking out one of the kennels, all of which were hosed down twice a day, James allowed me to wander round the centre looking at the other dogs – there must have been about fifty. In the next hour I befriended yapping Yorkies, a Basset/Irish Setter cross, a Pekinese and mutts galore. I was slobbered over by a St Bernard, almost shat upon by a Shih Tzu, who became over-excited to see me, and actually peed on by an over-enthusiastic Collie-cross pup that I made the mistake of picking up.

Smelling like a latrine, and covered with hair and drool, I bumped into Sylvia who, after snatching a makeshift meal on the run (a packet of crisps and a chocolate bar were all she'd had time for) was looking revived and was now on her way to the veterinary surgery to check on some Spaniel puppies that had come in the day before. I tagged along with her.

Rescuing animals, and in particular dogs, had been her obsession for as long as she could remember, Sylvia told me. At the age of two she was running an imaginary rescue centre for a pack of invisible dogs from her parents' house in Bromley, Kent, and would disappear down the road in pursuit of any real dog that happened to pass by. Worried that she'd get run over, her parents had bought her a Corgi, Kim. All went well until five-year-old Sylvia, who by now wanted to be a show-jumper, set up a series of hurdles and attempted to train Kim to jump them. Understandably, Kim refused – her short legs weren't exactly built for jumping – and from that point on, their relationship went downhill.

This didn't put paid to Sylvia's determination to work with dogs, and when she left school at fifteen and got a job, she used her first pay packet to buy herself another. When Chance, as she called him, was run over by a lorry and killed, Sylvia acquired a third dog, this time from Battersea Dogs Home. By then she also owned a Shetland pony named Lass: instead of asking her parents if she could have one, as other children might have done, she'd found a five-month-old pony she wanted, then dragged her father along to see it. Though he could ill afford it, her father bargained with the horse trader, a deal was done on the spot and Lass travelled home in the back of the family's Wolseley car with her head sticking out of the window, in true Thelwell-cartoon style.

Sylvia treated Lass as if she *were* a dog. Against her parents' wishes, she brought her into the house (having first put her own school socks on the pony's hoofs, so that she wouldn't leave a trail of hoof-marks behind her) and she even took her shopping on a leash. Tethered up outside Marks & Sparks in Bromley High Street while her thirteen-year-old owner went inside to buy her first bra, the diminutive Shetland pony attracted a big crowd of admirers who wanted to know what on earth she was doing there. When Sylvia came out, Lass compounded matters by snatching the carrier bag from her hands, shaking the bra out of it and chewing it up in front of everyone. It was a mortifying experience.

Owning pets was fun, but it wasn't enough for Sylvia. In 1983 she founded Brook Cottage Animal Rescue. In 1986 she built and opened a second rescue centre, in Edenbridge, Kent, which she named Last Chance Animal Rescue after her beloved second dog. Then, after helping set up a third animal rescue, this time in Israel, she moved to the United States when she ran yet another rescue centre, in Tucson, Arizona.

It was there that, in 1999, she met Bill VanAtta, a tall, gentle, baseball-cap-wearing Arizonan, at a ranch where they were both staying for the weekend. Though they liked each other instantly, Sylvia had her rescue work and Bill had his business, manufacturing synthetic marble for bathrooms – two seemingly irreconcilable worlds – so they parted company and went their separate ways. But not for long.

They married during the millennium year, and soon afterwards Sylvia began testing her new husband's tolerance by acquiring dogs – lots of them. Bill not only stood the course, he was won over to her way of thinking. He sold his business, and the couple took a job together running a so-called 'humane' animal refuge in North Carolina.

To their horror, when they arrived at the place they discovered that many of the unwanted animals were taken away to be destroyed, and that the methods by which the condemned were dispatched were not nearly as humane as the refuge's name had led them to believe: puppies and kittens were strangled, cats drowned and the dogs shot.

It was to prevent these animals from suffering more than necessary when they were put down that Sylvia learned to administer painless lethal injections. Years later, she still found it hard to forgive herself for this, for it went against every principle she held. However, while they were in North Carolina she and Bill also managed to save literally hundreds of dogs and cats, whose time at the pound was up, by driving them, sometimes vast distances, to other refuges that operated no-kill policies.

After ten months they came to the conclusion that they could no longer continue putting down healthy animals: it was just too distressing. Having persuaded the rescue to change its euthanizing policy, in 2003 they took the life-changing decision to return to Britain and set up a combined animal rescue centre and boarding kennels.

Crossing the Atlantic wasn't a simple task: by this time the VanAttas had acquired fifteen dogs of their own (including two wolf crosses), four cats and two horses, and had no intention of leaving anyone behind. It cost more than £25,000 to get them all inoculated, issued with pet passports and transported to England. This was a huge chunk of their savings at a time when the dollar–pound exchange rate was definitely not in their favour. After searching long and hard for the perfect premises, during which time they and their menagerie all lived together in one large horsebox – yes, humans, dogs, cats and even horses – they heard about some boarding kennels for sale in South Wales. On paper the premises looked perfect, and since they'd already been gazumped on several other properties (the market was sky-rocketing at the time), they went ahead and bought it sight unseen.

Sylvia was the first to visit the place. 'It was an absolute hole, really dirty and nasty,' Bill told me later. 'She rang me up in tears and said, "What have we done?"' But by then the contracts had been exchanged so there was no backing out of the deal. The VanAttas had to make the best of it.

It took them five years, most of Bill's retirement fund and an immense amount of hard work to transform what had been a ramshackle series of run-down buildings into decent kennels. It was typical of their dedication that, while nearly everything else on site was now finished, the cottage where they lived was still being modernized. The animals definitely came first.

Keeping the rescue centre going was an even more expensive business than setting it up, even though a local dog-food firm generously donated food. In order to make ends meet, Sylvia and Bill ran the small boarding kennels I'd seen at the front of the property. However, this made it complicated to register the rescue as a proper charity; instead, it had to be a not-for-profit business that relied on donations, adoption fees and money raised by a dedicated Friends organization to keep going. Veterinary bills were huge (couldn't I just imagine it!) because all the dogs that needed it were spayed, inoculated, microchipped and wormed when they were brought in. If they were sick, undernourished or injured, as many were, the vet might need to X-ray them, send off tests to laboratories, perform operations and/or prescribe drugs. Since the kennels were all heated in winter, and the dogs' bedding needed washing, as did the dogs when they arrived at and left the centre, the electricity bills were enormous. So were vehicle and transportation costs.

Sylvia's highest costs, however, were the staff's salaries. She firmly believed that exercise and attention were an integral part of the animals' rehabilitation; it wasn't enough just to feed them, and keep them warm, dry and clean. Consequently she employed eight full-time helpers who ranged from kennel manager James to Lisa, who ran the office. And, as I'd seen for myself, they were all working at full stretch.

By now Sylvia and I had reached the Portakabin that housed the veterinary surgery. Chris was in the small theatre, operating on some ten-week-old Cocker Spaniel pups who'd arrived at the rescue the day before with their mother, an ex-breeding bitch. Goldie, the male pup, was suffering from trichiasis, in-growing eyelashes that caused a great deal of irritation and pain and could eventually lead to blindness, while his tiny sisters, Lala and Laura, had heart defects, which had meant they couldn't be sold through the usual commercial channels. Chris had just neutered Laura, who was lying in a small cosy recovery cage while she came round from the anaesthetic. She'd just woken up, and Lala, who'd had the same op an hour earlier, was now trampling all over her. While Sylvia prepared another cage in which Laura could come round in peace and quiet, she allowed me to hold Lala.

'Oh, she's gorgeous!' I sighed as the floppy-eared bundle

of golden fur first licked my face, then snuggled under my chin. So far I'd avoided falling in love with any of the dogs, but this time I was smitten. 'Can I adopt her?'

'I'm afraid she's already been reserved,' Sylvia told me. 'She *is* lovely, isn't she? But you should see her mother – the poor darling's got the most horrible skin complaint.'

With visions of developing scabby patches, hair loss and disfiguring rashes – me, not the puppy – I quickly put Lala back into the recovery cage and ran to the loo, where I scrubbed my hands under a hot tap and scoured my face and neck thoroughly with some strong antiseptic wipes I found there. Still feeling unclean, I returned to the surgery, vowing to be more cautious with the dogs in future and not to get too sentimental.

But a few minutes later I was cuddling another tiny puppy, Mork, who had a big lump on the top of his skull where his cranial plates hadn't fused. Though he probably didn't have long to live, he didn't appear to be in any pain, so Sylvia said she was going to look for a quiet home where he could live out the rest of his days in peace.

And so the afternoon passed, as I fell for one dog after another. By the time I left the rescue centre I was cold and hungry and confused, and it was already dark. Too exhausted to attempt the long drive back to London, I booked into a B-and-B in Swansea, where I threw myself into the shower, then fell gratefully into a lumpy, unevenly sprung bed.

It wasn't the lumps that kept me awake until the small hours but the thoughts that were running through my head. Earlier on, when I'd called Sue to tell her I was staying in Wales overnight, I'd asked after George. Sated with roast chicken and blueberries, for which he'd recently developed a taste, he was apparently curled up in front of the open fire in her living room. Now I kept thinking of him, fast asleep in luxury, then of Vera and the other dogs at Many Tears, and the bad experiences that had brought them there; and finally of the unfortunates still trapped in unlicensed puppy farms or being abused by their owners.

I'd been so impressed with the work Sylvia and her team were doing that I should have felt inspired by it. Instead I felt useless and depressed. I really wanted to help by adopting a dog from them. But I had to be honest with myself: taking on a dog was, as I knew oh-so-well, an expensive business. That apart, there hadn't been one dog at the centre that I'd felt was just right for me – except for Lala, the tiny Spaniel puppy, and she'd already been reserved by a potential adopter. If I was to take on a rescue dog at this point in my life, with all the long-term commitment and problems that it might entail, I knew I'd have to fall for it in the same way I'd fallen for George ten years before.

Besides, there was George to think of as well. He was now an old boy of seventy-plus in dog-to-human-years who liked a quiet, lazy lifestyle and was set in his ways. Landing him with a big, wild, bouncy playmate, such as Vera or Muddle, was out of the question; he'd be terrified of it. If I were to get him a canine companion, I'd have to make sure it was as gentle and laid-back as he was. The idea was to make his life happier, not to upset him.

I'd talked to Sylvia about this earlier, and she'd suggested that I wait for a rescue Cavalier to turn up at the centre, as they did from time to time. On the face of it, this was a great idea. His own was the one breed that George invariably greeted on the Heath with pleasure, running up to any fellow Cavalier King Charles as if he instinctively knew that the bitch or dog with curly ears, fast-wagging tail and soppy expression was a distant cousin, maybe even a half-brother or -sister. Other Cavs greeted him in the same way. I'd always wondered how the breed managed to recognize its own. How did they know what they themselves looked like? By secretly studying their reflection in mirrors, perhaps? Maybe there was a Cavalier equivalent to the Freemasons' secret handshake – three wags to the left, followed by one to the right. Or perhaps they all gave off the same scent – a mixture of bad breath and fuggy ears, if George was anything to go by, not to mention the spectacular farts he was capable of producing, usually at the most inopportune moments, like when he was lying under the kitchen table and we were having dinner.

I'd never know the answer. However many years I had him, I'd never be able to plumb the depths – or were they the shallows? – of George's mind.

'Maybe you should try fostering dogs for a while,' Sylvia had gone on to say. 'That way you can find out whether having another dog around makes George happy.'

Fostering dogs? I'd only ever heard about people fostering children, so it seemed an extraordinary idea to me. Then I remembered that Billy, the puppy Hannah was about to adopt, was currently being fostered by a couple in Swindon. Sylvia explained that the couple were part of a nationwide network of volunteers, most of them already dog-owners, who took in her rescue dogs and looked after them until she managed to find them permanent homes. With the very popular breeds such as Cavaliers, this usually took only a matter of days, but with harder to place dogs, such as Rottweilers, Akitas and some crossbreeds, the process could take months.

While they were looking after them, fosterers taught their foster dogs the skills they'd need when they eventually moved into a permanent home, and their own dogs lent a hand by setting a good example. If the foster dogs had never experienced pet-life before, this usually included housetraining them, teaching them how to walk on a leash and how to socialize with people. Perhaps most important of all, fosterers helped dogs who'd been mistreated in the past to learn to trust humans again.

'Sometimes our carers fall in love with their foster dogs and decide to keep them,' Sylvia had added with a smile. 'We call them failed fosterers!'

'But don't you think George is a little too old to put up with a succession of strange dogs coming and going?' I'd asked.

She'd shrugged. 'Dogs are surprisingly adaptable, Judith. You never know, it might give him a new lease of life.'

The idea of fostering dogs hadn't immediately appealed to me. But as I turned it over in my mind at three o'clock in the morning I suddenly realized it was an inspired idea. If I fostered dogs, George would have a stream of canines to keep him company. Meanwhile, my nest wouldn't feel quite so empty when I had two pets to look after, and a brand new purpose: helping needy dogs on their way to a better life. I'd also be able to enjoy the pleasure of having another dog in the house without making a long-term commitment to it. And if, by any chance, I grew to really love it, I could always become a 'failed fosterer' and keep it.

I sat bolt upright in bed, grinning. My depression had lifted as fast as it had come. Yes, fostering dogs was the perfect solution to all my dilemmas, a way to have my Bonio and eat it, at the same time killing two birds with a handful of mutts.

8

Back in London, I allowed myself a rare phone call to Joshua to tell him I intended to become a canine foster mother.

'A canine foster mother? Doesn't that imply you're a dog?' the university student corrected me. 'Or, rather, a bitch. No offence, Mum. Well, great. But what is it?'

'I'm going to take in poor mistreated dogs – strays and ex-breeding dogs – that don't know one end of a house from another.'

'What do you mean, *dogs*? How many?'

'Just one at a time.'

'Where will you get them from?'

'The same place Hannah's getting her puppy – this animal rescue centre in South Wales.'

'Okay.' He sounded doubtful. 'Do you have to drive all the way there every time you want one?'

'No, no, Many Tears sends a van up the M4 most Sundays on a "foster-run", so all I have to do is choose a dog from the ones on their website. It'll be driven up to Reading and I'll pick it up there.'

'Like ordering stuff online, you mean?'

'No, not quite.'

'Then what happens?'

'Then I'll bring the poor thing home to live with us.'

'What? For ever? I'm not sure that George will like that. Having to share you, I mean.'

'Well, if it makes him unhappy, I'll stop.'

'Promise?' he said suspiciously.

'Of course. Anyway, each dog only stays for a week or two, maybe a month. It depends how long it takes for the rescue centre to find it a permanent home. And actually I think George might like having a friend of his own species around. He must be dreadfully bored all by himself. I'm sure that's why he sleeps so much of the time. When we have a foster dog, he can help it learn all about being a pet and I . . . Well, I'll look after it. Give it lots of TLC. And train and rehabilitate it, too, of course.'

There was a short silence. Then Joshua said, 'But you've never managed to train George properly, and we've had him for ten years!'

Which, oddly enough, was exactly what my sister said when I told her about my new project. It was reassuring to know that everyone had so much confidence in me.

Taking as much care over my answers as Joshua had over filling in his UCAS form the previous year, I completed a detailed fostering application form and sent it back to Many Tears. A week later I received a call from a woman named Amanda, who said that she was a home-vetter for the centre and that, if it was convenient, she'd like to come round that afternoon to meet me, inspect my flat and check whether I was suitable fosterer material.

Since George smelt like an old trainer I threw him into the bath and shampooed and groomed him. Then I spent the rest of the morning tidying up the clutter that had mysteriously proliferated throughout the flat, fluffing up the sofa cushions, swabbing the kitchen floor and de-dogging the lawn. As soon as I'd finished I realized the place looked far too tidy and clean for a dog-friendly home, so I scattered some dog chews in the corners, disarranged the sofa cushions and replaced some of the clutter to make the living room look lived-in rather than like a museum.

I needn't have worried. Amanda was warm and easy-going. She arrived with one of her own dogs, a Collie-cross named Rob, who immediately jumped onto the red-velvet sofa where George was sitting. Looking totally affronted – what the hell was this strange dog doing in our house and on his throne? – George immediately jumped down, flounced across the room and threw himself onto his special embroidered floor cushion. Not a good omen, I feared.

Meanwhile Rob continued to trample up and down the sofa. At one point I thought he was going to lift his leg on the arm, but I bit my tongue and said nothing in case Amanda wrote me off as too house-proud to be a dog fosterer. Luckily, after having a good sniff, he jumped down of his own accord and set about demolishing one of the strategically placed dog chews while George glared at him through narrowed eyes.

Instead of grilling me about my intentions as I'd feared she would (How many hours a day would my potential foster dog be walked? How often would I leave it alone? Would my expectations of its behaviour be too high, and what school – I mean puppy class – would I put its name down for?), Amanda simply chatted to me over a cup of tea. It was all very relaxed.

Afterwards, she had a quick look around the rest of the flat and the garden, where we both peered into the deep concrete pit behind the back wall. I explained that, three years previously, the couple who'd just bought the house behind me had decided to replace their entire back garden with a twelve-metre-long basement extension, and that Camden Council, in their wisdom, had granted them planning permission. It was out with the old frog pond, the well-stocked flowerbeds and the ancient apple tree I'd looked out on with such pleasure in the past, and in with the concrete mixers, diggers and, once they'd hit the water table, pneumatic drills, plus 24/7 all-night electric pumps. For two years the noise had been so unbearable that all the surrounding gardens, my own included, had been no-go areas. Three years on, the basement extension was still unfinished, and the former garden was a damp, gaping concrete hole crawling with builders, potentially lethal to any dog who cared to jump over my back wall.

'Mmm. I think you'd need to put up a higher fence if you wanted to foster large dogs,' Amanda commented. That was her only suggestion. Apparently I'd passed the home-vetting procedure with flying colours. 'Odds-on Many Tears will be calling you up this Sunday, asking you to take in an emergency case,' she said, as she left.

Thrilled to have been given the thumbs-up, I immediately went online and ordered six-foot-high trellis panels strong enough to cage in a cougar. 'Why not you order them from my cousin?' my builder Dobromierz complained, when I phoned to ask if he'd install them when they arrived the following week. 'He owns big timber business in Warrington. He would give you bargain price!'

I called the trellis company back and cancelled my order, then called Dobby again and said I'd like to order the stuff through his cousin instead. Half an hour later he called *me* back to say there was no problem, except that his cousin didn't stock trellis: they'd have to order it specially and delivery would take a minimum of eight to twelve weeks. I told him to forget it, and called back the original company to un-cancel my cancellation. They didn't seem very pleased to be getting my business again.

A few days later George and I drove over to see Hannah, who'd been to collect Billy from his fosterers in Swindon and had taken a week off work to help him settle in. The little Jack Russell-cross puppy was even more beautiful in the flesh than in his photo. Extremely petite, with a dear little pointy black-and-tan face, flopping-over pointed ears, and slender white legs ending in the tiniest paws I'd ever seen, he skittered around Hannah's kitchen fizzing with energy; by contrast, George resembled a giant fat, hairy sloth. And an unfriendly one at that. He cut Billy dead when the puppy nibbled his ears and tried to persuade him to play, then took refuge in an armchair, where he promptly fell asleep.

Hannah's minimalist house had been taken over by an array of furry dog-beds, ceramic dog bowls and plastic dog toys in primary colours. A big metal cage – a.k.a. a puppy crate – stood in her living room, there was a litter tray in the kitchen and what looked like vast panty liners spread all over the wooden floor. 'They're puppy training pads,' she explained, as she picked up Billy to cuddle him. 'Though he doesn't really need them. Do you, you clever boy? I've been taking him into the garden every few hours and he's practically housetrained already.' Billy responded by snuggling against her contentedly. Then he wriggled free, ran under the table and peed. Hannah laughed.

Out in the hall, a baby gate had been fixed to the bottom of the carpeted stairs to stop Billy going up to her bedroom.

'So, is he sleeping in the kitchen at night?' I asked.

'Oh, yes! I mean, I do put him in his puppy crate.'

'That's brilliant. And he doesn't mind going in it?'

'No. Not much.' Hannah smothered a yawn. 'He barked a bit on the first night. Until about two in the morning. Naturally he was missing his brothers and sisters.'

'Yes, naturally. So what did you do?'

'I ignored him.' She looked rather sheepish as she added, 'At first.'

'Then what? Did you end up taking him upstairs?'

'No! I told you, he's not allowed up there, and I mean to start how I intend to go on.'

'So what did you do?'

'I . . . well, I came down here and cuddled him for a while, then I went back upstairs.'

I had to admire her resolve. If only I'd had it when I'd first got George, my love life might have been completely different.

'But then he started barking again.' She yawned a second time. 'I thought I'd let him get on with it, but the trouble was he didn't stop. So in the end I came down here and slept on the living-room sofa so that he'd be able to see me through the open door.'

'I presume he calmed down then?'

'Sort of. After I'd brought the puppy crate into the living room, that is. And . . .'

'Yes?'

'And then moved it right by the sofa next to me.'

I suppressed a smile. 'So you're sleeping down here every night with Billy, are you?'

'It's only a temporary measure,' she said, somewhat defensively. 'If I'm firm with him he's bound to settle down in a few more days.'

'I'm sure he will,' I agreed. But I was lying. Something told me that Hannah was already on the same slippery slope with Billy that I'd been down with George. Perhaps it was mean of me, but I couldn't help finding the thought comforting. At least I wasn't the only person in the world who wasn't a natural when it came to training dogs.

9

Three weeks later, on a sunny Sunday morning, I was driving west down the M4 again.

This time George was sitting on the passenger seat beside me, watching closely as I pinched another Malteser from the glove compartment just in front of him. When he realized I wasn't going to give him one, he began to whine, so I patted him on the head and ran through all the reasons why he wasn't allowed one.

First, Maltesers were fattening and George was on a diet. Second, that last horrendous vet's bill had included more than three hundred pounds' worth of dental treatment. Last, and by no means least, I'd recently heard that chocolate contained theobromines, chemicals that were potentially poisonous to dogs. A single Malteser might turn out to be Death by Chocolate for him.

George answered with a volley of ear-splitting barks that seemed to indicate my reasoning was as riddled with holes as a bar of Aero. Point One: he'd been on a diet for seven years, yet had lost only half a kilo in total. Point Two: he'd had so many teeth out already that there were scarcely any left in his muzzle to rot. Point Three: on the subject of theo-whatsits, he'd once eaten an entire packet of chocolate money that had been destined for Joshua's Christmas stocking, and in more recent times had scoffed a plateful of Belgium truffles, which I had thoughtfully left out for him on the coffee-table. Moreover, apart from some sparkly turds containing the coins' golden wrappers, and a little extra wind (and what was a little extra, when he already had so much?), he'd suffered no ill-effects from those feasts.

With his round belly straining against his canine seat-belt, George stared longingly down into the murky depths of the glove compartment, wherein he knew lurked not only the Maltesers but also a selection of fluff-covered wine gums and squashed jelly babies, evidence of my shameful addiction to the tooth-rotting sweets of my childhood. Spoilsport that I was, I reached out and slammed the door on them. He lay down, sighing at the unfairness of life, and placed his twitching nose sadly between his paws.

Poor old George. I felt quite sorry for him. Little did he know what the day held in store for him. For we were on our way to collect our first foster dog.

The garden trellis had arrived and, after complaining that it was of much poorer quality than the kind his cousin would have ordered for me had I not been so impatient to get it, Dobromierz had erected it, thus turning my country-cottage garden into a dog-safe environment that could have doubled as a maximum-security prison yard. Now all I had to do was select the right dog to go into it. There'd been plenty of variety on the Many Tears website, to which I'd developed an addiction that rivalled the one to sweets. I scanned through it every day – not once, not twice, but at hourly intervals – to see if any new dogs had arrived in Llanelli. At the same time, I'd catch up on the stories of dogs who'd been at the centre for some time: Vera, for instance, who'd recently been adopted; her old kennel-mates Muddle and Blossom, who were still waiting for

'for-ever' homes a month after my visit; and the easier-to-home breeds like Cavaliers and Labradors, who seemed to come and go from the website in a matter of minutes.

Since it was part of a fosterer's job to post updates of their charges on the website, I'd also been able to keep track of all the dogs that were currently being fostered by other people. It was amazing how quickly most of them adapted to being wanted and loved, perhaps for the first time in their lives. Even serious behavioural problems seemed to improve within a matter of days of their going into foster care.

'When we first brought Roberta back with us, she was terrified of everything and everyone, including us,' one such update had read. It was about a German Shepherd that, before arriving at Many Tears, had been locked up alone in a shed all her life. Now she was temporarily living with a foster family in Gloucestershire. 'She snarled at our other dogs, and ran behind the sofa, shaking, whenever anyone came into the room. Even food wouldn't tempt her out, though she was clearly starving. What a difference a fortnight has made! Roberta now follows me around the house all day long, and can't stop wagging her tail. Yesterday she played in the garden for the first time, along with the rest of our pack, and she's made a special friend of our Rottie and cuddles up to him in the kitchen at night – when she's not cuddling up with us on the sofa, that is! She's an adorable girl, and desperate to please.'

Another update was about a West Highland White Terrier who'd been a stud dog all his life and had arrived at the centre with dreadful skin problems and infected ears: 'Dylan has been with me for five weeks now,' his fosterer had written, 'and his health is only just starting to improve. We apply cream to his coat every day, and it's slowly starting to thicken up, but the vet says his ears have been so neglected that he has permanent hearing loss. He's just beginning to trust us a little, and will even take treats from our hands once in a while. Now and then, when he thinks we're not looking, he shows flashes of being a cheeky chappie who loves to roll about in the mud with our other dogs. He's a brave boy who's trying hard to overcome his problems and he needs a quiet for-ever home where his new owners will be loving and very patient with him.'

Inspired by these reports, I couldn't wait to get started. But what dog would be most appropriate for me to foster? I ruled out the very large ones on the grounds that they'd be too much for old George to cope with. That left the smaller dogs, of which there were plenty. There was Jimmy, a little black crossbreed who'd been abandoned in a dustbin; and Flake, a three-year-old Westie bitch who'd been bred from so many times that her teats were almost touching the ground. Bobo was a cute Manchester terrier who'd had one front leg amputated after being knocked over by a hit-and-run driver, and Coco Puff was a tiny Shih Tzu who was blind in one eye. Knickerbocker, a Springer Spaniel that had been abandoned by her former owners, had already been sent to another foster home by the time I applied to foster her, and Jitterbug, a six-year-old Cavalier with a heart condition even worse than George's, was on the point of being sent to me when some kind soul applied to adopt her.

Then there was Bailey, a six-year-old Border Terrier. The poor thing was horribly disfigured. Both of her ears had been torn off, a long scar ran right across her face and she had an eye missing. The expression in the remaining eye was of deep resignation, as if she'd been ill-treated since the day she was born and had long ago given up hope of a better life.

'Poor old dog. She must be the ugliest in the world,' Joshua emailed back, after I'd sent her details to him. What on earth could have happened for her to end up in such a state? Had she been tortured by humans, set upon by Pit Bulls or used for illegal dog fights? Filled with fury that anyone could mistreat a dog so, I immediately phoned Many Tears and volunteered to foster her. If I didn't give Bailey a chance, maybe no one else would.

But it turned out that, far from being the victim of torture, all her scars had resulted from fights she had started. Bailey was a little terror, and couldn't possibly be homed with a novice fosterer like me, or a submissive old soul like George.

It was back to the website where, after a couple of days, I spotted Tulsa, an ex-breeding Cocker Spaniel with extra-droopy ears. Her expression was sweet, and the blurb described her as 'kind and gentle'. My application to foster her was accepted, and I was all set to go.

I was only twenty-four hours from Tulsa's arrival when Sylvia VanAtta called.

'I really want to make sure that your first experience of fostering is a good one,' she told me, 'and I'm not at all sure that Tulsa is the right dog for you to start with. I just bathed her myself, Judith, and she didn't react at all. I'm afraid the poor thing's a bit of a zombie, bless her. A lot of the ex-breeding bitches are like that because they've been shut up in sheds or pens all their lives and they've never had to relate to humans. Sometimes it takes them months to respond, and I'm worried that in the meantime you'll find dealing with this one so upsetting that you'll be put off fostering for ever.'

My protests that I could cope failed to convince her. 'Look,' she continued, 'I've got some lovely five-year-old Bichon bitches going out to foster tomorrow. One of them is particularly lively and affectionate, although she's an ex-breeding dog, too. She's completely unsocialized. She's never lived in a home so she knows absolutely nothing about it, so you and George will have to teach her everything. Actually, she's been promised to another, more experienced fosterer, but if you like I'll try to swap things around and get him to take Tulsa instead.'

I was grateful to Sylvia for her thoughtfulness, of course I was, but at the same time I also felt rather miffed. It was as if she'd already sussed out that, unlike her other foster carers, I wouldn't be able to handle anything difficult.

Near Reading I turned off the M4, doubled back towards London, and pulled into the motorway service station where Sylvia had told me I was to rendezvous with the foster van. She'd said to wait in the caravan and lorry section, which was usually deserted on a Sunday, and as I sat there in my parked car, staring out of the windows at the bare tarmac, I felt as nervous as a drugs-dealer at the end of a supply chain, waiting for an important cocaine drop.

But it was too late to be anxious about what I'd taken on: the white Transit van I'd seen down at Many Tears had just drawn up in a big empty bay near me. For a moment the driver and I regarded each other warily through our respective windscreens. Then we smiled and got out.

'Hi. Are you from Many Tears?'

'Yes, love. I'm Neil. And you must be . . .?'

'Judith. I've come to pick up a Bichon called Inch.'

By now, a few other cars had driven into the lorry park and pulled up nearby. Their drivers and passengers – all obviously experienced fosterers – greeted each other as if they were old friends and strolled over to the van. While they clustered around him, talking and laughing, Neil opened up the doors and let out the smell of freshly washed dogs. I scanned the wall of puppy crates for the one I'd been promised. There she was – a small, sad-looking bundle of fur, with dark unhappy shadows underscoring her almond-shaped eyes.

Neil unfastened her crate door and gently prised her out of her compartment. She didn't struggle, but neither did she seem eager to leave it. 'She's a right little darling,' he said, as he handed her to me, along with a bag containing some paperwork and a sack of food. 'You certainly won't have any trouble with her. She'll be as good as gold.'

I held her tightly. The last thing I wanted was for her to wriggle out of my arms. But the little Bichon was far too scared by what was happening to jump ship. She was rigid with fear.

As I carried her carefully back to the car, George peered through the side window at the object in my arms – no doubt hoping it was edible. When I opened the back door and he realized it was another dog, his jaw literally dropped. Poking his head through the gap between the front seats, he watched, amazed, as I eased Inch into the metal puppy crate that was jammed onto the back seat (I'd got it from Hannah on semi-permanent loan: apparently Billy no longer needed it because he'd learned to sleep in his bed in the kitchen. Or so Hannah had told me. I suspected otherwise.)

Once inside the crate, Inch's legs slowly buckled under her and, without looking at me, she sank down onto the blanket I'd put in. 'Don't you worry, I'm only locking you up in here for an hour at most,' I promised, as I slid the bolt shut. 'I'll let you out as soon as we're home.'

When I got back behind the steering-wheel George pulled his head through the gap in the seats and gave me an astonished look that asked, 'What the hell is going on?' Instead of launching into a long explanation that he wouldn't understand, I patted him on the head, started the engine and pulled out of the lorry park.

He'd work out what was happening soon enough.

I arrived home fifty minutes later to find two large leather shoes abandoned just inside the front door and an empty pizza carton on the kitchen table. My heart lifted. I called Joshua's name and, a few seconds later, he came pounding upstairs from the garden floor. Although he'd popped home once or twice since starting at university, he hadn't been back for the past fortnight and, as always, I felt ridiculously pleased to see him.

He told me he'd come to collect a book he needed. 'And I want to see the new dog, of course.' He frowned at the bundle I was clutching. 'What happened to poor old Scarface?'

'Bailey? It turned out she had a habit of attacking other

dogs. Hence the scars. So I applied to look after a dear old Spaniel.'

'That's not a Spaniel.'

'No. Many Tears suggested I foster this one instead. Isn't she adorable?' I stroked Inch's tense neck. 'She's a Bichon Frisé. Apparently that's French for a curly-haired little dog. I Googled the breed last night and it turns out they're descended from the Barbet, a kind of water dog. They were once bred in Tenerife and then they were a sailor's dog, which became popular in France in the late sixteenth century and . . .'

By this time Joshua's eyes had glazed over: having a history fanatic as a mother had put him off the subject for life. 'Why don't you put her down and let her run around?' he suggested. 'She must have been cooped up all day.'

I lowered Inch gently onto the kitchen floor, and we waited to see what she'd do. She didn't. Or, rather, she remained glued to the same spot, trembling with fear. I really felt for her. Since being given up by her breeder a week before, she'd have been moved from place to place, and from kennel to kennel, not realizing she was going to be treated lovingly by humans, perhaps for the first time in her life. Then, just as she'd got used to being at the rescue centre, she'd been plucked out of her kennel, shut in a dark van, taken on a long journey and handed over to me, yet another stranger. How scary was that?

I took a good look at her. She was nothing like the pedigree Bichons whose photos I'd seen on the Internet. They'd all been cute, bright, snow-white, curly-tailed pom-poms of soft curls with grins on their faces. Inch was more like a grubby shorn lamb, with an over-large ribcage and a thick, straight, woolly baton of a tail, which was lowered right between her legs. Instead of being white, her coat was a dingy cappuccino colour, stained espresso brown around the paws, and the curls on her back were so thin that you could see right through them to the sore skin underneath. Her belly sagged, probably the result of having to give birth too young to countless litters, and her teats were long and dark from suckling the pups she'd been forced to have. After years of servitude, the expression on her face wasn't so much blank as deeply exhausted. Although she was relatively young – at five years old, just half George's age – Inch had the air of a down-trodden bag lady who'd long ago lost hope of life improving and could scarcely summon the will to keep breathing.

After a few minutes of standing in the same place, she sighed deeply. Then, like a dusty automaton that had been stored in a cupboard for a hundred years and had only just been dusted off and wound up, she very slowly started to move. First her vacant eyes flicked sideways. Then she gave a small sniff. Lowering her little nose towards the ground, she put one cautious brown paw slowly in front of the other and crept around the margins of the kitchen, paying extra special attention to the spot on the hearth where I always placed George's food bowl. I had the feeling that she'd never had so much freedom to explore before and, in a limited way, she was almost enjoying herself.

Which was more than I could say for George. By now he'd thrown himself down on the floor midway between me and Joshua, and was watching the newcomer with a scowl.

'That's our new foster dog, George,' I explained, bending down and stroking his long curly ears. 'She's had a pretty bad time in the past, so I want you to be kind to her and help her to learn how to live in a house.'

Just then Inch looked up and registered George's existence. A dim light flickered in her eyes, like that of a dying torch bulb, and she crept slowly towards him. Instead of getting up to greet her, George shrank back. Raising his aristocratic nose high in the air, he scuttled off to his favourite bed, jumped into its fake-sheepskin depths and sat down in it with a possessive, defiant air.

Inch followed him over to it and, again cautiously, climbed in beside him. If she was planning to cuddle up she had another think coming: my King Charles wasn't into physical contact with the *hoi-polloi*. Rather than get up close and personal, he immediately retreated to his special throne, the red-velvet sofa. No sooner had he settled there than Inch left the dog-bed, wandered over to it and, after contemplating it for a moment, jumped up beside him. Nostrils wrinkling in disgust, George slid back onto the floor and padded across to his special embroidered cushion beside the fireplace, only to find Inch following him yet again.

'Look at her tail. It's getting quite high,' Joshua observed as, having ousted George from the cushion, too, she proceeded to pursue him under the kitchen table, where he'd taken refuge. 'That's not a good sign, you know.'

'Surely a raised tail just shows she's happy to be here.'

'Haven't you watched *The Dog Whisperer*, Mum? A high tail shows she's dominating George. I mean, look at *his* tail – it's right down between his legs now! I hope she's not going to boss him around too much,' he added protectively, as our Cavalier scuttled back to his basket once more, with Inch still on his heels.

'No chance. George has been the boss around here for years.'

'I'm not so sure. Shouldn't you put her in the garden?' he asked, as Inch diverted to sniff the living-room hearthstone in a slightly more than curious manner. I dived to pick her up – but it was too late: she was walking through the puddle and heading for the living-room rug, leaving a trail of wet footprints in her wake.

I cursed myself for not having taken her out into the garden sooner; I'd quite forgotten that she wasn't housetrained. Without saying a word to her – for she wasn't in the wrong, I was – I got out some antibacterial spray, grabbed a mop, bucket and some kitchen roll and thrust my hands into a pair of Marigolds.

Little did I know that, for the next six months, they would rarely be out of them.

Fostering rescue dogs would turn out to be an unforgettable experience, not only because I'd grow to love all the dogs I took in but also because I'd spend a good part of the time on my knees with my hands encased in yellow latex, mopping up puddles and clearing up messes. Other Many Tears fosterers boasted on the website that their charges learned to be clean in a matter of days, even hours, but, like dog discipline, housetraining clearly wasn't my strong point.

I'd soon be wondering what was.

Afterwards, I decided to take Inch outside before anything worse than a puddle occurred. This meant getting her downstairs to the back garden. Since she wouldn't be coaxed into leaving the room by herself – in fact, she wouldn't even make eye contact – I called to George to come with me and, reluctant to be separated from her kind, Inch crept slowly after him. But when we reached the end of the hall, she ground to a sudden halt. Like a rambler who suddenly finds herself on the precipice of Beachy Head, she stared down the stairs as if she'd never seen anything so treacherous.

She probably hadn't. She'd never lived in a house before – for all I knew she'd never even been inside one. An everyday thing like a staircase was as unknown a phenomenon to her as human affection. She had no idea what this canyon was for, or how to manoeuvre herself down it, and no amount of gentle persuading on my part would make her try.

From his perch halfway down the stairs, George stared back up at her with a smirk of *Schadenfreude*. So, the coward was too frightened to follow him down! Glorying in his superiority, he scampered back up to the hall, circled her, then ran back downstairs again, barking boastfully. Still too frightened to follow him, Inch looked away.

My instinct was to pick her up and carry her to the lower ground floor, but Joshua stopped me. My role as a foster mother, he reminded me, wasn't simply to baby and pamper Inch, it was to teach her to do things herself. 'Leave this to me, Mum,' he said.

First he got me to fetch one of the many dog treats I'd bought in preparation for Inch's arrival. It was a pungent sausage, thin as a pencil and as pink as the Spam of school fritters past – and smelling rather like them. After snapping off a chunk of it, Joshua walked down a few stairs so that his hand was level with Inch's face. Like some kind of Svengali, he wafted the sausage in front of her nose. At first she resisted but, after a minute or so, the smell proved too tempting and she leaned forward over the top step and tentatively took the treat from between his fingers. As if she feared he was going to snatch it away, she then withdrew and sucked it slowly into her mouth. Once she discovered it was good to eat – better than that, scrumptious – she swallowed it.

'Good girl!' Joshua broke off another piece of sausage, this time holding it slightly further away from her nose. As she craned towards it again, Inch slowly inched to the very edge of the top stair. Joshua let her have the treat, then repeated the process.

'That's it! Clever girl!' On his third attempt, one of her front paws slid down onto the first tread and, with a little help from him, the rest of her body followed.

Another chunk of treat followed. Then another. And so the two of them progressed, step by step, chunk by chunk.

Meanwhile, once he realized what was going on, George ran manically up and downstairs beside them, clamouring for a treat. By the time the three reached the lower ground floor, the packet was almost empty.

'What *is* this stuff?' Joshua muttered, as George practically bit his fingers off in an attempt to collar one of the last nuggets. 'It's totally addictive. It's like crack for dogs.'

He'd successfully got Inch down to our bedroom level, but even a last chunk of canine crack couldn't lure her into the back garden. Was she scared of the great outdoors, or terrified that if she went through the french windows she'd never be allowed back in? Deciding that she'd already coped with more than enough new experiences for one day, I picked her up, carried her outside and put her down on the lawn. Unlike George, who was rooting around in the flowerbeds, Inch stood exactly where I'd put her, staring into space, just as she had upstairs in the kitchen.

It suddenly occurred to me that Inch might never have been in a garden before, never seen trees, never stood on grass. For all I knew, she might have spent her entire life penned up indoors. She simply had no idea what anything was, or what was expected of her. She was bewildered, overcome.

I scooped her up again, and kissed the top of her head. Even though Many Tears would have shampooed her when she left the rescue centre, she still reeked of neglect. The changes she'd experienced were too much to take in and she looked exhausted. As I carried her back into the house, she tucked her brown-stained muzzle under my chin and snuggled against me like a frightened child, whimpering softly.

A wave of love swept over me. I already knew that, when the time came, I'd find it hard to give Inch up.

10

''Bye, Mum. Remember, *you*'re the one in control.'

'Of course I am!'

'And whatever you do, don't let Inch sleep in your bed-room. You know what happened with George.'

These were my son's parting words as he headed off later that evening. I assured him I knew exactly what I was doing, but inside I felt as nervous as when I'd first brought him home from the Royal Free Hospital, aged four days and five hours. Then Udi had been there to help look after him, and having had two children before he'd already known how to change a nappy, how to tell whether a baby needed feeding, even how to persuade it into a Babygro when it didn't want to wear one. All marvellously reassuring.

This time I only had George to help me with the new arrival. And if his behaviour of the last few hours was anything to go by, the King of the Canines wasn't going to put himself out. When it came to looking after Inch, I was on my own.

There was always the canine crack to fall back on. It had worked so well in teaching Inch the art of negotiating stairs that, before the evening was out, she'd even managed them once or twice by herself. Every time she succeeded I congratulated her with another nugget of sausage. And, so that George didn't become jealous, I had to give some to him, too. God knows what was in it, but by bedtime both dogs were running after me with their tongues hanging out.

Determined to start off as I intended to carry on – *I'm in control* was my new mantra – I heaved the puppy crate into the study, arranged a thick fleecy blanket inside it, and, firmly but gently secured Inch into it for the night. Reverting to the petrified creature I'd picked up at the motorway service station earlier that day, she made no protest. Still, the last thing I saw as I shut the study door on her and George were her eyes, staring through the bars in the direction of my departing figure.

I lay awake for a long time, waiting for either or both dogs to start barking, but neither made a sound. How stupid of me to have been so anxious about dog fostering, I reflected smugly, as I drifted in and out of sleep. Though he hadn't welcomed his new canine companion with open paws, George hadn't actually rejected her yet. As for Inch, she was settling down already. Looking after rescue dogs was a cinch.

A blood-curdling cry woke me around half past five. I jumped out of bed and threw open the study door. George was right behind it, scratching desperately to get out. Inch was standing up in her cage, staring through the bars like a mad creature, and the booming noise was coming out of her mouth. Though she was a toy-sized dog she possessed an opera singer's vocal capacity – not a sweet Katherine Jenkins soprano, but a booming baritone like Willard White. And much as I admired Willard White's voice, when the same level of sound emerged from the muzzle of a small, off-white dog, the effect was more like something you'd witness in a horror film than on-stage at the Royal Opera House. What came to mind was that scene in *The Exorcist* when the demon speaks through twelve-year-old Regan's mouth.

Overnight Inch had changed from a passive statue into a fiery little devil. As soon as I unbolted the crate door she flew out and ran from room to room like Beelzebub, with a rather mystified George following her. I picked her up, carried her into my bedroom and stroked her back, but just as I thought she was calming down, she spotted her reflection in my wardrobe mirror and the opera scenario began again. Realizing she was probably desperate to go outside – after all, to my knowledge she'd only done one puddle since she arrived – I rushed into Joshua's room and unlocked the french windows so that I could let her into the garden. By the time I'd opened them, she'd already peed on the carpet.

I ran up to the kitchen, snapped on my Marigolds, fetched bucket and water, blotted up with kitchen roll, then sponged the carpet with shampoo and stain remover. After that I threw on a coat, shoved my bare feet into the nearest shoes to hand – my Kurt Geiger ankle boots – and, since she froze when she saw the french windows, carried Inch outside. Shivering in the cold morning air, I stood beside her petrified body until, ten minutes later, she pooped on the lawn. No sooner had I bagged up the business, along with three other rosettes that had appeared overnight courtesy of the local foxes, than George followed suit at the edge of a flowerbed, so I shovelled that up too.

It wasn't yet six o'clock, but there I was, out in the drizzle, naked but for a coat and a pair of black patent killer heels, having already cleared up five lots of shit and one puddle. Make that two, because the moment I carried Inch back inside she peed again, this time in the hall.

Up in the kitchen, she hovered around my feet while I measured out her breakfast. Though I knew she'd have been well fed at the rescue centre, she stared at the bowl as if she was starving. George, who usually only showed that level of excitement over steak leftovers, followed her example: canine competition was having an effect on him already. I put their bowls down a metre apart, and guided Inch to hers. But while George was fastidiously picking off the topping of chopped chicken, Inch vacuumed the lot like a Dyson on full power, then head-butted George out of the way and got stuck into his.

I was amazed to see her move so fast. So, I think, was George. Too well-mannered – or was he too much of a wuss? – to tell her where to get off, he looked shocked, and waited for me, his servant, to intervene. I obliged by guiding Inch gently to one side, but as soon as George started eating again she dodged back and knocked him away a second time. Then a third.

Food dominance, that was what the experts called it. Or maybe it was dominance full stop. The terrified little dog who'd arrived the day before seemed to have meta-morphosed overnight into a lamb-sized ladette, who not only stole George's breakfast but before the morning was out had nicked his favourite bed, too.

One didn't have to be a trained animal behaviourist to understand where she was coming from. She'd probably spent her entire life fighting for her share of a communal eating bowl and sleeping on bare concrete, as I'd heard many commercially farmed breeding dogs did. Now that she'd found a plentiful source of food and somewhere comfortable to lay her head, she had no intention of giving them up. While the King lay nearby on the hard wooden planks, staring at her reproachfully, Inch stretched out in his basket's soft, well-padded depths and rested. And rested. Her off-white curly coat would have been indistinguishable from the fake sheepskin lining, had it not been for the gentle rise and fall of her chest.

That afternoon, Sue popped in unexpectedly, and found me still in my dressing-gown. 'What's the matter? Are you ill?' she said, as she swept through the front door, chic in full makeup, hoop earrings and a fake-leopardskin trench coat.

I ran a hand through my unwashed hair. 'I haven't had time to get dressed yet.'

'Why not?'

I sighed. 'You have no idea how much hard work looking after an extra dog involves,' I explained, 'what with all the clearing up, and the feeding, and the floor scrubbing, and taking her out into the garden every five minutes to try and house-train her, and all the love and attention and cuddles she needs. There doesn't seem much point in getting dressed anyway because I can't take her out for a proper walk.'

'Why?'

'Because even though she's five years old she's never been taken out before, and she doesn't know how to walk on a leash. And I can hardly take George out without her, can I?'

'Why not?'

'And leave Inch all by herself on her first full day here? No way!'

'Well, you wanted to do this,' she said, all sympathy as usual. Then she sniffed. 'What's that smell?'

'What smell?' I trailed after her into the kitchen, sniffing. 'You're imagining it.'

'No, I'm not. Ugh! It's disgusting.'

'How dare you?' I sniffed again, and this time I caught it – the sweet but cloying smell of neglect that clung to Inch's coat. Sue was right, damn it. Annoyingly, she usually was. 'It's Inch.'

'Your foster dog? Is that its name? Didn't you bath it when it arrived?'

I remembered the anti-flea shampoo I'd bought from my local pet shop a few days before in preparation for her arrival. It was still in the cupboard under the sink where I'd put it when I'd brought it home. 'It doesn't matter, because the rescue centre washes all the dogs before it sends them out to foster homes.'

'Well, I'd bath her again if I were you.' She shuddered. 'She's probably got fleas.'

'Of course she hasn't!'

'Where is she, anyway?' I pointed at George's basket, where the fluffy cream lining suddenly opened its eyes and blinked at us. 'Oh, she's *sweet*!' Like a queen greeting one of the great unwashed, Sue bent down and gingerly touched Inch's head with a gloved fingertip. The Bichon's vacant eyes slid away. 'Adorable! Why was she at the rescue centre?'

'Her owner didn't want her any more, probably because

she couldn't have any more puppies. You see, she'd been a breeding bitch. You know, forced to mate and have litter after litter.'

'You mean a sex slave? How appalling!'

'Isn't it? You can pick her up if you want to.'

'No, thanks.' Though she loved George, and spoiled him with copious amounts of food whenever he visited her house, Sue wasn't really a pet person. Years before she'd adopted a kitten from a rescue centre. On the first night, she'd decided she couldn't cope with it being dependent on her so she'd given it to me the following day. 'How's darling George taking it?'

As if he knew she was talking about him, darling George picked himself up off the floor and, looking unusually downcast, plodded slowly over to greet her. Inch raised her head and watched him, then climbed out of the basket, walked over to Sue and body-butted him out of the way. Seizing the opportunity, George ran back to reclaim his basket. But just as he was climbing in, Inch barged past him. The dance continued as George ran back to Sue and Inch followed him. This time, as she climbed out of the basket, I spotted a small brown speck crawling across the furry lining.

'Oh-oh!'

'What?'

'Look! That! There!'

Keeping at a safe distance, we both squinted into the basket. Sue was right yet again: Inch did have fleas. And although she'd only been here for twenty-four hours there was scarcely a single square foot in the house where she hadn't slept, crept, rolled, or sat since she'd arrived, both sofas included. Female fleas laid around fifty eggs a day, which meant that there were probably fifty eggs already scattered around my flat waiting to hatch out into fifty larvae. In a few days' time, these would metamorphose into fifty pupae from which would later emerge fifty fully fledged adult blood-suckers. If these all went on to procreate at the same rate for, say, a couple of weeks, their numbers would soon rival the population of the People's Republic of China.

In the few seconds I'd taken to work this out, Sue had picked up her handbag and fled, leaving me to deal with the looming infestation. Itching already, I threw on some clothes, drove to the vet's and bought an armful of anti-flea products, some for George and Inch, others for me and my home. On the way back I stopped off at a supermarket to acquire a trolley-load of industrial-strength gel air fresheners. At home, I positioned these strategically around the house in their sleek plastic containers, as if they were sculptures on Easter Island. Choking on their various scents, which ranged from Caribbean Lime Mist to Floral Bouquet and Cotton Fresh, I shut both dogs out in the garden and, holding a J-cloth over my nose so that I didn't poison myself, sprayed every corner of every room with insecticide.

All that was left to do then was to treat both dogs and bath Inch. She shook with fear while I doused her in warm water and anti-flea shampoo and kept up a reassuring monologue, promising her that everything was soon going to be all right. No matter how much shampoo I used, and how many rinses I gave her, the dark stains on her feet and muzzle would not come off.

*

As I dropped to my knees at nine o'clock that evening to mop up the fourteenth accident of the day – this one in the downstairs hall – I reflected that dog fostering had already fulfilled one of the functions I'd hoped it would: it had cured me of empty-nest syndrome. Here was one bereft parent who was no longer wandering around the house, wondering what on earth to do with herself now that her precious offspring had left home. I simply hadn't time to think about Joshua.

I felt ashamed at how badly I was coping. What was wrong with me? Looking after one extra dog should have been no trouble at all. However, she seemed to take up even more of my time and energy than my baby son had done years earlier. She was only a tiny dog, but in my mind little Inch had already morphed into Foot, or even Yard. And if I didn't get on top of the situation soon, I might well have to rename her Square Mile before the week was out.

I was losing control. Of her. Of the housetraining. Of George. Of the whole caboodle. After only thirty-six hours of being a dog fosterer, I was already wondering if I'd bitten off more than I could chew.

I'd make a new start tomorrow, I promised myself, as I finally crawled into bed and slathered hand cream over my detergent-chapped fingers. What I badly needed was a good night's sleep.

But the dogs had other ideas.

11

When Sue and I were children, our father often took us to London Zoo on a Saturday morning. More often than not, our first stop was the seal pond and its slithery doe-eyed inhabitants, our second Bernard Lubetkin's art-deco penguin pool, where we'd watch the comical maître d's in their black-and-white dinner suits dive off the Busby Berkeley walkways into the cold blue waters below. After a short stop at the Children's Zoo, to pet the rabbits, dare each other to touch the slithery snakes or stop the goats eating our coat buttons, we invariably ended up at the primates' house to pay homage to the zoo's most famous inhabitant, Guy the Gorilla.

A Western Lowland gorilla from French Cameroon, Guy had arrived at London Zoo on Guy Fawkes Night in 1947, which was how he'd got his name, and he remained there until 1978, when he died of a heart-attack during a routine dental operation. For most of this period he lived in isolation in two small, thickly barred cages, one indoors, the other outside, linked by a metal shutter and bare but for an old tree trunk and a raised sleeping platform, bolted to the wall. When it came to ideas about animal welfare, the 1960s were positively Victorian.

Though he was only five foot four inches tall, Guy appeared massive. He weighed in at around thirty-four stone, had a nine-foot arm span, and enormous beefy biceps and thighs. Atop his bulging weightlifter's shoulders sat a massive, noble head with flaring nostrils, a high, domed skull and prominent, glowering Neanderthal brows. The total effect could have been as terrifying as King Kong, the fictional monster who'd sent my thirteen-year-old future father diving for cover beneath a cinema seat when he'd first seen the movie back in 1933. However, Guy's eyes shone with a rare and kindly intelligence. Despite all he had to endure in a lifetime of captivity – not least loneliness, boredom and the humiliation of being gawped at by on-lookers such as myself – he was a gentle giant who, when birds flew into his cage, was known to let them land on his dinner-plate-sized palms and gaze at them as if he'd never seen anything so miraculous.

A big sign on the side of the cage warned the public not to feed Guy, who lived mainly on a diet of fruit and vegetables with a few crunchy insects thrown in. One day, however, the gorilla, who was sitting in his outdoor cage when we arrived, lazily scratching a thigh with his long pointed fingernails, looked up and saw my father, who happened to be eating an apple. Guy stopped what he was doing and pointed at it. My father held the apple up and, to our astonishment, Guy nodded. After having a quick look to make sure that the keeper wasn't looking, Dad hurled his half-eaten apple through the bars. Guy caught it and polished it off.

Thereafter, even though it went against the rules, my father would bring an apple for Guy whenever we visited to the zoo. And in time Guy learned to spot him in the crowd. When he saw us approaching he'd sit back on his haunches, gesticulate at the bars, and wait for Dad to throw him his snack.

One rainy Saturday morning we arrived to find Guy shut up in his indoor cage. He looked bored and more than usually frustrated, as he paced up and down, manoeuvring his huge body across the concrete floor on clenched fists. The moment he spotted my father in the crowd he rocked back on his hefty haunches and beckoned with his right hand for my father to throw the apple to him. But there was a problem: the bars separating Guy's indoor cage from the public were covered with security glass, and getting the apple through to him seemed like Mission Impossible.

Dad spread his hands to indicate that there was no way he could do it. Guy glanced up at the top of the cage, then beckoned again, this time using his other hand. We looked up to where he was pointing: there was a hole in the glass, big enough to throw the apple through.

My father was an accurate shot and, a moment later, sent the apple sailing through the hole. As it tumbled into his cage, Guy reached up and caught it. Then he settled down to eat it – but not before he'd acknowledged the gift with a gracious nod.

From then on, we all felt very differently about visiting Guy. It now seemed a crime that this highly intelligent animal was locked up year in, year out, with absolutely nothing to do except stare back at those who stared in at him as if he was a monster in a freak show. In the end, his lonely imprisonment in that cage lasted until 1971 when he was moved to a more humane, purpose-built pavilion. Later he was joined by Lomie, a female gorilla from Chessington Zoo with whom it was hoped he'd mate. (He didn't. Perhaps he was past it by then, or perhaps he didn't want to inflict the kind of boredom he had suffered on any future offspring.)

It was because of Guy that I grew up hating to see animals in captivity. A single bird in a cage, such as my grandmother's budgie Joey, was enough to make me unhappy.

Which perhaps explains my aversion to puppy crates.

For those who've never heard of them, puppy crates are plastic-floored metal cages used to transport dogs and puppies safely from one place to another. Back in the 1980s Barbara Woodhouse, the Joyce Grenfell of dog experts, also advocated their use as a training tool. Unlike her catch-phrase 'Walkies!', which, thanks to her TV series, *Training Dogs the Woodhouse Way*, was soon on the lips of practically every dog-owner in the country, Mrs Woodhouse's ideas about puppy crates were slow to take off. Nowadays, however, they seem to be coming into vogue.

By confining a puppy to a crate overnight and for a few hours every so often during the daytime, the theory goes, the owner is satisfying their pet's need for a private refuge or den while helping to reduce separation anxiety and destructive behaviour. Even more important, since dogs and puppies are, by instinct, averse to soiling the place where they sleep, a puppy crate can be an extremely effective housetraining tool. Confine a puppy to its crate for a few hours, and it will apparently cross its back legs and wait for you to let it out rather than relieve itself.

I'd never even considered crate-training George, and I have the feeling that his breeder, Mrs Coleman, would have shown me the door of her cottage if I'd as much as suggested it. However, when it came to looking after Inch, even I, who hated the idea of locking animals up in confined spaces, had to admit that having a safe place where I could put her on occasions might be a Sensible Thing.

To have let Inch trample all over the car while I was driving her back from Reading would have been utterly irresponsible and positively dangerous, for instance, so I'd put her in Billy's old crate for the journey. She'd slept in it quietly on her first night with me, but her second night was a different matter. Now that she'd tasted freedom – room after room of it, complete with no end of comfy dog-beds and sofas – my foster dog had no intention of being shut up in a confined space ever again. And who could blame her?

So, when I put her in the crate at bedtime, Inch began to bark, in her baritone fashion, and bark. Since I'd been through similar things with George a thousand times before, I decided to ignore her, shut the study door on both dogs, and went to bed. Soon I heard a terrible crashing noise. I ran back to find Inch throwing her whole body against the bars, as if she was determined to smash through them.

Frightened that she'd do herself an injury, I opened the crate door, whereupon she shot out like a bullet and, without wasting a second, made for the dog-basket where a very fed-up George had been trying to get some sleep. When Inch climbed in beside him, he retreated to the day-bed, from which heights he glared down at her sullenly.

Once more I shut the study door on both dogs. George would just have to put up with the minor inconvenience of sharing his royal quarters. But he wasn't having it. He wanted out, and the moment I got back into bed he was scratching at the study door. Then *he* began to bark. Encouraged by him, Inch joined in. I clamped a pillow over my ears, stuck my head under the duvet and waited for them to stop. When they didn't, I took the only possible course of action for one who needs a good night's sleep: I let them out.

Allies in victory, they immediately made a beeline for my bedroom, where they curled up quietly on the floor, George in his special place between the bedside chest and the wardrobe, Inch just beside my bed. I took one look at them, and decided to leave them there. Crate-training would have to start again tomorrow.

Apart from George's loud snoring and Inch's heavy breathing, all was quiet and I drifted off to sleep. But at about two o'clock in the morning a strange rhythmic thumping noise woke me up. I snapped on the light to find that Inch was manically scratching herself. Then she writhed around on the carpet. Then she rubbed her back against the wardrobe doors, rattling them. As I watched, it occurred to me that 'Inch' was the wrong name for her. She should have been called 'Itch'.

It was the fleas. The treatments I'd given her earlier hadn't killed off all the bloody things yet. I did feel sorry for her – and even sorrier for myself. Eventually she settled down again and, praying that the peace would last, I finally fell asleep – only to wake up at three thirty to discover that she'd had diarrhoea just behind my bedroom door.

As I cleared up, I realized how stupid I'd been to let an unhousetrained dog have the run of my bedroom. Like it or not, she'd go back into the crate until morning. Inspired by Hannah's efforts to crate-train Billy, I dragged the wretched thing into the bedroom and put it beside my bed. Surely Inch wouldn't complain about being locked up for a couple of hours if she was right next to me.

Whatever had made me think that? By five that morning

I'd stopped caring about the carpet and let her out again. This time an exasperated sigh issued from George's corner. Having apparently given up all hope of any decent kip while the newcomer was in the same room, he picked himself up and voluntarily plodded back to the study to spend the rest of the night alone.

I felt like joining him. But there was no point: Inch would have followed us.

12

A week after she'd come to live with us, my foster Bichon was looking more like an ordinary dog. Her coat was thickening, her dull eyes, while still refusing to meet mine, looked a little less vacant and, thanks to the anti-flea shampoo I'd used repeatedly, the brown stains on her paws and around her mouth had faded, as had the smell of neglect.

Inside, though, she was damaged goods. However well or ill she'd been treated in the past – and, from her behaviour, I could only presume it had been the latter – life as a breeding bitch had deeply scarred her, and it was clearly going to take more than a few weeks of my TLC to put this right.

She was making progress, but slowly. She'd already attached herself to George, and modelled her behaviour on his, and that had to be a positive thing. When he barked, she barked; when he sat, she sat; and when he nagged for food, so did she. On reflection, perhaps he wasn't the best of mentors. However, at mealtimes Inch was dominant, almost aggressive, towards him. Once she had polished off the contents of her bowl in a matter of ten seconds – literally – she still pushed George away from his before he'd made any inroads at all. I longed for him to take the initiative and scare her off with a bark or a snarl, but that wasn't in George's nature: when it came to standing up for himself, my dog was as soft as a fluffy pyjama case. That being so, I resorted to scooping Inch up just before she head-butted George out of the way of his breakfast and putting her on my lap. She immediately stiffened, almost as if she expected me to hit her. But as I stroked her back or scratched her ears and she realized that I wasn't going to hurt her, her spine, legs and neck would gradually relax, and she'd snuggle against me like the small woolly lamb she so resembled.

Her dominance had, of course, extended to George's sleeping arrangements. Whatever dog-bed, sofa, chair or even lap he lay down on, Inch would make her way over to it, sit down next to him and, centimetre by centimetre, gradually stretch out her limbs until she'd pushed him off. It was almost as if, having been an underdog all her life, she'd suddenly found herself in a position of power and was determined not to revert to type.

Like a disturbed child, she suffered from separation anxiety, and couldn't bear to be parted from me – not for a second. Day and night, as if her life depended on it, she kept one eye on me at all times, though she still wasn't brave enough to look directly at me: it was always a sidelong glance that avoided meeting my gaze. I suspect she felt that, were she to lose sight of me for so much as an instant, this peaceful period of plenty she now found herself in might turn out to be an illusion, and she'd wake up back in the nightmare of the puppy farm.

In the cause of keeping me within her sightline, Inch fought sleep like a trooper, although she couldn't beat it all the time. As she lay near my desk, or on the kitchen floor, watching me work or cook, her dull eyes would gradually blink closed and her head droop slowly onto her paws. Even then, she'd start awake at the slightest sound, such as the tap of George's claws on the floorboards, and the whole cycle of trying to keep herself awake would begin again.

Poor George. With the newcomer taking up so much of my time, he simply wasn't getting the amount of attention he was used to. Once top dog in our household, he'd been thoroughly demoted, I'd almost say dethroned, by the determined, neurotic, sad-faced Bichon, and he wandered around the house looking as bewildered as a king in exile.

Outdoors, though, he still ruled. The little usurper had lost none of her terror of the garden, which was making housetraining her nigh impossible. She still peed indiscriminately wherever she happened to be standing: in the bathroom, under the kitchen table, in my bedroom and even on the stairs. The downstairs carpet had become a marshland of big damp patches criss-crossed with narrow dry paths, and I'd developed some kind of detergent-related eczema on my hands from mopping up – those Marigolds never seemed to be in the right place at the right time. Since the kitchen was open-plan with the living room, there was no waterproof corner to which I could confine Inch until she'd learned better and, even as a place to keep her out of trouble, the crate was a no-go area: she looked so terrified when she saw the dreaded thing that I collapsed it and stowed it away behind the living-room door. The only solution I could think of was to spread newspapers all over the floor, but with two dogs and one human walking about on them all day long they never stayed where I put them. George liked tearing them up and eating them, and Inch managed to miss them every time.

How did one housetrain a dog? Since George had come to me fully housetrained, I hadn't a clue. During the ten years I'd owned him my bookshelves had gradually filled with tomes on dog behaviour and training methods – most of them as yet unopened and unread. Now I dusted them off, and devoured every paragraph I could find about housetraining. Soon I was so well versed in the theory that I could have written a PhD on the subject. But since most of the literature referred to housetraining puppies, rather than adult dogs, I wasn't much better off.

The old-school dog trainers advised rubbing a puppy's nose in its puddles and smacking it gently with a newspaper when it messed indoors, advice I rejected as totally un-suitable for a nervous rescue dog. Instead, I decided to do what the modern experts suggested. As far as I could tell, this could be summarized in five short words: praise good behaviour, ignore bad. One was never to tell off one's pet for doing a puddle in the house, as that would only reward what was attention-seeking behaviour. Instead, one must step over the puddle as if it didn't exist, and clear up the mess when the dog wasn't looking. I found it hard to see how the dog would learn that such behaviour was undesirable unless one told it so in no uncertain terms, but those were the rules. I followed them slavishly.

Day and night, come rain or shine, I also took Inch out into the garden at intervals in the hope that watching George do his business there might inspire her to do hers. It didn't. Instead of doing what came naturally to most dogs – which would have been to explore the smells and sights on offer, then add to them herself – Inch froze with all the terror of an agoraphobic who suddenly finds herself standing naked in the middle of Wembley Stadium. While George charged frantically in and out of the flowerbeds, barking at the squirrels and watering everything in sight to show Inch who was really boss, I did my bit to encourage her by tramping round in slow circles, at the same time making loud sniffing sounds – God knows what the neighbours thought of me. My efforts might have won me an Oscar for dog impersonation, but they had no effect whatsoever on Inch, who trailed after me with a blank expression, her thick stubby tail tucked between her legs as she shadowed my footsteps. Despite George's demonstrations she hadn't a clue what was expected of her. And, short of joining in and demonstrating myself, I'd no idea how to help him get the message across.

I'd succeed in time, I assured myself every night, as I crawled, exhausted, under the duvet, the needy newcomer curled up on one side of me and George on the other – by now the odd flea bite or puddle in the room seemed a small price to pay for a few hours' precious sleep, and luckily there was no man around to go hysterical at sharing the bed with two canines. As the late Barbara Woodhouse had maintained, there was no such thing as a difficult dog, only an inexperienced owner. And, though I could hardly claim to be *that* after ten years of dog ownership, I obviously still had as much to learn as my foster dog did.

We were not destined to learn it together.

Just ten days after I'd picked her up from the van at Reading, someone applied to adopt Inch. It was the middle of the afternoon when I heard the news, and I was working in my study. George was asleep on the day-bed beside me and my little Bichon – for so I already thought of her – was sitting on my lap, with her paws on the edge of the desk. When Lisa, the Many Tears administrator, broke the news to me, I automatically tightened my grip. 'So soon?' I heard myself say. 'But Inch has only been with me for a short while. I'm not sure she's quite ready to go yet.'

'I know,' Lisa said, her voice cheerful but understanding at the end of the phone. 'I'm sorry for you that a permanent home's come up so quickly on your first time as a fosterer, but I'm thrilled for Inch, naturally. And it sounds as if it could be just the right place for her, Look, could you phone the woman up now and talk to her? And do tell her all about Inch's bad points, as well as her good ones, so that she gets a really rounded view of what she'd be taking on. We find that it's best if we're honest and upfront with potential adopters. If she's still interested after that, call me back and we'll arrange for one of our home-vetters to go round to her house and check her out in person.'

She gave me the woman's telephone number and hung up. I looked down at Inch and, as she snuggled trustingly against me, I felt that apple swell in my throat, just as it had three months before when I'd dropped Joshua off at his university hall of residence. I choked it back, kissed Inch's head, then, feeling oddly hostile towards whoever she was, took a deep breath and called the would-be adopter.

The voice at the other end of the line was so warm and friendly that my antagonism instantly melted away. Heather, as she was called, said that she was delighted to hear from me as she'd fallen in love with Inch's photo on the Many Tears website and now couldn't wait to get the adoption process under way. She explained that she lived just outside London with her family. She and her husband had two teenage sons and a male Bichon, Casper. In addition, her sister owned another of the breed, and her mother had two more. If she was allowed to adopt her, Inch would become the fifth member of the pack, and part of a large extended family of people and dogs.

'You do understand that Inch isn't housetrained?' I said discouragingly. 'And she does have problems relating to people. In many ways she's not what you'd call a normal dog.'

'The poor little thing,' Heather commented, in an unperturbed voice. 'One of my mother's Bichons is ex-rescue too, so I do know about the problems they can have.'

In case she didn't, I listed them all, in graphic detail: Inch's fearfulness, her incontinence, her dominant behaviour with George and her inability to settle at night unless she was on my bed. But rather than put Heather off, I only succeeded in convincing her that she could offer Inch the perfect home.

I began to think she might be able to. And when she and her husband came to pick Inch up a few days later, with their own Bichon in tow, I was sure of it. Casper was as well groomed and turned out as any pooch you'd see at Crufts, and his owners obviously doted on him. And I had a feeling Inch was going to as well, because the moment she saw him, she actually ran up to him, her stubby tail wagging as she recognized one of her own kind. And while we humans politely introduced ourselves by shaking hands with one another, the Bichons got straight down to some serious bottom-sniffing, then began to chase each other around the room.

The couple sat down at the kitchen table, with the friend who'd driven them to London, and while I made tea, Heather scooped Inch up in a motherly fashion and proceeded to cuddle and kiss her. 'Tomorrow will be her shopping day,' she told me. Though she and her husband weren't wealthy, spoiling their pets was one of their greatest pleasures: they were going to take Inch out and buy her a few of life's necessities. A pink collar, leash and halter to contrast with Casper's royal blue ones, a pink dog-bed and, last but not least, a few pretty pink clothes. Clothes? 'Just some T-shirts and coats,' Heather assured me. 'Bichons suffer from the cold, you know, particularly when they've just been clipped.' From now on Inch, like Casper, would be visiting the canine beauty parlour for a cut, blow-dry and 'peticure' every six weeks.

Half an hour later, as she was carried away down the garden path by Heather's husband, Inch peered over his shoulder and gave me a tragic glance. For the very first time since I'd had her, her eyes gazed directly into mine. She looked desperate, as if she was begging me not to let these strangers take her away. In the past fortnight she'd slowly learned to trust me. Now, just as she was getting used to me, George and her new surroundings, I was betraying her by handing her over to yet more strangers and a future of which she knew nothing.

I felt a sharp stab of guilt, but it was short-lived. In the past couple of weeks Inch's life had undergone a transformation akin to a fairy tale. Her years as an exploited breeding bitch were well and truly over, and she was going to a home where she'd be cherished and adored for the rest of her days. From now she'd be part of a pack of happy, doted-on members of her breed, and her life would be that of a pampered pooch, with lashings of love, daily walks in the park, trips to the beauty parlour – oh, yes, and shopping expeditions for clothes. What could be nicer for her than that?

A foster mother's role wasn't to keep her charge for ever, I reminded myself, as I shut the front door on her. It was to look after her for a short while, prepare her for the outside world, then let her go. Despite her drawbacks, not least among them the puddles, I'd grown very attached to my foster Bichon in the past fortnight, and I was certainly going to miss her, much more than she'd miss me. While I'd always remember her, she'd begin to bond with her new owners in a matter of hours and she'd soon forget me.

Thanks to the rescue centre, Inch was in wonderful hands. Safe hands. Heather's hands. The very best.

13

Just before Christmas, Joshua returned from his hall of residence, and our home was once again filled with noise, music and dirty laundry. I was happy again. A few days before the twenty-fifth, Tabby and Nathaniel came over and we decked the tree together. Unpacking twenty years' accumulation of gaudy baubles and lights from the cardboard boxes in which they'd been stored since the previous January was, as usual, a bitter-sweet reminder of Christmases past, and of Udi, whose favourite time of the year this had been. Here was the exquisitely made Santa bauble he'd brought home from one of his shopping expeditions to Liberty's, and here the musical Christmas lights he'd picked up for a fiver in our local street market; they flashed in six different combinations in time to fourteen different tunes. There was the metre of tacky gold tinsel with which he'd always decorated the Christmas-tree holder, and there – infinitely precious to Joshua and me – was the plain green bauble that still bore the scorch-marks of the Great Fire of 1995. Coming from Austria, where it was customary to put real candles on the Christmas tree, Udi had always insisted on them, and usually watched the flames like a hawk. But, rather the worse for wear in the middle of the New Year's Day party we threw that year, he'd wandered off and left a single candle burning, with the result that the entire tree had gone up, almost taking the house, and our guests, with it.

We still missed Udi terribly – we always would – but in the years since his death we'd learned how to enjoy ourselves without his mercurial presence in our midst. This year's celebrations were particularly enjoyable because Hannah brought Billy to stay over on Boxing Day. With two pooches curled up on the sofas with us, or begging for turkey leftovers, or asleep in front of the fire, the celebrations turned into a minor dog-fest, and the house felt warm and homely.

Not so when Joshua went back to university during the first week of January. As George and I rattled around in the otherwise lifeless flat, I went down with a bad dose of post-Christmas blues. My thoughts turned to getting a new foster dog, and between writing paragraphs of my novel, I found myself searching the Many Tears website again.

I soon found something to raise my spirits: three photographs of irresistible honey-coloured bundles, all with pink noses and flattened-back floppy ears. The description under the first read:

> *Millie is a 5½ month old female Labrador puppy. She has come in from a breeder with her brother and sister, Winkle and Wiggle, and they are all about as mischievous as can be! After their baths they bounded about like spring lambs. Millie has never lived as an only dog so would be happiest if homed with an existing dog. She is very small but makes up for her size with her huge personality!*

The Labrador Retriever is by far the most popular breed of dog in the world. The Finns and Swedes adore it, as do the Australians and Americans. Here in Britain it's way ahead of the competition: in 2008 more than forty-five thousand pedigree Labrador puppies were registered with the British Kennel Club – that's more than twice the number of the breed's nearest rival, the English Cocker Spaniel, and four times the number of registered Cavaliers.

As well as being country dogs who can hunt, retrieve game and track, Labradors' clever minds and good natures make them perfect guide dogs for the blind, explosives sniffer dogs for the army, and assistant dogs for the disabled. In the 1990s, one such Lab, by the name of Endal, became assistant to Royal Navy Chief Petty Officer Allen Parton, who'd sustained serious injuries during the Gulf War. Despite his own debilitating joint condition, Endal learned to obey hundreds of spoken or hand commands from his master, including helping with the shopping, loading a washing-machine and opening train doors. He could even operate an ATM machine, use a chip-and-PIN card, *and* put the plastic back in his owner's wallet when he'd finished with it. That wasn't the half of it. When Parton was knocked out of his wheelchair by a passing car in 2001, Endal pulled his unconscious owner into the recovery position, retrieved his mobile phone from underneath him and pushed it against his face, then covered him with a blanket and ran to a nearby hotel to raise the alarm. In recognition for this act of heroism, he won several awards, including the PDSA Gold Medal for devotion to duty – the animal equivalent of the George Cross.

So much for a Labrador's intelligence. With their big grins, waggy tails and mellow temperaments, these dogs also make the ultimate family pet, and since the part of north London where I live is packed with school-age children, it's also prime pet Lab territory. Take a walk on Hampstead Heath at any time of day and you're likely to see at least half a dozen bounding through the woods with their owners, wagging their tails with the wild enthusiasm of football fans waving their team's colours, and grinning with delight simply because they're out and about with the one or ones they love.

As for Labrador puppies . . . Can anyone who's ever seen those lavatory paper commercials be immune to the magic of these delightful roly-poly creatures? Is there anyone who hasn't wanted to cuddle one? Anyone who hasn't longed for their own gambolling bundle of mischief to play with? Fostering one of these pups from the Many Tears website would give me a once-in-a-lifetime opportunity to enjoy these incredible pleasures, while knowing I was helping the rescue centre at the same time. No lifelong commitment necessary! It was a win-win situation.

But which of the three siblings should I opt for when they all looked equally adorable? In the end I went for Millie because she was the smallest. A sophisticated woman like me knew that size didn't matter. In fact, when it came to dogs, the smaller the better, as far as I was concerned. Why? Because one of my ex-boyfriends, Alex, owned a lolloping great Lurcher. Although he was as tall and skinny as a skimmed-milk latte, Rocket Ron, as he was called, ate like a horse and shat like a . . . Well, let's just say that the small plastic bags I used to clear up George's messes wouldn't have sufficed to clear up Ron's. No. For those you needed a full-sized JCB Loader.

So, a big Labrador, no. But a very small Lab puppy? That I could handle – or, rather, manage with a hand spade.

In a flurry of excitement, I sent Many Tears a begging email, and the following day they replied: yes, I could foster Millie – if they didn't manage to find her a permanent home before the next foster run, which was in ten days' time.

From then on I was like a child outside a toy shop, desperately in love with a stuffed animal I'd seen in the window and terrified that someone would go in and buy it before I'd had the chance to play with it. Wicked as it was, I prayed that no one would come forward to adopt Millie just yet. I wanted her to go to a lovely for-ever home, but not until I'd had the pleasure of fostering her. Convinced she'd be snapped up, I looked at her entry on the website ten times a day, just to make sure that the red 'Reserved' sign hadn't been posted above her name. But although her siblings had found potential owners by the following Thursday, Millie still remained available. When, on Friday morning, I received a phone call to tell me I could pick her up from the foster van in two days' time, I literally jumped up and down with excitement. That toy in the shop window was to be mine.

Later that day George and I went with a walk in Highgate Woods with my friend Elizabeth and her dogs, Flynn and Molly. Instead of throwing her arms into the air and screaming, 'Hallelujah!' when I told her the news, Liz stopped short in the middle of the path. 'You're fostering a *what?*'

'A Labrador puppy.'

'Oh! But . . .'

'But what?' I narrowed my eyes at her, ready to take offence. 'I suppose you think I won't be able to cope with a puppy?'

'I didn't say that!' She didn't have to: her expression said it all. She walked on, and, somewhat put out, I followed her. Since she was one of my most pet-friendly friends I'd expected a little more enthusiasm from her. 'It's just that, well . . . Surely you've read *Marley and Me*? Labs can be a real handful.'

'Not this one,' I said, with certainty. 'Apparently she's very small. And she looks so cute!'

'Flynn was cute and very small once upon a time,' she murmured, as we watched her leggy, tall, madcap Collie hare off into the distance in pursuit of a squirrel. 'That's why we fell for her. When we got her home she immediately doubled in size. And she tore up our duvet the first week we had her. We're still finding the feathers in our bedroom.'

'I doubt Millie will even be able to reach my duvet, let alone destroy it.'

Elizabeth nodded, but as we walked on I could sense she wasn't convinced. 'I thought you found the last foster dog a lot of work. George didn't particularly take to her, did he?'

'Well, no. But Inch was an adult ex-breeding dog. She had serious problems, the poor darling. A happy little puppy who hasn't spent years being ill-treated will be much easier to housetrain. And she won't be able to push George out of the way, because she'll be smaller than he is. Honestly, I do know what I'm letting myself in for this time.'

'You do know?' she reflected back at me, in a calm voice that made me feel like one of her psychotherapy patients.

'Okay, okay, I know what you're thinking!' I snapped.

'What?'

146

'That I'm sublimating my desire for love by falling in love with dogs!'

She burst out laughing. 'Actually, I was wondering what to make the hordes for supper – shepherd's pie or pasta with tuna. But since you've brought the subject up yourself . . .'

'The truth is,' I confessed, 'I've still got a bad case of empty-nest syndrome. It's all very well being free, but I don't know what life's *for* now that I haven't got to look after Joshua on a day-to-day basis. No one needs me any more, Liz. Even though I try and keep busy, I have far too much time on my hands.'

Elizabeth had two teenagers, a six-year-old, a husband, all those pets to look after, and a full-time job. She never had a minute to spare. No wonder she gave a wistful sigh and said, 'It sounds like bliss! Aren't there any men around to cheer you up?'

'Oh, I've given them up for good. And even if I hadn't, who would I ever meet at my advanced age? And where would I meet them?'

She shrugged, as if she had no idea. But five minutes later she suddenly said, in a very casual way, 'I was at a lecture at the Freud Museum the other day – you know the place? In Maresfield Gardens? Where Sigmund used to live? Well,' she went on, 'they're apparently staying open late tonight and throwing some sort of social event. For unattached people. Aged fifty plus.'

I looked at her in horror. 'You mean a *singles* night? For *wrinklies*? Surely you're not suggesting I go to it?'

'Of course not! Well, not *go* in the sense of go with the intention of meeting someone.' She gave me a sidelong glance. 'I just thought it might make a good newspaper or magazine article for you to write. Or give you inspiration for your novel. Maybe you should think about it.'

A large, red-brick Edwardian building in a residential street in south Hampstead, the Freud Museum is the house where Sigmund Freud and his family settled after fleeing the anti-Semitic tyranny of Nazi-annexed Austria in the summer of 1938. Exceptionally, and through the influence of high-placed friends and admirers, the family were allowed to take their personal effects with them when they left Vienna, including their books, furniture and Freud's collection of antiquities, which numbered some two thousand pieces and ranged from small Greek and Roman sculptures to Ancient Egyptian burial masks.

At the time of their flight, Freud was eighty-two years old and in the late stages of oral cancer, for which he had a total of thirty operations. In order to make settling in as easy as possible for him, his new study was laid out exactly as his old one had been: his books were rearranged on their original shelves, his favourite antiquities were lined up on his desk, and the carpet-covered couch upon which his patients lay down to be psychoanalysed was placed against a wall, with his armchair out of sight just behind it – the great professor didn't like to be stared at by his patients while he was working.

Although Freud died in the house a year later, 20 Maresfield Gardens had remained the family home until the death of his youngest daughter, Anna, in 1982, by which time she herself had become a highly respected psychoanalyst and, with Melanie Klein, the co-founder of psychoanalytic child psychology. It was Anna's wish that the house where she'd lived and worked for the past forty-four years be turned into a museum that would honour her father and his ground-breaking ideas on the interpretation of dreams, psychosexual development, the ego and the id, and the importance of the unconscious mind. Since it opened in 1986, the Freud Museum has become the nearest thing that exists to a shrine to psychoanalysis. Visitors come from all over the world to see it although, ironically, many Londoners aren't even aware that it exists. It's a hidden gem, and one of the city's best-kept secrets. To enter it is to step back into pre-war Vienna – particularly in Sigmund's study, which, thanks to the foresight of Anna and her mother Martha, has remained untouched since the day he died.

Not, you'd think, the obvious venue to hold a singles night.

But you'd be wrong.

Why had I let Elizabeth talk me into going? I asked myself, as I stomped down the hill from Hampstead village, dressed in a sober black trouser suit and sweater, an outfit more suitable for a funeral than a night out. There wasn't going to be anyone there worth meeting – not that I wanted to meet anyone. Even so, the nearer I got to the museum the more nervous I felt, and the lower my self-esteem plummeted. I'd never been to a singles night before. All the women there were bound to be younger, cleverer and more attractive than I was, while all the men – well, they'd either pair off with the younger women or be desperate misfits, even potential murderers, who couldn't find a date any other way.

By the time I'd reached Maresfield Gardens I needed less to mingle with the single than a session on Freud's couch. But there I was, in the museum's spacious parquet-floored hallway, amid a crowd of friendly, ordinary human beings of around my age, none of whom looked desperate. And before I had time to say 'Oedipus complex', someone had handed me a glass of wine and, with everyone else, I was playing Psychobingo, a game that entailed going up to total strangers and asking them personal questions so I could tick off the boxes on a bingo card. Had I met anyone here who suffered from insomnia? Someone who checked the locks twice before they went to bed? Someone who rode a vintage motorbike? Or someone who owned a pedigree dog? It turned out that I was the only person present who had one of those, so nobody else could tick that particular box on their card without first meeting me.

Suddenly someone called, 'Full house!' and Psychobingo ended. By now my embarrassment at being there had evaporated. Perhaps because of the beautiful, intimate setting and the pianist who was playing jazz on the mezzanine, this didn't feel like a cattle market but a classy house party where everyone present was throwing themselves whole-heartedly into playing psychologically themed party games, among them Free Association Football, Psychosexual Pursuits and Phobia Charades.

In Phobia Charades, two people got together to mime a phobia, the name of which they either picked out of a hat or chose themselves, and the people standing around them had to guess what it was. I'd heard of the obvious ones such as agoraphobia, claustrophobia and arachnophobia, but I'd no idea there was such a thing as oikophobia (not fear of oiks, as one would have thought, but of home surroundings), chronomentrophobia (fear of clocks), pogonophobia (fear of beards) or – even though I, like most women, suffered from it – rhytiphobia (fear of getting wrinkles). Watching two total strangers get together to act out hagiophobia (fear of holy things) and chiraptophobia (fear of bats) had us all in fits of laughter. Then it was my turn and I was paired off with a tall, attractive man, with the silvery-grey hair of one in his sixties but a much younger-looking face. I'd noticed him in the dining room earlier, but hadn't yet talked to him. He suggested that, if I didn't have a phobia in mind, we pick one out of the hat.

'Okay, it's something called isolophobia,' he muttered to me, out of earshot of the others, as he unfolded the small piece of paper.

'Great.' I looked up into his eyes, which were startlingly blue. 'But what *is* that?'

He looked serious for a moment, then cleared his throat. 'Apparently a fear of being alone.'

Tell me about it, I wanted to say. Freud's couch in the adjacent room suddenly seemed more inviting than ever, as I realized that here was another phobia I secretly suffered from. After taking a few seconds to work out a scenario – the man was to walk away from me, at which point we were both to look terrified at being by ourselves and not recover until we got back together and clasped hands – we threw our inhibitions to the wind and acted it out so well that everyone guessed the answer immediately.

'Well, I must say you were very convincing,' the man said afterwards.

'So were you.'

'Yes, well . . .' He smiled disarmingly. 'I'm afraid I'm a bit of a closet isolophobe.'

'Me, too,' I confessed.

As we drifted up the grand oak staircase together, past the faded small table and armchairs on the small mezzanine where Sigmund's wife Martha used to sit and read in the mornings, I told him a little about myself, and he did likewise. His name was Matthew, he was an engineer and, coincidentally, a widower. His wife had died two years before, after a long illness, so he was now the sole parent of their grown-up daughter. So, we had widowhood in common, and it turned out that he and I lived within five hundred yards of each other. Although we were practically neighbours, we'd never seen each other before. Most peculiar.

By now we were on the first floor where we opened the door of a designated 'Dream Room'. Inside, small groups of people were sitting around discussing their dreams and nightmares and what they might mean.

'And then this armed soldier marched into the church – but he wasn't exactly a soldier, more of a policeman, really – and I began to scream. Except it wasn't so much a scream as a song,' a woman was confiding.

The people around her leaned closer.

'Do you remember what song it was?' one asked earnestly.

'I *think* it was a Christmas carol. Something like "Away in a Manger". But it *might* just have been Robbie Williams's "Angel".'

Another woman raised her eyebrows and asked her, in all seriousness, 'And what exactly does Robbie Williams signify to you?'

This was all too heavy for me, and obviously for Matthew

as well, because he grimaced at me and, struggling to keep straight faces, we rushed back out into the hall and closed the door. 'I'm not sure I'm up to that,' he said, with a grin, as we went back downstairs, where one of the organizers asked us if we'd like to play 'Dr Freud Will See You Now'. This wasn't exactly a game, rather a two-minute session for two people in Freud's study, which was otherwise closed for the evening. When the couple were alone in the room they could either remain silent or say whatever they liked to each other; it was entirely up to them.

We stepped inside, and the organizer closed the door on us. Although we'd been talking quite easily till then, we immediately clammed up, perhaps because we were over-awed by the atmosphere. With its heavy, drawn curtains and dim lighting, Freud's study was both beautiful and mysterious. Time seemed to stand still in it. The walls were lined with his books, and display cabinets were crammed with his vast collection of antiquities. His couch – surely one of the most iconic pieces of furniture in the world – stood against one wall, covered with rugs and cushions, as if waiting for the next patient to lie down on it. Most atmospheric of all, the great man's desk was just as he'd left it, with his round wire-rimmed glasses resting on the blotter and his special chair, which rather resembled a Henry Moore sculpture, pushed back a little, as if he'd just got up from it and stepped outside.

Though I could hear muffled voices through the closed door, the silence in the room grew deeper and more preg-nant by the second. Suddenly Matthew turned to me and asked, 'Look, would you like to have lunch with me some time?'

I gulped and said, 'Thanks. That would be nice.'

He immediately took a slim diary from his inside jacket pocket, flipped it open and said, 'How about next Sunday?' We quickly exchanged telephone numbers. Then the study door was opened from the outside. Overcome with a sudden urge to get away, I told him I had to leave, grabbed my coat from the rail in the outer hall and ran.

It wasn't until I was halfway home that I remembered I was due to pick up Millie from Reading on Sunday. Brilliant – I'd already blown it. I stopped in the street and texted Matthew an apology, saying I'd have to cancel. Instead of texting back, he immediately phoned me. I could tell he was still at the museum because I could hear voices and laughter in the background.

'Am I to take it you've changed you mind about seeing me again?' he said. 'I'd rather you told me if that's the case.'

'No, honestly. It's just that – well, I'd completely forgotten that I have to pick up my new foster dog then.'

'I see.' Then, after a short pause, he said, 'Actually, I don't. I'm completely mystified. You did say a foster *dog*?'

'Yes. It's a kind of rescue dog.'

'I didn't catch that,' he said. 'Hold on, let me get out of this crowd. That's better. Sorry, what was that?'

'I have to drive down to Reading on Sunday and pick up a rescue dog,' I explained again.

'Ah.' After a short pause he went on, 'Do you make a habit of picking up waifs and strays from the Home Counties?'

'This'll be my second time. It's rather a long story.'

'Well, if you still want to meet up some day, maybe you can tell me about it.'

'Okay, I will.'

Then Matthew said, 'I don't want to seem pushy, but would you by any chance like some company on Sunday? When you drive down to collect the dog, I mean. Hello? Hello? Are you still there?'

I'd been struck dumb. I cleared my throat. 'Yes, I'm still here,' I croaked. 'Let me get this right: did you just suggest that you'd drive down the M4 with me on Sunday?'

'If that's the route you're taking.'

'Um, it's to a motorway service station.'

'This sounds more enticing by the minute.'

'And I won't be stopping there for very long.'

'Now you're putting me off.'

'Just in the car park, you see, to pick up my dog from a van. Then I'll be driving it straight back to London.'

'Right. If I tell you that's the best offer I've had in a long time, you'll know what my social life is like. Fine. I'll come along for the ride.'

'No, you can't! I couldn't possibly ask you to do that!'

'Actually, you haven't asked,' he pointed out. 'I offered.'

'Yes, but . . . You can't really want to come with me. It'll be so boring for you!'

'Funnily enough, Judith,' he said, and I could almost see him smiling, 'I think I know what I want better than you do.'

I walked the rest of the way home feeling shell-shocked. This man, a total stranger, had just offered to come for a ride in the car with me *on canine business*. How different was that from Zach who'd refused to help out with George in *any* way, even after we'd been going out for years?

One thing was certain: Matthew wasn't, like my ex, suffering from cynophobia, a morbid fear of dogs.

It was a shame I'd renounced relationships for ever. Because I might just have met the Perfect Man.

14

The following Sunday morning, Matthew turned up outside my house just as I was trying to force Hannah's puppy crate into my hatchback. He had such a friendly smile that I instantly forgot to be nervous, and he earned himself extra points by making a great fuss of George.

'Are you absolutely sure about coming with me?' I said, as I collapsed the crate for the fourth time at the expense of my fingers, and tried to angle it through the back door.

'Why else do you think I'm here?'

'You don't know what you've let yourself in for.'

'I like an adventure. Look, can I help you with that cage?'

I had my pride. Ten years of coping on my own, and a lifetime of being a feminist, had made me pretty self-sufficient. I could change a plug as well as the next man, assemble flat-pack furniture in a fair approximation of the finished article, and hang pictures without smashing my thumbs – though the walls sometimes needed replastering by the time I'd finished. In the far-off days when I was a twenty-year-old art student living in Manchester, I'd even taken car maintenance evening classes, so that I could service the old banger I then owned without recourse to male mechanics. Every Wednesday night the elderly instructor would wheel an ancient tea trolley into our classroom bearing an assortment of greasy automobile parts arranged on it like a selection of dainty cakes. He'd pick them up one by one and, in a quavering voice, announce that this bit was a crankcase, that bit a camshaft or a piston, and this was a Big End, then show us how to clean and repair them. Sadly these disembodied parts bore no relation whatsoever to anything I could see under the bonnet of my old Morris 1000, and when it eventually rolled to a halt on a bypass near Salford it was because of a flat tyre.

My flatmate and best friend Jud, who was with me when it happened, helped me push the old crock onto a nearby garage forecourt, where a couple of burly Mancunians in oil-stained overalls came rushing out of the workshop and kindly offered to change the tyre for us.

'Thank you very much,' I said, 'but that won't be necessary. My friend and I are perfectly capable of changing it by ourselves.'

'Are you now, love? Fancy that!'

Painfully slowly, and with much recourse to the handbook, Jud and I assembled the jack. By the time we'd finished, half a dozen smirking mechanics had surrounded us, all with their arms smugly crossed over their chests. 'I don't think you should put it there, love,' one tutted, as I got down on my knees and carefully positioned the top of the jack under the door frame.

'I do know what I'm doing, you know.'

'You do, do you? Right-oh, then.' He sniggered.

Fuming, I violently cranked up the jack and waited for the side of my Morris to lift off the ground. It didn't. Instead, there was a terrible crunch and the door frame buckled at the bottom. Could this be right? I wondered, as I kept cranking. A second later the top of the jack burst through the rusty floor between the driver's pedals. It took all six men plus a large winch to prise it out. I didn't just lose face, I lost my car, too, because the driver's door never shut properly after that.

Perhaps it was the memory of this incident that made me accept Matthew's help in getting the collapsible puppy crate into the car. He put it on the pavement, examined it for a moment, eyed the car door, then simply slotted it in, God knows how.

'Now why couldn't I do that?'

'Well, I do happen to be an engineer,' he said modestly. 'Compared to building an oil rig that was quite simple.'

We set off, with George crammed into the back seat between the crate and the door, and on the drive down the M4 I explained about Joshua going off to university, my empty-nest syndrome and my new venture as a dog fosterer. Matthew said he'd felt just as upset when his daughter had gone to university – and his wife had still been alive at the time. He was so warm and interesting, so easy to talk to, that by the time we reached the service station where we were due to meet the foster van I felt I'd known him all my life. Certainly long enough to admit that I was ravenous.

'Me, too. Did you bring anything to eat, by any chance?'

'Ah . . . well . . .' I'd brought dog biscuits for George, a bowl and a bottle of tap water, plus some treats for him to share with Millie when we got her, but absolutely nothing for us humans. For some reason this made Matthew laugh. 'I see where your priorities lie!' he said. Leaving George in the car for a few minutes, we raided the shops next to the motorway restaurant. Then, armed with sandwiches, crisps and sweets, for which it turned out he, too, had rather a penchant, we sat in the car in the otherwise deserted cara-van and lorry park and munched through the lot.

'I can't believe we're doing this,' I said, as I fed the crust of my egg-mayonnaise-on-wholemeal to George, who'd stuck his head through the gap between the front seats at the first sniff of food, and was watching every bite I took as if it were his last chance of eating, ever. 'Picnicking on junk in a motorway car park.'

'Mmm.' Matthew swallowed his mouthful of chicken-tikka wrap. 'I have to say this wasn't quite what I had in mind when I suggested Sunday lunch. But it's certainly different. I feel like an undercover agent staking out a spy-ring.'

After we'd eaten we took George for a walk around the perimeter of the car park. Unwilling to waste energy walking when it could have been better expended nagging for more food, he lifted his leg on the nearest shrub then immediately pulled to go back to the car. Determined that he should get some exercise, I urged him on – an arduous task until we passed an overflowing litter bin, whereupon he did a double-take, shot sideways and, before I could stop him, pounced on a large McDonald's takeaway bag. One violent shake sent its congealed contents flying across the already litter-strewn tarmac – and Matthew's extremely well-polished shoes.

I glared at George furiously. It wasn't enough for him to have got rid of Zach: he was obviously intent on wreck-ing my chances with anyone else. Not that I thought of Matthew in that way, of course.

'I'm so sorry!'

'Don't worry, it's no problem!' He produced a tissue from

his jacket pocket and wiped off the ketchup and chips. 'I'd better clear the rest of this up before someone else steps in it.'

Public-spirited, as well as good-humoured? I threw myself at his feet. 'No, no! I'll do it.'

'Here, let me help. It looks like the aftermath of a gruesome pub fight.'

'Yes, but to George it's a Michelin-starred meal. Drop that!' I commanded, as George fell on a half-eaten burger. 'I said drop it!'

But in two gulps it had gone, and some cold chips followed in its wake. So fussy about what he ate at home, when it came to garbage in the street my picky pooch turned into an industrial-strength vacuum-cleaner, indiscriminately sucking up anything within reach. Including, on this occasion, the melted remains of a McFlurry and the soggy lipstick-stained cigarette butt that happened to be floating in it.

By now, several other cars had pulled up near us, each containing a puppy crate. When their doors opened and the occupants got out, half of the passengers appeared to be dogs. There was a German Shepherd, a Dalmatian bitch, a Jack Russell and a couple of handsome mutts – all beautifully kept, and, as I found out when the foster van pulled into the car park and I talked to their owners, all ex-Many Tears rescue dogs who'd been adopted by their 'failed' fosterers.

Matthew took George's leash from me and led him back towards the car, leaving me to collect my puppy. As the driver unlocked the van doors, my fellow fosterers and I clustered around them, like parents waiting at the school gates to collect their kids. In contrast to the dogs in the van, all of which were overawed by or even terrified of what was going on, the humans were terribly jolly and upbeat. One took a Cairn Terrier, another a Westie with sore skin. The Dalmatian owner led away a gleaming but scared Pongo to match his Perdita, and the Jack Russell owner took an emaciated Yorkie with hardly any hair.

Which left one dog in the van: mine.

I frowned at it curiously. 'Er, I think there's been a mistake. I was to collect a small puppy.'

'Millie, wasn't it?'

'Yes.'

He gave a shrug towards the crate. 'That's her, love. Why? Is something wrong?'

'No, no. Of course not.'

'Let's get her out, then, shall we?' He opened her crate door and quickly clipped a leash to Millie's collar. For a moment she hesitated, then left her temporary prison and leaped down onto the tarmac.

I caught my breath. Yes, this was indeed the beautiful Millie, whose photograph I'd fallen for. But the 'very small' five-month-old puppy I'd imagined was, in reality, a very big five-month-old puppy. She was at least twice the size of George and about the same size as a year-old lion cub, which, with the exception of the floppy triangles of her ears, was exactly what she looked like, with her broad leonine nose, slanted hazel eyes, huge fat paws, and teeth as white and jagged as a Himalayan range in winter.

I took the leash from the driver, wound it several times around my hand and, after patting and stroking her big head for a minute, to which she responded with a quick, nervous glance, I slowly guided her across the tarmac towards my car. She didn't so much walk as prowl alongside me, placing one front foot slowly in front of the other, her shoulder muscles rippling beneath her thick yellow coat. After every few steps she stopped and glanced at me apprehensively – though not, I admit, quite as apprehensively as I glanced back at her.

With much pulling forwards on my part, and tugging backwards on hers, we eventually reached the car. Matthew got out to help me. 'No, no!' I said quietly. 'I think it's best if you stay where you are! I don't want to make her any more frightened than she already is.'

He nodded. 'Okay. I hadn't realized I was so scary.'

Figuring that Millie must be thirsty after the long drive up from Wales, I carefully opened the back door, took out George's empty bowl and filled it for her. She sniffed at it suspiciously, had a few laps, then deliberately tipped over the bowl with the remaining water – had I but known it, it was a portent of things to come.

'Are you sure you don't want a hand getting her in here?' said Matthew, from the front seat, where I noticed that George had just insinuated himself: he was now sitting square on his lap.

'No. I can manage.'

But could I? Putting Inch into the car had been a matter of tucking her under one arm. Doing the same with a great big scared lioness – correction, Labrador – was something else. A car was a virtually unknown quantity to Millie, and she reacted as if all kinds of horrors awaited her inside it. I tried coaxing her, pushing her, even tempting her with a lump of Magic Sausage. But each time I thought I was succeeding she pulled back at the last minute and reared up on her leash. Scared that she might run away if I didn't take decisive action, I eventually resorted to grabbing her around the waist and heaving her onto the back seat, after which I shut myself in next to her and quickly guided her head into the crate. After I'd pushed the rest of her body in – it barely fitted – and shot home the bolt on its door, she turned around and looked at me through the bars as if her worst fears had been confirmed.

'I thought you were getting a puppy?' Matthew remarked.

'I was. She is. She's just a little larger than I expected. No worries.'

'Look, George! This is your new companion!' He attempted to turn George's head so that he could see the new arrival. But, keeping his back ramrod straight, my Cavalier stared resolutely out of the windscreen. He knew perfectly well that there was another dog in the back of the car, but he was damned if he was going to acknowledge it. Perhaps he thought it might dematerialize if he didn't.

He'd soon get used to Millie, I reassured myself, as I slipped into the driver's seat. And, daunted as I was by her size, so would I.

I glanced over my shoulder to see how she was doing. With her head touching the crate roof, her nostrils sticking through one side and her thick tail sticking out of the other, she looked like Alice in Wonderland after she's eaten the cake and grown into a nine-foot giant. But, unlike Alice, there was no golden key in the crate to help Millie escape from it, so after turning in circles a couple of times, she resigned herself to being super-sized and lay down on the blanket. As she curled up into a tight ball her kohl-rimmed eyes flashed at me. She looked scared, but also rather hopeful, I thought – as if she'd summed me up and decided she could trust me. The next moment she tucked her pink nose underneath her back legs and went to sleep.

She remained that way until we got back to London. While Matthew followed with George, I led my puppy slowly up the garden path and into her temporary home. Just inside the front door, she crouched and christened the doormat. Matthew stared in dismay at the stain spreading across the coconut coir. Then he handed me George's lead.

'Right. Okay. Well, if you think you can manage from here, I'll leave you three to get better acquainted. Thank you for a . . . a . . . an unforgettable experience,' he finished.

'You're welcome. Any time you want to do it again . . .'

'I'll remember that.'

I grinned at him, and he smiled back. Then he walked down the garden path, frowning at the dandelion-infested overgrown lawn as he passed it, and left the premises, closing the peeling front gate firmly behind him.

I had a hunch I'd never hear from him again.

15

My lion cub slept quietly in the crate all night long. Like Inch, she woke very early the following morning, and roared to be released.

Out in the garden, she watched George do a puddle, then followed suit – a very encouraging sign, which I instantly rewarded with praise and a dog biscuit. Since she balked at the idea of coming back into the house, I heaved her in through the french windows. Perhaps in the hope of getting another dog biscuit, she immediately peed again. After I'd cleared that up, she followed me into my bedroom where I threw myself back into bed and she peed for a third time. Needless to say, no extra biscuits were forthcoming.

Eventually Millie lay down on the floor beside me with her nose between her front paws and her back legs splayed out behind her, looking to all intents and purposes like a lion-skin rug. But every few minutes she got to her feet and stared at me. After a while she sidled forwards and laid her muzzle on the duvet. When I stroked it, her front paws soon followed. Then the rest of her. As she crawled onto my chest, her long tail wagged like a metronome. She was irresistible.

Unable to get back to sleep, I took her upstairs and fed her. She demolished her breakfast at top speed, and then, since George had just gone to sleep on the sofa, she jumped into his small, furry basket and curled up in a tight ball; how she managed to squeeze her big, roly-poly body in there, I'll never know.

I brewed some coffee and put out a bowl of cereal for myself. Since the weather was mild and a watery sun was

shining, I opened the balcony doors, which overlooked the garden. A breeze blew in, bringing with it the song of blackbirds and finches. Millie, meanwhile, had woken up, uncurled herself and stretched out her long limbs in a delicious yawn, revealing her soft pink belly. Her head lolled backwards over the side of the basket, and her upside-down eyes gazed across the room at me, alight with a rather naughty expression.

A moment later she scrambled to her feet, padded over to the table and rested her nose on my knee in an endearing gesture. And as she looked up at me with her big brown eyes, a wonderful feeling of peace flooded through me. Oh, the joy of Labrador ownership! In less than twenty-four hours, this gorgeous lump of puppy-flesh had turned my empty nest back into a real home again. I felt as settled and complacent as a country squire on a Sunday afternoon, dozing in his leather armchair in front of a log fire with his gun dogs lying at his feet. All that I lacked to complete the picture were a glass of sherry, a copy of the *Telegraph* and, last but not least, my own stately pile to sit in.

Millie must have intuited what I was thinking, because the next moment she walked over to the fireplace, arched her back and very kindly produced one for me.

As the smell filled the kitchen, complacency changed to panic. I knew better than to tell Millie off – she was only a puppy, after all, and it was my job to train her – so I knelt down in front of the hearth to clear up. A second later I heard a loud slurping coming from behind me. I swung round. Millie's paws were on the table, and her head was in my cereal bowl.

'Get down!'

She scrammed, sending the cereal bowl crashing to the ground and a thick flurry of soggy corn flakes splattering over the recently upholstered kitchen chairs. As I ran for a sponge to mop them up, Millie hopped back to the hearth and trampled through her as-yet-to-be-cleared-up mess.

By the time I'd picked the cereal off the chairs, cleared away the squashed pile and swabbed the floor clean of dirty-protest paw prints, I didn't feel much like eating break-fast. As for Millie, she'd long since squeezed herself back into George's basket, and was now fast asleep again, blissfully unbothered by the havoc she'd caused. Ghastly as the mess had been, I couldn't stop smiling.

What is it that makes us humans so indulgent towards our dogs? Why do we love them so much? We really do treat them as if they were part of our family. And that's what they are to us: members of our pack. They're our best friends, our brothers and sisters, our indulged children. We confide in them, cuddle up with them, share our jokes and even our beds with them (at least, we do when there's no spoilsport around to object). We take our dogs on holiday with us, and we even arrange our holidays around them. We worry about them when they're ill, and if anything terrible should happen to them, we're devastated.

Most extraordinary of all, we willingly excuse in our dogs the kind of anti-social behaviour we wouldn't tolerate for a moment in people – snarling at us, for instance, or digging up the flowerbeds, the occasional nip, and even farting in public. 'Oh, the poor thing can't help it,' we say indulgently. 'He's just a dog, bless him.'

Dog and Bitch have been Man's Best Friend, and Woman's too, since time immemorial. Just how long is still a mystery: scientists and archaeologists date our relationship back to anywhere between twelve thousand and a hundred thousand years ago. No one will ever know exactly what started it off, but I'd take a calculated guess that, somewhere along that broad timeline, a fur-clad *Homo sapiens* tossed a meaty bone to a hungry *Canis lupus*, the dog's ancestor, and a symbiotic bond formed between them.

Since then, *Canis lupus*, the wolf, has gradually evolved into *Canis lupus familiaris* – the four-hundred-breed-strong domesticated species of dog that exists today. During that time, dogs have learned to communicate with us in a way they don't even communicate with each other. Instead of nipping our necks or sniffing our bottoms, as they do with their own kind, they look directly into our eyes, listen to our spoken commands, and read our body language and emotions in a sophisticated, highly intelligent way. It's not just that meaty bone they're after nowadays: as anyone who's ever patted a stray or visited an animal rescue centre will tell you, dogs seem to crave an emotional bond with humans, too.

Today there are reckoned to be in the region of four hundred million dogs in the world (some eight million of those are in Britain – that's one for every 7.6 people). There are pet mutts living in shanty-town slums in Africa, and pedigree pooches living in palatial mansions in Saudi Arabia. There are working dogs sniffing out snakes in the tropics, and dogs pulling sleds in the Arctic. Dogs have even been sent into outer space (the first dogstronaut was a Russian mongrel called Laika, who went into orbit in Sputnik 2 in November 1957; sadly, she never returned).

Why, of all other animals on earth, have people formed such a strong and lasting bond with this one species? According to recent scientific research in Sweden, the answer doesn't lie in our hearts but in our brains. Stroking a dog has been found to trigger the hypothalamus to make oxytocin, the so-called 'love hormone' or 'cuddle chemical' that women produce after giving birth and when breast-feeding their babies. As well as provoking a maternal response and helping us to bond with our offspring, oxytocin increases feelings of trust and empathy, reduces fear and stress levels, and even lowers our risk of having a heart attack. (The hormone has also been linked to sexual arousal, but in this context the less said about that the better. It would certainly give new meaning to the phrase 'heavy petting'.)

You don't have to touch your dog for your hormones to get going. Apparently just looking at it is enough to do the trick. Over the millennia in which the sharp-faced wolf has evolved into the domestic dog in all its myriad guises, it has gradually developed, or has been interbred to have, the facial features we find attractive in our own babies, among them a high forehead and big eyes. These infantile features are even more pronounced in puppies, which probably explains why we go so gooey over them, finding them cute and funny no matter how destructive they are.

Millie was no exception. Her limpid brown eyes were surrounded by hazel rims that made them look twice the size; it even gave them a fashionable smoky appearance, as if they'd been outlined in kohl by makeup artist Jemma Kidd. Above them rose two pale, surprised suggestions of eyebrows, and a high forehead framed by the largest, floppiest Labrador ears I'd ever seen. Several shades darker than the rest of her coat, which was the clotted cream colour known as yellow in the breed, they were smooth, pliable and compulsively caressable; you almost wanted to nibble them.

One stroke of those huge velvety triangles and my hypothalamus went into overdrive. In my eyes – correction, brain – Millie wasn't simply a Labrador, she was a *Labradorable*. And I adored her.

Now that George was ten years old, I'd quite forgotten what fun puppies were. All but the most unruly adult dogs were trained to control their behaviour and reactions, but with a puppy there was no filter between their emotions and how they expressed them, or between their desires and what they did – more so, perhaps, in the Labradorable than in any other breed.

When Millie explored the flat it was with the wild enthusiasm of a child let loose in Hamleys. As she scampered around at top speed her tail thrashed double-time behind her, like a toy sword, felling everything from a vase of flowers on the coffee-table to a pile of papers on a windowsill and the bottles I'd lined up in the hall for recycling. Rather than try to curb her enthusiasm, I took the easier option – the one I'd adopted when Joshua was a toddler – of moving anything breakable, dangerous or chewable out of her reach.

On the sofa, Millie was Indiana Jones exploring the Temple of Doom. Resting the outsized paws she had yet to grow into on top of the seat cushions, she'd dig her leonine muzzle underneath and between them, and push them aside. Then she'd jump up into the space she'd created and, with a flick of her nose, send the back cushions flying over the top and on to the floor behind. Head down, she snuffled in the crevices in search of hidden treasure – a lost biro, a stale crisp or a petrified half-biscuit that had been festering there for years. Whatever it was, she swallowed it, then licked her lips with satisfaction, revealing her sharp white teeth.

As I was to learn over the next month and a half, Millie was a creature of extremes. She didn't so much eat as vacuum up her food with an industrial strength that made Inch seem slow by comparison. Rather than lap from her water bowl, she wallowed in it, drenching the kitchen floor. Instead of running after a ball, she'd take off like an Exocet missile, overturning chairs, tables, and sometimes even George as she homed in on her moving target. When she'd exhausted herself, she'd fling herself at full power on to the sofa or into a dog-bed – or even into mine – and a split second later be dead to the world.

Her first encounter with the staircase was as traumatic as Inch's had been. But, thanks to dog treats, she mastered it within hours. After that, there was no stopping her. Like a child at Disneyland, who insists on riding Magic Mountain time and again, she ran up and downstairs endlessly, just to re-experience the thrill of it. Within a day or two she was taking the treads faster than an aerobics instructor in a step class – with the result that she often ended up tumbling down it.

The stone steps out in the back garden were another such challenge. At first she trod down them cautiously. Then she took them two at a time. By the end of a week she had realized she had no need to use them all: why bother, when it was much more fun to run along the patio, launch herself off it and belly-flop down onto the grass? Soon a wide, muddy landing strip stretched right across the garden, cutting my lawn into two unequal halves. I hadn't the heart to stop Millie jumping because she was enjoying herself so much. I'd reseed the lawn when she went to her 'for-ever' home – if I could ever bear to part with her, that was.

Inch had been terrified of the back garden, but to Millie it was an adventure playground filled with fascinating sights, sounds and smells. While George picked his way carefully through the somewhat overgrown flowerbeds, stepping daintily between the shrubs, she marauded after him, chewing leaves, digging up specimen plants and flattening everything she came into contact with – including George. When she attempted to apologize for her clumsiness by kissing him better, my Cavalier took refuge beside me on the garden bench. He wasn't hurt, only put out to have his quiet ramble so rudely interrupted. His eyes would glare up at mine, as if to say, 'When is this bloody nuisance going home?'

Millie meant no harm: she just wanted a playmate. She'd been used to sharing a kennel with puppies of her own age. Now she was billeted with Victor Meldrew, and she simply couldn't understand why he looked so disapproving all the time. She followed him from room to room in the hope of getting him to join her in a wrestling match or ball game. She tempted him to wrestle her for dog chews. She hid behind doors to ambush him, and ran in dizzying circles around him. But he never obliged by joining in.

Poor George. Millie was so much bigger and heavier than he was. Heavier still after a few days on double rations. The cup of dry rubble moistened with water I was supposed to feed her didn't seem nearly enough for a growing puppy, so I gradually increased the amount every day. But however much I gave her, Millie was still hungry. Like most Labs, she was a bottomless pit. By the time I'd put her bowl down, she'd not only have emptied it but have licked it dishwasher-clean, after which she'd run over to George's bowl and nudge him firmly out of the way.

I tried bribing her to sit while George finished his supper. But my success only lasted as long as a packet of treats did, unless she made off with the whole bag. Once, when I grabbed her collar to stop her knocking George away from his food she ended up pulling me, and the chair I was sitting on, across the room and into the kitchen hearth, where his bowl was.

I decided that the simplest thing was to separate them at mealtimes. Since this was pretty difficult in an open-plan flat such as mine, I ended up feeding Millie on the wrought-iron balcony that led off the kitchen, while George ate inside.

By the time I'd tempted her out there, put her bowl down, shut the doors and put down George's food, my Labradorable had already finished everything in her bowl and would be standing on her hind legs with her giant front paws resting on the glass, peering in at me with a pleading expression on her face. When I refused to open the doors, she leaped up and down, barking loudly, and looking like a demented jack-in-the-box.

The moment George had finished, I'd open the balcony doors again. Millie would charge back in, head straight for his bowl and, tail wagging, clear up any scraps he'd left behind. Showing no resentment, she'd then follow me back down to the study. While George rested on the day-bed, she'd lie on the floor beside my desk, and fall asleep with her big lion's head on my feet.

I was wallowing in the bath at eleven thirty on Saturday morning when the doorbell rang. I climbed out, threw on my dressing-gown and, followed by Millie, who'd been waiting outside the bathroom door for me, ran upstairs to answer it.

Matthew was standing on the threshold, carrying a Flymo and an extension lead. I don't know which of us was more horrified to see the other.

'Hi. I thought . . .' His voice trailed off. Until I registered his expression I'd totally forgotten that I had a brown Dead Sea mud mask plastered all over my face. 'Oh. Oh, I'm disturbing you,' he went on. 'I'm sorry. I stupidly presumed you'd be up by now.'

With my left hand I grabbed Millie's collar to stop her charging outside while with the right I pulled my hair over my face in an attempt to hide the mud. 'I'm a bit slow about getting going these days,' I said, sounding and looking like a ventriloquist's dummy – the mask had hardened around my lips, which made it almost impossible to move them.

I watched him struggle to keep a straight face. 'You look . . . very fetching. But – if I might say so – not exactly politically correct. A bit like a Black and White Minstrel. Or Al Jolson in *The Jazz Singer*.'

'Please don't make me laugh,' I said, through gritted teeth. 'The mask will crack, and my face will fall apart.'

'Sorry. I really should have telephoned before I turned up. But I was in the middle of doing my garden when it suddenly occurred to me that you might want a hand with that front lawn. So I just unplugged my mower and, well, I walked up here.'

He'd come to mow my lawn? Then he really was the perfect man. Had I been able to move my facial muscles I'd have burst into tears of gratitude.

While George rooted around in the front flowerbed, Matthew plugged in his mower and set to work. Meanwhile, taking Millie with me, I ran downstairs, rinsed off the mud mask, threw on some clothes and brushed my hair. By the time I emerged from the house the dandelions had gone the way of the Amazon rainforest.

'Would you like me to do the back lawn now?' Matthew asked, as he wiped his brow with the back of his hand. And when I managed to choke out another thank you he said, 'Come on, George!' and took him and all the equipment around the side of the house.

I donned my gardening gloves and, accompanied by Millie, de-dogged the knee-high grass before he began. Unfortunately, one of the dogs must have immediately replaced what I'd taken away because, halfway through mowing, Matthew stepped in something. Instead of storming off, never to be seen again, he merely groaned and said, 'Oh, shit!'

'Yes, literally. I'm so sorry.'

'Don't worry. I'll just wash it off. Where's your hose?' I bit my lip. 'You do have one?'

I explained that I'd purchased a new hose several months before to replace the old one, which had sprung a leak the previous year. However, the new one wasn't working yet. He looked mystified. 'How can a hose not work? Surely the water just goes in one end and comes out the other.'

'You'd have thought so. But the reel is one of those rewindable things and it's so complicated that I haven't managed to put it together yet. It has lots of connectors and springs that I can't make sense of. Neither could Joshua, and he did physics A level.'

'Would you like me to have a go?'

'No, no, I'll manage it. One of these days.'

'I'm sure you will.' He glanced down at his filthy shoe.

'However, I could use it right now. So why don't you let me take a look at it?'

He brought the half-assembled plastic reel from the side of the house, then asked me if I still had all the pieces that went with it. I said I did, somewhere, and disappeared inside where I eventually located them behind a box of light bulbs at the bottom of the airing cupboard; how they'd got there, Heaven only knows. Matthew lined up all the bits on the garden table, pored over the illustrated diagrams and, once I'd furnished him with a couple of screwdrivers, put the whole thing together. It took him a good hour, but he made no fuss. He said I shouldn't feel stupid for not having been able to do it because the diagrams were bloody useless; it really was extremely complex.

Once he'd got it working he washed the dog shit off his shoe, picked up his Flymo and went home.

I was glad he hadn't asked to come into the house because I couldn't possibly have let him see it, considering the state it was in.

16

'Fucking hell, what is problem?' Dobromierz said, in fault-less builder's English. 'Burst pipe?'

'No.'

'The drains is blocked?'

'No.'

'Bloody bath overflow this morning? Leaking tap, perhaps?'

'Not exactly.'

'But the carpet! Is fucking wet!'

'Yes, Dobby, I'm well aware of that, thank you.'

'And the smell! Damp, yes. But also something rotten!'

After an absence of two months, my builder had just returned to begin the much overdue job of repainting the exterior windows. This time he'd brought his seventeen-year-old nephew Marek, who'd just arrived in England from Gdańsk. They had found me on my knees in my dressing-gown in the downstairs hall, surrounded by a sea of sodden, scrunched-up kitchen roll. There was a bucket of soapy water beside me and, as usual nowadays, my chapped hands were fetchingly encased in Marigolds.

'I've got a new foster dog,' I admitted. 'She arrived about ten days ago.'

Dobby snorted. Then he shook his head and spoke to Marek in Polish. I don't know what he was saying, but I have a feeling it wasn't complimentary, because Marek rolled his eyes and gave a short, mirthless laugh. 'So, last one – Foot – is not enough trouble for you?' Dobby continued.

'She was called Inch. And she wasn't any trouble. She just wasn't housetrained. That wasn't *her* fault.'

He jerked his stubbly chin at George, who was sitting quietly on the bottom step of the stairs, twitching his tail and looking as if butter wouldn't melt in his mouth. 'And what His Highness think of this new lodger? He likes it?'

'Ye-es. She can be . . . well, a bit exuberant for him at times. But she's only a little puppy.'

Just then there was a loud noise overhead, as if the ceiling upstairs had collapsed. The next moment Elsa the Lioness came thundering downstairs so fast that she tripped and tumbled down a few steps. Instead of proceeding in a ladylike fashion once she'd caught her balance, she sprang into the air and, legs outstretched, soared over George's head like a 787 skimming the Hounslow rooftops as it approached the runway at Heathrow.

George ducked, then flinched as, a split second later, fifteen kilos of yellow Labrador flew through the open door of Joshua's room and crash-landed in the middle of it.

There was a moment of silence, in which I was terrified that Millie might have injured herself. But, no, she was fine, as usual. Having picked herself up, she shook herself violently, then, tail wagging, bounded over to George, pushed her grinning face into his and gave him a wet, sisterly lick. Disgusted by such familiarity, the King of the Canines turned his head away. Millie must have thought he was offering her his ear to kiss, because she poked her nose underneath it. This time George squealed, as if he was being savagely attacked.

'Pull yourself together, George. And leave him alone, Millie! You know he doesn't like it.'

As she turned her head to look at me, she spotted Dobby and Marek. Her smoke-rimmed eyes widened as if she'd never seen any creatures so handsome as the portly builder and his thin, pasty-faced skinhead of a mate, and a second later she hurled herself at them.

Though he was a reliable builder, Dobby was a miserable sod. In the three years since he'd started doing odd jobs around my house I'd never once seen him smile or heard him say anything cheerful. Now his face broke into a wide grin. '*Ah! Ty byku Jeden!*' he growled, taking Millie's head in his hands and shaking it firmly but playfully from side to side. 'What an animal!'

The next moment Millie's eyes lit on the pile of kitchen roll next to me. She threw herself at it, and began to rip it to shreds.

'No!' I said, as she chewed a mouthful. 'Don't do that! I've been mopping up your puddle with it! Drop it, Millie!'

She swallowed it. I wasn't surprised. The longer she lived with me, the less notice Millie took of my admonishments. Life was much too much fun at the moment to waste a second of it listening to me.

Dobby took her face in his hands again and patted it lovingly. 'Now, this is *real* dog,' he said, as she grabbed the sleeve of his jumper and gave it a playful pull. 'The kind we have back home!'

'She's great, isn't she? But not *quite* housetrained. As you can see,' I added, as she suddenly let go of Dobby's sleeve, sniffed the bit of carpet I'd just finished scrubbing clean, then crouched and gave it her signature rinse. Sighing with resignation, I dunked the J-cloth I'd just wrung out back in the bucket of detergent and began scrubbing the area again.

Millie darted forward, grabbed the end of the soapy cloth, and tried to wrestle it from me. 'I'm trying to train her,' I gasped, as I struggled for possession of it. 'Let go! I mean, I take her out to the lamppost regularly, and I put her in the garden every half-hour. She does a puddle every time. Let *go*! Then she comes straight back in and immediately does another. It's easier to deal with upstairs, because the floors are all wood. Stop it, Millie! Okay, you win! Take it!'

Head held high in victory, she trotted into my study with her blue-and-white booty hanging from her mouth and dripping all the way. Having turned to give me a quick look, she jumped on to the day-bed, and proceeded to bury it under one of the cushions. 'I need the kind of dust covers my grandmother used to have,' I shouted over my shoulder, as I ran after her. (My paternal grandmother, Sarah, had once boasted to my father that her twenty-five-year-old sofa, which had been shrouded in plastic covers since the day she'd bought it, still looked as good as new. My father had retorted that this was because she'd never let anybody actually sit on it.)

Dobby stopped smiling, and scratched his inch-long salt-and-pepper hair. 'Dust covers is bloody old-fashioned, Judith. You need more contemporary solution. I think I have it. You leave to Dobromierz, eh?'

So saying, he gabbled to Marek in Polish again, Marek

gabbled back, and the two disappeared through the side door with their van keys, leaving their toolbox behind.

I didn't see them again until lunchtime, when they returned bearing what appeared to be a metre-wide roll of cling-film.

'See this? Is builder's carpet protector,' Dobby explained, as they got down on their knees and, accompanied by high-pitched squeaking and ripping noises that sent both Millie and George into a frenzy of barking, began to unpeel the sticky-backed transparent film and pat it down over the hall carpet. 'Fucking good. We use all the time. Is self-adhesive and water-repellent. From now on all puppy accidents stay on surface, so carpet stay clean.'

This was a brilliant solution to the puddle problem – although in Millie's case the word 'puddle' was something of a misnomer. Hers were more like lakes. Windermere, for example. On occasion Lake Michigan, even. She produced alarming amounts of pee with even more alarming frequency. I was beginning to think they should call the breed Lavs, not Labs. No wonder they used them to advertise toilet tissue. Perhaps I should train her to carry an Andrex roll around her neck, in the same way that a St Bernard carried a brandy barrel. Then, as it unravelled behind her, she could clean up after herself.

Dobby had come up trumps. In a matter of minutes, the old blue carpet in the downstairs hall, study and Joshua's room was transformed from the damp marshland it had recently become into a squeaky-clean shiny pool. Walking across it was like walking on water, except that the surface was bone dry and crackled like bubble-wrap underfoot. I considered this an insignificant price to pay for puddle-proofness.

'I do your bedroom now?' Dobby asked as, hands on hips, he surveyed his good work. 'We have enough protector left.'

'No, thanks. Not for the moment. I've decided to keep Millie out of there in future. There has to be one room in the house that's an entirely dog-free zone.'

'How you manage that, tell me?' I pointed through my open bedroom door to a big flat cardboard box that was leaning against the wardrobe doors, as yet unopened. Dobby stomped in there and examined it. His lips curled in a sneer. 'A *baby gate*? For the *dog*? Huh! In Poland, it's enough we just say, "No!" and shut door on them. Dogs are meant to obey.'

I explained that I'd already tried shutting the door on Millie. She'd barked and yelped and scrabbled at it so plaintively that I'd given in every time. Consequently, she'd spent the last six nights doing her lion-skin rug impersonation at my bedside. Even though I'd now put down an old duvet for her to sleep on, I'd found her head on the pillow next to mine when I'd woken up the previous morning. As my mother had remarked when I'd told her about this, it was high time I imposed some discipline on my foster puppy. Otherwise I'd end up having the same trouble with her that I'd gone through with George.

Inspired by Hannah's efforts to stop Billy going upstairs, I'd gone down to John Lewis's baby department in search of the gate, figuring that if Millie could see me, but not actually get to me, she might happily sleep in the hall outside my bedroom. While I was standing between the cots and buggies, surrounded by heavily pregnant women, a salesman had come over to advise me on which model to choose. 'What age is, um, your toddler, madam?' he'd asked loudly.

Too embarrassed to say that I'd wanted it for a dog, I'd answered, with some truth, 'She's just five months. But she's very precocious.' Everyone turned and stared at me. I knew what they were thinking: that I was old enough to be a grandmother.

The model I'd ended up with was an 'easy fit' number that needed no screws or drilled-in fixings; you simply put the metal frame in a doorway, and the special 'power frame' expanded to fit the width, much in the same way that a telescopic shower-rail fits over a bath. Since it was so easy to put up and take down, I hadn't bothered to open the box and assemble it yet. To be honest, I rather enjoyed getting out of bed in the mornings and warming my feet on my living rug.

Apart from her indiscriminate peeing and her sleeping habits, Millie really was the perfect dog. Or she would have been had she not enjoyed eating quite so much. As well as the double rations I was giving her, she helped herself freely to the bread from the breadboard, apples from the fruit bowl, roast chicken from the counter, and a large tomato and mozzarella salad I'd put on the kitchen table when a couple of friends came to supper (she got stuck into that when I went to open the front door to them).

Millie was just a girl who wanted to chew. It was the non-food items I really worried about. An old MP3 player, for instance. And the TV remote she'd stolen from the sofa. Half of one of the dog baskets. A so-called indestructible plastic doormat that lived in the garden. A wheel on my desk chair (it hadn't helped that I'd been sitting on it at the time). A wine-soaked kitchen sponge (wine-soaked, because I was clearing up the remains of a bottle of red she'd knocked over). Knickers nicked from the open washing-machine door. My one pair of Prada shoes (I'd picked them up at a sale in Glasgow years ago, and though I'd seldom worn them – they were far too uncomfortable for that – I'd felt more stylish for knowing I possessed them). I hadn't even realized that some of these objects were missing until they'd reappeared in pieces, in piles of dog shit in the garden – and sometimes even in the house. What could they be doing to her digestive tract?

Living with Millie was like living with a hyperactive toddler who wasn't wearing nappies. It was a good thing that my brain was awash with so many bonding hormones because I forgave her everything. Besides, I knew her so-called 'naughtiness' was no more than normal high spirits. What she really needed was a playmate and exercise – lots of it – to tire her out. However, since she hadn't had her final vaccinations, Millie wasn't allowed to mix with other dogs yet, so for the time being the house had to be her playground, a pensioner pooch her playmate, and her only trips out to George's lamp-post, where I took her every hour for a little leash- and housetraining. Luckily this frustrating situation was due to end in three days' time, when she was to go to the vet's for her final jabs.

I was getting excited at the thought of taking her and George to the Heath for their first proper walk together. In fact, I couldn't wait.

But I would have to.

17

'Do you think Millie's all right?'

'Why do you ask?'

Matthew rested his knife and fork on his plate and frowned. 'She seems to be coughing rather a lot, doesn't she?'

It was Thursday night, and I'd invited him over for supper to thank him for the lawn-mowing, an act of camaraderie that was way beyond the call of duty. So far the meal had been a disjointed affair because I'd had to take Millie out into the garden every fifteen minutes or so to ensure she didn't disgrace herself, or me, in the kitchen. It wasn't just a matter of letting her out there, but also of staying outside with her: in the short time she'd been with me, Millie had become as attached to me as I'd been for years to my favourite brand of waterproof mascara – if it wasn't within reach day and night, I felt as if the bottom was falling out of my world.

So far Matthew had been remarkably patient about my absences from the kitchen. He'd even come into the back garden with me once or twice. A laid-back temperament was obviously one of his many virtues, along with warmth, generosity of spirit, tolerance, a willingness to mow lawns, and a dry sense of humour that rather matched my own. In fact, from what I'd seen so far, the man had so many virtues that I was beginning to suspect that, far from being perfect, he must be hiding a dreadful vice or secret from me: a penchant for wearing turquoise shell-suits, perhaps, or a conviction for GBH.

This was hard to imagine when I looked at his kindly face, which, in that instant, simply showed concern for the puppy that was currently sitting beside him, as George was beside me, their noses twitching as they gazed up hopefully at the edges of our plates.

Suddenly Millie put her head down, retched violently, then coughed up a gob of bubbly spittle and deposited it on the floor. Matthew and I both stared at it with dismay. Then I reached for the kitchen roll. Foaming sauces might be all the rage among Michelin-starred chefs nowadays, right up there with roast faggot purée or tripe-and-rhubarb trifle, but I didn't feel that Millie's contribution to my plain roast chicken made it any more appetizing than it already was. Quite the reverse.

'I noticed she was coughing a lot when I mowed the lawn the other day,' Matthew said, discreetly lifting his feet to allow me to spritz under them with anti-bacterial cleaner. 'It's got much worse since then.'

It occurred to me that this was true. Millie had coughed now and then ever since I'd picked her up from the foster van, but I'd thought nothing of it, particularly since it usually occurred after she'd been sprinting around the house like Kelly Holmes. I assumed she'd just overreached herself, or that all the rushing about had made her thirsty. However, now that Matthew had brought my attention to it, I realized that her cough had got awful in the last couple of days.

Five minutes later, we were sitting side by side in my

study with the dogs on our laps, Googling 'kennel cough' on my computer. The disease, we learned, was an infection of the upper respiratory tract, which, while rarely life-threatening in itself, could lead to serious complications, such as pneumonia, particularly in dogs suffering from immunosuppressant illnesses, or in unvaccinated puppies (what about half-vaccinated ones? I wondered). Among the symptoms of kennel cough were occasional gagging, retching, coughing up phlegm, a watery nasal discharge and sneezing.

With the exception of a temperature and a wheezing chest, Millie had them all.

'Did the rescue centre vaccinate her against the disease?' Matthew asked.

'I think so. But I'll have to confirm that tomorrow.'

'I presume that George has had a jab?'

I bit my lip. My Cavalier's other inoculations were all up to date, but this was one illness I'd never had him vaccinated against. Now I could have kicked myself.

Reading the rest of the article didn't make me feel any better. Kennel cough was highly contagious, and the contagious period could last for months. On top of that, the virus or bacteria quickly spread from dog to dog by means of physical contact, surface contamination and/or airborne bacteria. This meant that every time Millie coughed, sneezed or even breathed, millions of germs were being flung out around her for George to ingest. If he hadn't caught the virus from her by now he soon would.

The evening fizzled out. My mind wasn't on anything but the dogs' health, and Matthew went home early. Later, while Millie coughed and spluttered on the floor beside my bed, and George gave the occasional sneeze from the study, I lay awake worrying about all the what-ifs that could happen to them. Kennel cough might be a mild illness in most cases, but to me it had suddenly become as potentially fatal as the H_5N_1 bird-flu virus. The thought of Millie becoming seriously ill was dreadful. And if George caught it from her, I'd never forgive myself.

At eight o'clock the following morning, still panicking, I described Millie's symptoms down the phone to Sylvia at Many Tears.

'Yes, it does sound like kennel cough,' she said calmly. 'The poor little puppy. Well, I wouldn't worry, because she was vaccinated against it when she arrived here. We do get outbreaks from time to time, like all rescue centres. It'll probably pass in a couple of days.'

In that 'probably' there lurked a panoply of possible disasters. 'But what should I do? It's very contagious, isn't it?'

She got my measure: 'If you're worried about George catching it from her –'

'No, no!'

'– well, of course you *could* send her back to us, but that won't make any difference, because if George was going to catch it, he's probably done so by now. If I were you, I'd just keep Millie indoors and give her a teaspoon of expectorant twice a day. And a vitamin C pill. Oh, and if you want, you can put a few echinacea drops into her water bowl to help build up her resistance. I'll pop some antibiotics in the post to you, but don't give them to her unless she really seems to need them. Is she ill in herself at the moment?'

I gazed over at the lioness, who was dribbling Joshua's

football around the living room faster than Wayne Rooney at Old Trafford. 'Not exactly.'

'Then I don't think you have much to worry about. The most important things are to keep Millie in, and to keep her quiet.'

Keeping her in was easy: since she hadn't yet had all her jabs, I'd been doing that already. But keeping her quiet? A five-and-a-half-month-old Labrador with more fizz than a bottle of Lucozade Sport? How, exactly? The only thing I could think of was giving her back the packet of herbal sleeping pills that I'd wrested from her jaws in the nick of time that morning.

First, I had to get the medicines Sylvia had suggested. Which meant going out to the local chemist. Which meant leaving Millie on her own for half an hour. Since she'd arrived, I'd been a virtual hermit. With some difficulty I now persuaded her back into the puppy crate in the kitchen – the one place where I knew no actual bodily harm could come to her when I wasn't with her – then I clipped on George's lead and walked him quickly into the village. Relishing this rare opportunity to be alone with me, he forged ahead without protest.

Even before we turned back into our road fifteen minutes later, I could hear a banshee-like howling rending the air, a noise so terrible that even George froze. I didn't have to guess where it was coming from because six or seven strangers were standing on the pavement outside my house, staring at it. As I manoeuvred past them with George, they glared at me.

'Is that your dog in there, making that noise?' one woman demanded.

'Yes.'

'You really shouldn't leave it locked up alone for hours on end!' said a man.

'But I haven't!'

'People like you should be banned from keeping animals. I feel like reporting you to the RSPCA!'

Just then, a loud bang augmented the howls, and the woman tutted some more. I opened the front door and rushed into the kitchen, only to find that the puppy crate was no longer in there. It was in the living room, where Millie had managed to move it, having first kicked out the plastic base tray and put her feet through the bottom bars. She was now lurching around in it like Hannibal Lecter in a full-body mask, howling and coughing as she crashed into the furniture.

I rushed over and freed her. Not one to hold a grudge, she fell on me gratefully.

18

The expectorant and vitamin C weren't the instant cure I'd hoped for. As for the echinacea in Millie's drinking water, after one sip she clamped the bowl rim between her teeth and ran through the flat with it, sloshing water everywhere – a new trick, but one she was to repeat frequently from then on.

What with that and the pools of slimy saliva she was coughing up all the time, it was wet, wet, wet in the house. And let's not forget the puddles. The carpet remained dry, thanks to the transparent plastic protector. However, it was almost impossible to spot the lakes sitting on top of the shiny surface so I kept stepping in them.

Was it because she wasn't well that it was taking Millie so long to get the hang of housetraining? Or any training, for that matter? The Many Tears website was full of updates from other fosterers, claiming that the dogs they were looking after didn't mind being home alone for a couple of hours, and that they slept all night in the kitchen without barking *and* that they had been '99% housetrained!!' within a week of coming to stay with them (it was the double exclamation marks that really got to me). Round my way, however, the status quo was still as it had been on the day Millie had arrived: she peed and pooped everywhere, and she couldn't bear to be separated from me, day or night. I comforted myself with thinking that Labs were particularly hard to train.

Then Hannah called to ask me what she called a 'huge favour. You see, I've just booked to go to Spain for a few days, in a few weeks' time. And I was wondering if . . .'

'Yes?' I prompted, when her voice petered out.

'Well, if you could possibly look after Billy while I'm away . . . I know it's a lot to ask, but he's just got used to living with me, Judith, so I don't want to put him in kennels. Nor do I want to leave him with someone he doesn't know.'

'Of course I'll have him, darling. This house is already Dog Hall. One more isn't going to make any difference.'

'Thank you so, so much! That's a weight off my mind. I'll do the same for you, naturally, if you ever want anyone to look after George. Oh, yes, and you won't believe what happened this morning,' she went on. 'I was walking Billy in Richmond Park when he started playing with this beautiful Labrador puppy. I got talking to its owner, and he told me he'd adopted her a fortnight ago. From Many Tears!'

'No!'

'Yes. And guess what? The dog's name is Winkle – and he's Millie's brother.'

'What an incredible coincidence!'

'I told him all about Millie, and he said Winkle's got exactly the same sweet nature.'

'That's amazing! Did he, um, happen to mention house-training?'

'Ye-es.' She sounded hesitant. 'But I'm not sure I should tell you what he said. It might upset you.'

'That's ridiculous. How could it?'

'Because Winkle's already one hundred per cent clean in the house.'

I had to stop myself slamming down the phone.

I decided to call George's vet, Howard, for some professional advice. First I mentioned Millie's kennel cough. Like Sylvia, Howard said I shouldn't worry too much. 'It's usually a self-limiting disease, dear, like the common cold. It should go away in a few days,' he reassured me, before reiterating what Sylvia had already told me: that George would either have been infected with or become immune to the virus by now. 'Any other little problems?'

It all came out in a rush: Millie's separation anxiety, her sleeping habits and, last but certainly not least, the housetraining. In no uncertain terms, but with all the charm of the Irish, Howard told me just whose fault all these things were. Mine.

'The trouble is, Judith, you're feeling sorry for Millie instead of showing her who's in charge. The reason why she gets so worried when you leave her is because she doesn't feel *safe*. And that's because *you* haven't made her *feel* safe. You haven't given her a safe place to be in, have you? You haven't crate-trained her!'

'I did try.'

Howard sighed. 'Did you *force* her into the crate, or have you made it into the most *marvellous* place, a place where she really wants to be, more than any other place?'

'How do you mean?'

'A crate should be a dog's hideaway, you know. It's your job to make her love it.'

I laughed. 'That's impossible – no dog likes being locked up in a metal cage!'

'On the contrary! For a start you should keep the crate in a place where Millie feels most comfortable.' Like on my bed? I thought. 'Then pick the right time to put her in there. After you've been playing for a while and she's tired out would be ideal. And don't reward her by letting her out if she starts crying or tries to escape. Wait till she stops complaining.'

That could be Doomsday. I explained about going to the chemist the day before, and the lynch mob outside my house threatening to call the RSPCA.

'That's just because you left Millie in the crate too soon, didn't you? You've got to make her feel at ease in it first. So, dear, always *feed* Millie in her crate. Every time you give her a *treat* it should be in there, too, with the door open. The crate should be the place she keeps her toys, because she *wants* to. And when you go out, you should hang a blanket over it, perhaps, to make her feel even more secure. Think of a fox. What does it do when it feels frightened? It retreats to its dark den! So, there you are!'

According to Howard, crate-training – or confinement-training, as he called it – was also the answer to the housetraining crisis.

'After meals you should take your puppy out into the garden to eliminate, then, if she doesn't do anything, bring her back in and put her straight in the crate,' he explained, so patiently you'd have thought he was talking to a complete idiot. 'Then take her out and put her back in the garden. If Millie still doesn't eliminate, it's back in the crate again. Then leave her out, if you can supervise her, or put her back in it, if you can't, then take her out to have a play. Later, take her out into the garden, then put her back in the crate for a while, followed perhaps by another spell of playing . . . Supervise her . . . Put her in the crate . . . Take

her out . . . Put her in . . . Take her out . . . In . . . Out . . .
In . . . Out . . .'

By the time our conversation ended I was thoroughly confused. Was I meant to put Millie in her crate *before* I took her into the garden or afterwards? Before or after mealtimes? At night or only in the mornings? When she was good, or when she'd been bad? And how was I to make the dreaded Guantánamo cell a place she really wanted to be in? Perhaps I should hire an interior decorator to turn it into a fashionable pad for her. Install a shag-pile carpet or American oak flooring. A fully sprung bed with memory-foam mattress, or a Japanese futon. Plantation shutters or made-to-measure velvet curtains with matching pelmets. Which of these many options would Millie prefer? Was she a minimalist type with a thing for retro sixties sofas, or would she rather have shabby-chic, duck-egg-blue dis-tressed bars and a vintage Laura Ashley chintz armchair instead?

Whatever the décor, I had a feeling that this was one den Millie had no intention of getting used to. Even a pile of sausage treats failed to tempt her back into the dreaded thing of her own free will (though not George, who wolfed down the lot). A few days later it ended up flat-packed behind the living-room door, where I'd stowed it when Inch was around.

As for the peeing, I'd either have to put Millie in nappies, or housetrain her by some method. Maybe hypnosis would work. With any luck Paul McKenna would soon write a best-selling book about it: *I Can Housetrain Your Incontinent Puppy*. Maybe he already had. Until then, I'd just have to resign myself to clearing up after my Labradorable fifty times a day. And when I went out for a short while, I'd just have to give her the run of the flat with George, and hang the consequences.

Matthew called, and said he knew it was short notice, but would I like to go to a concert at the Festival Hall in two days' time? The London Philharmonic was playing his favourite Brahms piano concerto and he'd love me to hear it. I said yes.

'But I'll have to cancel,' I told my mother, when she dropped in to see me.

'Why, dear?' Mum was seated on the sofa, with George perched on the edge of her knees like a ship's figurehead, and Millie by her feet, gazing up at her adoringly. Like me and my late grandmother Laura, Mum loved dogs; they seemed to sense it, and always worshipped her back. 'Go out and enjoy yourself!'

'But I'd be out for hours. I can't possibly leave Millie by herself for that long. She'll go berserk.'

'She'll have George with her, won't she?'

'And she'll probably flatten him – without meaning to.'

My mother looked aghast. 'You're not really going to turn down a date –'

'He's just a friend,' I interrupted.

'– because of your foster dog?' she continued, as if I hadn't spoken. Millie blinked up at her, and Mum stroked her quivering nose. 'She looks as good as gold to me, bless her. Don't you think you're being a little *overanxious,* Judith?' And this from the veritable Queen of Worry, a woman who still warned me to 'Be careful!' every time I crossed a road. 'Why, there was a story in the newspaper today about a mother who left her three toddlers alone on a beach while she went to a shopping centre! The tide came in, and the poor things nearly drowned.'

'And your point is?'

'Millie and George are *dogs*, not children! They'll be fine in the house without you for a couple of hours. If you're so worried, why don't you ask Joshua to come round and dog-sit for you? He likes dogs. I'm sure he wouldn't mind.'

Taking my mother's advice was not a habit with me. If it had been, I'd never have become a dog fosterer, because when I'd told her what I was intending to do, she'd answered that I was mad even to think about it: the dogs would ruin the carpet. So far she'd resisted the smug satisfaction of saying, 'I told you so!' so I guessed I owed her one.

'Make yourself look respectable before you go out on this date,' Mum couldn't help adding, as her eyes swept over me. 'You're covered in dog hair.'

The promise of a full fridge was enough to lure Joshua back from university for an evening, so I went off to the Festival Hall feeling carefree. Matthew and I even stopped off for something to eat afterwards, and then he dropped me home with a quick peck on the cheek.

Panicking about what might have happened in my absence, I rushed inside to find Joshua and a crowd of his friends chilling out in the garden with beer and takeaway pizza, and everything in the kind of glorious disorder that one expects when there is a group of nineteen-year-olds around.

As for the dogs, they were being made a huge fuss of by everyone. George was too busy begging for pizza crust to take any notice of me, but when Millie spotted me she ran over, wagging not just her tail but her whole body. She looked happier than I'd ever seen her. As if she was really part of the family. As if she belonged with us.

A lump rose in my throat, and I found myself wondering if I oughtn't to adopt her. Then Joshua came in from the garden and said, 'Mum, I *love* her! Can we keep her?'

'I don't know. I'm not sure it would be fair to George. She treats him like a helicopter landing pad.'

'She just wants to play with him.'

'I know. But she doesn't know her own strength. Besides, there's the training problem. She's not leash-trained yet. Or housetrained. And she hates being separated from me, even for five minutes. I can't go to the loo without her scrabbling at the door.'

'I thought *you* were supposed to be training her. It's not hard – she's no trouble at all. Look, if you want her to stop doing something, you just have to bark at her, like this.' Joshua demonstrated. Millie immediately jumped to attention and sat obediently in front of him. I was impressed: a term and a half at university, and my son had turned into Cesar Millan, the well-known TV 'dog whisperer'.

'It's the housetraining that really gets to me,' I went on. 'Millie pees and craps everywhere. All the time. There are days when I just can't cope with it.' I sighed. 'What do you think I should do about it?'

My son gave me a withering look. 'Stop complaining,' was his brief answer.

I gasped. 'Excuse me?'

'Stop complaining, Mum. You wanted to foster dogs. Did you really expect it to be a picnic?'

'No, but . . .'

'And, anyway, what sort of foster mother gives up at the first hurdle? You're always telling me that life's tough, and that nothing worthwhile ever comes easily. So, I suggest you just get on with it.'

Talk about your own words coming back to haunt you.

Joshua was right, though. I had to get on with it. And that meant exerting some control. So, after he and everyone else had left that night, I put Millie's duvet in the hall outside my room, and when she tried to come in I barked at her, just like he'd done, and sent her running out. Two minutes later her head reappeared, so I barked again. After I'd repeated this five or six times she suddenly got the message and settled down quietly to sleep in the hall.

Smug with success, I went into the bathroom to take off my makeup. By the time I came out, Millie had stolen back into the bedroom. As had George. He was stretched out in his special spot between my bedside chest and the wardrobe, and Millie was curled up into a tight ball next to him, with her eyes screwed shut, as if to make herself invisible.

When she heard me come in, she opened one eye and looked up at me hopefully.

My heart melted. 'You win,' I whispered, as I bent down and kissed the top of her head.

19

A fortnight later, the situation was definitely improving. Or so I was trying to convince everyone.

'How's life at Battersea Dogs Home?' my sister asked, when she phoned.

'Much better, thanks! George hasn't come down with kennel cough, Millie's no longer choking up gobs of saliva, and she's really settled in.'

'Is she sleeping in the study with George at night yet?'

'No, but . . .'

'Is she still peeing everywhere?'

'Yes, but . . .'

I could almost hear Sue shudder. 'How can you stand it?'

'I don't know. I guess I love her. And I think I'm getting the hang of housetraining her at long last.'

'Fascinating.'

'Take this morning. She performed the moment I let her out into the garden – such a good girl! It's now midday and we haven't had a single accident indoors yet. I think I've learned to anticipate when she needs to go so that I can get her outside in good time. Oh, and guess what? She buried her first bone in the garden yesterday! She came out of the bushes looking really proud of herself. I bet anything you like that's a milestone in canine development.'

There was a short pause. Then Sue gave her special

sibling sigh. 'I can't believe you just said all that! You're beginning to sound like those mothers who drone on and on about their toddler's potty training, or boast that they're reading Shakespeare at nine months old. Only much, much worse because Millie's a *dog*.'

'Bitch,' I corrected.

For some reason my sister took umbrage. When I explained what I'd meant, she calmed down and asked, 'Any potential adopters on the horizon yet?'

'No. Actually, I'm quite glad. Despite the mess, I love having Millie around. She's so sweet.'

'Humph. Well, for your sake, I hope they find someone to take her soon. Otherwise you're going to be a lost cause. By the way, can you look after Jessica's goldfish for a week when we go away over Easter?'

I said I would.

It wasn't just Millie who was changing. Something positive was happening to George, too. I'd first noticed it in the garden one morning when the two dogs had joined forces to chase off a squirrel. Afterwards, Millie had run in circles around George, barking and spoiling for a play-fight. To my amazement, he'd actually responded by play-fighting back. The subsequent wrestling match had only lasted three or four seconds but it was a huge improvement on George's usual reaction, which was to squeal and run to me for protection.

As if he'd suddenly discovered his inner dog, George had then pounced on a clump of crocuses and, snorting loudly in truffle-pig mode, started rooting underneath it for – what? Truffles, I suppose. Or ants. A few moments later Millie had joined him in the search. The wallflowers were well and truly trashed. Any sorrow on my part to see them disappear underpaw (they were, after all, the only proper flowers in the garden) was more than outweighed by my delight that the two dogs were getting on so well. Petals were ephemeral, but the seeds of canine friendship, if carefully nurtured, might well sprout into something lasting.

Since then, George had dropped his grumpy-old-man act. Instead of looking disapproving as Millie crashed around the flat, bringing down everything in her wake, he trailed around after her with admiring eyes, as if he were impressed by her behaviour. Sometimes I suspected that he was actively urging her on. His table manners seemed to have changed for the better, too. At mealtimes, he skittered around my feet in anticipation, then dived into his bowl as soon as it was put down. Even rawhide dog chews, which had never interested him before, took on a new fascination once Millie had pre-masticated them into a soft, slimy mush more suitable for his old gums.

So, my fussy dog was getting into second-hand dog chews! At this rate he'd soon be picking up mouldy old tennis balls on the Heath and carrying them home. Could it be that the King of the Canines was stepping off his pedestal at last and embracing real life, as lived by canine *hoi polloi*? Why, one night I even spotted him curled up on the sofa with Millie. What next? I wondered. Would my pampered pooch and my foster dog soon be sharing the royal dog-bed?

As for my own king-size model, I still had that to myself – when the dogs weren't curled up beside me. But things were moving on apace with Matthew, too: George and Millie were growing closer, and so were we. Both of us were cautious about changing the platonic nature of our friendship but, as in a teen magazine of the early 1960s, our friendly pecks on the cheek had progressed into proper kisses – and even the occasional clinch.

Now he'd come over for dinner again. We'd eaten, we'd drunk, and since Millie had just had her final inoculation and was officially allowed out in public, we had taken both dogs for a walk around Hampstead. As we approached my doorstep I realized it might well be time to utter the five words that could possibly catapult our burgeoning relationship much further along the commitment line. I hesitated for a moment, then blurted them out: 'Would you like a coffee?'

'Hmm. That would be nice.'

Five minutes later, we were on the way downstairs to my bedroom – all four of us. I was leading, with Matthew behind me and Millie and George bringing up the rear. When he got to the bottom step, Matthew stopped.

'Interesting carpet you have down here,' he commented, surveying the shiny blue sea of plastic protector. 'Can I walk on it, or will I sink?'

The plastic squeaked underfoot as I steered him into my bedroom, with the dogs still hard on our heels. George discreetly went straight over to his usual place, between the bedside chest and the wardrobe, but Millie sat down beside us. I regarded both dogs warily. What was I going to do with them while Matthew and I were – how shall I put it? – otherwise engaged?

Matthew stepped closer, slipped his arms around me and kissed my neck. Surreptitiously, I peered over his shoulder. George had settled down to sleep, but Millie was sitting right behind Matthew, grinning up at me inanely and wagging her tail as if she wanted to join in.

'Is something wrong?' Matthew murmured.

'No.'

'You seem a little tense.'

'Not at all! I just . . .'

'Mmm?'

Since George was flat out and there were more pressing matters to deal with at that precise moment, I decided to ignore him. But Millie . . .

'I'm . . . just going to put this creature in another room. I don't want to corrupt her morals. After all, she's only a puppy.'

As we broke away from each other, Millie sprang to her feet, ready to join in the next part of this interesting game. Instead I coaxed her into the study and firmly shut the door on her.

'Feeling more relaxed?' Matthew said, when I came back.

'Much.' He took me in his arms again and kissed me. The romantic mood was suddenly interrupted by a loud snort from the corner. 'Perhaps I'd better put George in with her.'

'That might be sensible.'

Disgruntled to be woken up so soon, George trailed after me at a snail's pace. As soon I opened the study door, Millie charged out and bolted back to the bedroom.

'Now, at last, I have you all to myself,' Matthew said, when I eventually returned from returning *her* to the study.

But for how long? I wondered, as we fell fully clothed

onto the duvet. I knew it was only a matter of minutes until either or both dogs started complaining. Sure enough, my ears soon picked up a whimper, then a lone loud bark, then the scratch of a paw on wood. Then all three sounds together. Matthew and I tried to pretend it wasn't happening, but before long it sounded as if a dozen giant rats were trying to scratch their way through the woodwork.

'Damn! This is hopeless!' I muttered.

Matthew grimaced. 'Rather off-putting, yes.'

'Sorry.' I disengaged myself, ran out into the hall semi-dressed, opened the study door and hissed, 'Shut up, you two!' then slammed it. 'Sorry, Matthew.'

He smiled. Rather thinly. We were just managing to recapture the mood when, as if she were a paid-up member of the morality police with a CCTV camera trained on us, Millie started to wail like a siren. And to bark. Woof, wail, woof, wail, woof, wail . . . On and on she went. 'Maybe it'd be better if I let her out of her crate and left her to roam the hall,' I murmured.

Matthew sighed as I scrambled out of bed in my underwear. 'Will that do any good, do you think?'

Released from Cell Block H, the two prisoners smirked at me victoriously. George ran upstairs, where he knew I wouldn't follow him, but Millie dashed back into the bedroom. Tail wagging, she leaped onto the bed – and landed right on top of Matthew.

'Get off!' I shouted. 'Now, out! I said OUT!' Chastened, she bounded into the hall with her tail between her legs and threw herself onto her duvet, which I'd just put down there. 'Stay!' I commanded. Millie rolled over onto her side and bent her front paw, displaying her belly in a show of submission. I melted. 'Good girl! Lovely girl! Now stay where you are, darling!' Her tail thumped.

I firmly closed the bedroom door. A minute later, it flew open, and she reappeared in the bedroom.

Matthew sat up. 'How the hell did she manage that?'

'There's been something wrong with that catch for ages. Now it must be completely broken.'

'Do you want me to take a look at it?'

'Yes, please. But not right away,' I added, as he stood up. 'Look, I'm terribly sorry about all this. The thing is, Millie's become so attached to me since she arrived – I guess she's suffering from separation anxiety.'

'Mmm.' I had the distinct feeling that Matthew was already contemplating separation of another kind.

'I know! Why don't I put up the baby gate? That way we can keep her out of the room, but the door will still be open, so she'll be able to see us through the bars.' I jumped out of bed yet again.

'Okay. Do you want a hand with it?'

'No, no, I can do it. It's an expandable thing, so it won't take me a minute to fix up.'

I was right: it didn't take me a minute, it took twenty. How was I supposed to know that the bloody thing was a self-assembly kit? By the time I'd got all the pieces out of the box and worked out which plastic screw and metal bar fixed to which, and in what order, Millie had carted most of the cogs off to the study and buried them in the dog-bed. She looked extremely pleased with herself. At least one of us was getting some pleasure out of the evening.

At last the baby gate was assembled. Now all I had to do was fix it *in situ*. Easier said than done, because the expandable sides were too big to fit in the narrowest part of the door frame, and yet were too small for the widest part. I eventually managed to wedge everything in place using some old books – oh, yes, and Matthew who, fed up with giving me instructions from the pillow, had eventually got out of bed to help.

I clapped my hands with satisfaction. 'There! Perfect. That should do the trick.'

'You're forgetting something.'

'What?'

'That.' Matthew pointed to the far side of the bed, where Millie was lying on the floor, penned into the bedroom with us.

'Aha!' I clicked open the middle of the baby gate, grabbed hold of her collar and ushered her out. 'Sit! Stay! Good girl!'

Back in bed, Matthew and I tried to pick up where we'd left off. But it was difficult to recapture the mood, particularly since Millie was now standing on her hind legs in the hall with her front paws on the baby gate's top bar, watching our every move. Every now and then she whined or barked at us. Whatever it was we were attempting to do, she was determined to be a part of it.

Suddenly she bent her back legs and vaulted the gate like an Olympic athlete, sending it crashing to the ground.

'Well, this is a novel form of birth control,' Matthew muttered.

'What do you mean?'

'*Canis interruptus*. I guess she'll just have to stay in here,' he continued. 'Let's hope she goes to sleep – before we do, I mean.'

But Millie had no intention of sleeping. Overcoming the obstacle course of the baby gate had excited her so much that she now crouched in the corner and . . .

'Oh, no!' I shot out of bed too late to stop her. 'Bad girl!' I shouted, near to tears. 'This is the last straw!'

'If only it was, it'd be easier to clear up,' Matthew remarked. 'Tell me, why didn't you get your builder to put down the carpet protector in here as well?'

'Because I didn't think I'd need it!' I sniffed. 'Because I intended to keep the dogs out of here!'

'How, exactly?' I pointed to the broken baby gate. Matthew suppressed a laugh, then got out of bed, came over to me and kissed away my tears. 'Do you have any of the carpet protector left?' I nodded. 'Well, why don't we lay it now?'

'But . . . ?'

He shrugged. 'I think any other kind of laying will have to wait for another occasion. I'm not sure I'm up to it now.'

Five minutes later – once I'd mopped up the puddle and dried the wet patch with my hairdryer – Matthew and I were on our hands and knees, in our underwear, unrolling the super-sized sticky cling-film and patting it down with our hands. It was a thin, transparent film with a yellow cast to it, which looked rather like latex. The kind that condoms are made of.

Matthew must have had exactly the same thought because he suddenly said, 'I've heard of safe sex but this is ridiculous!'

And we both fell about laughing.

20

A few days later, a couple in Oxfordshire saw Millie's photo on the website and applied to adopt her. Despite my rose-tinted description of her, a week later they dropped out. The search for her 'for-ever' home was back to square one.

By now Millie no longer needed rescuing – I did. She was idyllically happy, but I wasn't coping at all. I could repeat the mantra Joshua had told me until I was blue in the face, but the truth was that I was NOT in control – definitely not of Millie, not really of George, and certainly not of my own life any more. No, the boot was firmly on the other foot in my house. Or, rather, the other eight paws.

Though I'd employed more forms of bribery than a corrupt politician, Millie still hadn't got the hang of house-training. Oh, she knew all about relieving herself outside in return for a titbit of chicken. Yet the moment she returned to the house, she'd pee again. And again. And again. Maybe she was hoping to get chicken every time.

Hannah suggested I try using the puppy training pads that she'd used when she'd first got Billy, so I bought a packet of fifty. 'Keep your puppy dry! Protect your carpets!' the manufacturer claimed on the packet. Not in my house they didn't. Though I scattered the plastic-backed super-absorbent squares everywhere, Millie presumed they were for tearing up, not for doing her business on. She missed them every time.

When I was a child, I'd always longed for a Change My Diaper doll: you fed her water via a baby bottle, and a moment later the liquid came trickling out of her bottom. Now, at long last, I had one. Except this one was alive, and the water didn't come out of her nether regions in a cute little trickle, it gushed out like a power shower.

Could the frequency with which the shower went on be normal? Worried that it wasn't, I consulted Many Tears, who suggested I put a little cranberry juice in her drinking water along with the echinacea. This had no effect other than to turn Millie's urine a fetching rose pink. Next I took her to the vet to be checked out: Howard could find nothing wrong with her. As far as he could tell, she was fine: 'If you'd only followed my advice and crate-trained her . . .' He sighed wistfully. 'Now, if she'd been my puppy, I'd have had her clean within a week.'

Judging from the updates that most other fosterers were posting on the Many Tears website, so would they. Whereas all I could say in *my* website updates was that Millie had a wonderful nature and I loved her to bits; as for the housetraining, it was still 'a work in progress'.

How long could I continue like this? My work had ground to a complete halt. My open-plan flat just wasn't cut out for incontinent animals. I couldn't help but love my Labrador puppy – how could anyone resist such a bouncy, joyous bundle? – but looking after her had completely taken over my life. That tax-bill deadline was looming, and even though my Polish builders spent most of each day they were at the house throwing balls for Millie, they had nearly finished painting the exterior windows, which meant I was going to have to pay them.

Loath to admit defeat, I soldiered on. Then, one afternoon, after clearing up four puddles in less than forty minutes, I could stand it no longer. Desperate for some head-space, I locked myself into the upstairs bathroom, which had a big window behind the bath. Given that Dobby and Marek were around the side of the house, and the dogs were inside it, this was the only place where I was guaranteed some peace and privacy.

I turned on the taps, poured in some rose-scented bubble bath, stripped off and sank into the steaming depths. There was a big cedar tree outside the window and, since no one could see in, I pulled up the Venetian blind and gazed out into its dark green branches. Time to myself at last!

Then I heard a snuffling at the door. I took no notice. When something scratched at the woodwork and clawed at the door handle, I ignored that, too. The scratching turned into battering, interspersed with barking. I attempted to pretend that it wasn't happening. But it was as if the residents of Troy were trying to fool themselves that the Achaean troops weren't besieging their gates.

After a while all went ominously quiet outside. Then I heard something topple, followed by a loud crash. I got out of the bath and flung open the door to find a framed photo from the hall wall lying smashed on the floor. As I did so, the Trojan Dog barged past me into the bathroom, where she threw herself down on the mat, wagged her tail and gazed up at me hopefully.

I locked the door, shutting her in with me. 'Now stay exactly where you are, Millie, and please, please, don't bother me. I'm trying to think.'

Millie obeyed – for all of ten seconds. Once I'd sunk my

neck deep into the foamy depths and she couldn't see me, she jumped up and stuck her head over the side of the tub, to make sure I was still in it. As if she thought I might need help in washing myself, she put her paws on the side, leaned over and aimed her tongue at my neck.

I couldn't resist scooping up a small handful of bubbles and balancing them on her muzzle. She tossed them away with a shocked sniff, then leaned forward over the bath and poked her nose deep into a big cloud of them. Then she sneezed, sending the bubbles flying.

At that moment I heard a male voice in the garden. A few seconds later, the top of a ladder appeared against the window. I jumped up and, dripping water, reached for a towel. But before I could step out of the bath and grab it, Millie leaped joyfully in with me, sending a cascade of water gushing over the rim. As she sploshed up and down, wagging her tail, the top of Marek's head appeared at the window, followed by a hand holding a paintbrush and, finally, his face. His eyes swept over the dog and my naked body. Though his cheeks flushed purple, he nodded at me as if it was the most natural thing in the world to see me stark naked, sharing my bath with a dog, and then he quickly disappeared from view.

Matthew had been away on business since the bedroom fiasco. Now he was back and, amazingly, given the circumstances of our last meeting, he was on the phone asking when he could see me.

'Is there anything you'd like to do this weekend? Any films or plays you might like to see?'

'Well . . .'

'An art exhibition on Sunday?'

'I'd love to. Only . . .'

'What? Just say it, Judith.'

'I'm not sure I can get out of the house for very long.'

There was a pause. Then Matthew said, 'You mean, because of the dogs?'

I sighed. 'I'm sorry. George isn't the problem. In fact, since Millie's been here he seems to have changed from being King George the Bad into King George the Good. But the thing is, I don't see how I can leave him alone with Millie. She keeps jumping him. It's only a game, but she doesn't understand how much bigger and heavier she is. And she goes so berserk whenever she's separated from me.'

'Only then? Well, here's an idea. Why don't we take them out with us somewhere?'

'That's a good joke. To see *The Madness of King George*, perhaps, or *Reservoir Dogs*?' I scoffed.

'I was thinking more of a walk in the country. Followed by a pub lunch.'

I wanted to hug him for making such a generous suggestion. But he wasn't there to hug, and if he had been, Millie would only have nosed between us and stopped me. 'That is *so* nice of you! Thank you! But can you imagine what Millie might do if we took her into a pub? It'd be like rolling in a leaking beer barrel. Look, what if you came round here instead – that is, if you can bear to again?'

'I'm not sure I should risk it.'

'I'll make lunch in the garden, if it's nice enough, and we could take the dogs out for a walk to Kenwood afterwards. Millie's leash-training is certainly coming on.'

'I can see that this is one of those exciting offers it's impossible to refuse,' Matthew said. 'Who knows? I might even bring my Flymo, and give the lawn another trim.'

Laughing, I put down the phone, then gave a deep sigh. What Utopian planet had this wonderful, easy-going alien come from? And by what stroke of luck had he ended up hanging around with me?

Anxious to impress him for once, I scrubbed the flat clean, de-dogged the lawn for the hundredth time that week and, pestered by both dogs, who kept jumping up for scraps while I was cooking, prepared a special Sunday roast. Since the spring weather was terribly mild, I decided that we'd have an *al fresco* drink first, and maybe even eat outside, if it was warm enough. After he'd mown the lawn, of course (this was one gift horse I had no intention of looking in the mouth).

The garden table was on the small terrace underneath the kitchen balcony. I laid it with a pretty tablecloth and crockery, and even placed a small jug of daffodils in the middle. The scene was set for a bucolic lunch, which I hoped would go some way to making up for our last disastrous evening together. I was determined that nothing should go wrong this time.

As Matthew stepped out of the french windows and into the garden, his first view was of my Cavalier lifting his leg on one of the wooden chairs. Since George had never done such a thing before, I could only presume that he and Millie were co-conspirators in a plot to get rid of my new suitor before anything serious came of the relationship. I could have killed him.

'Well, this is a great start!' I said, as I ran for the garden hose. 'It's a good thing you put this together the other week.'

'Give it to me. I'll do it,' Matthew said, as I aimed the spray at the offending puddle.

'No, no, I will!'

Who was more of a control freak – Matthew or me? I wondered. But before we could fight over possession of the spurting hose, Millie snatched it out of my hand and jumped down the garden steps onto her landing strip, decapitating a clump of narcissi in the process. The moment she let go of it, the hose snaked up, drenching her and George, with cold water. As if he'd been stung by a bee, George ran off into the house, looking horrified, but after the initial shock Millie ran in and out of the spray with all the delight of a child.

Since the lawn was now far too wet to be mowed, I poured out two glasses of wine, and Matthew and I sat down to talk in the thin April sunlight. It was all very idyllic until George came back out of the house, jumped up on the bench and tried to squeeze himself onto Matthew's lap, leaving muddy paw prints on his crisply ironed trousers. 'Never mind,' he said. 'These are only my old gardening things.' Somehow I didn't believe him.

Exhausted by her shenanigans, Millie stretched out on the sun-warmed York stone with her head on my feet and went to sleep. This touching gesture, guaranteed to melt my heart, was marred only by a spectacularly pungent fart that wafted upwards on the breeze.

When we'd finished fanning the air with our napkins, I went upstairs to finish preparing lunch. Millie woke up when I moved, and came with me. I took the roast lamb out of the oven – it looked perfect – and pushed it to the back of the kitchen counter, well out of canine reach. In order to distract the circling shark for a few seconds I threw her a dog biscuit, then popped out onto the wrought-iron balcony, and called down to Matthew, 'It won't be long.' By the time I came back in, Millie was on one of the kitchen chairs, her nose twitching as she leaned precariously towards the roast. When I shooed her away, she ran to her water bowl, wallowed in it, then picked it up in her mouth and ran into the living room, splashing waves of water everywhere.

'Put that down!' I hissed.

'Everything all right up there?' Matthew called.

'Yes, fine.' I threw the as-yet-unread Sunday papers onto the floor to soak up the puddles.

'Are you sure you don't want a hand?'

'No, no. Stay down there!' I called.

What a mistake.

While I was on my hands and knees, mopping up, I glimpsed Millie scampering out onto the balcony. I breathed a sigh of relief: she'd left the lamb alone, and I was confident that there was nothing out there she could destroy.

I was wrong: there was my burgeoning relationship with Matthew.

'What the hell . . .?' he suddenly shouted. I heard the noise of pouring liquid followed by the sudden scrape of a chair and a disgusted 'Jesus Christ!'

I jumped up. Millie was crouching on the balcony, peeing through the metal lattice – just above where Matthew had been sitting.

21

The following Friday I heaved Millie into the car and, while she lay across the back seat contentedly chewing a meat-filled marrow bone, I drove her to Southend-on-Sea. My heart ached. I felt as guilty as if I'd been going to tie her up in a sack and drop her off the end of the town's famously long pier. What I was actually doing was taking her to a new foster home.

In other words, I was getting rid of her. The events of the previous Sunday had made me see what everyone around me had known for ages: that, although George was getting used to her, I couldn't cope with my Labrador pup any more.

Neither could Matthew.

'Golden showers,' he'd muttered, as he'd come out of the bathroom, where he'd washed his hair and changed into a clean shirt of Joshua's. 'That dog may be into so-called *water-sports*, but I'm certainly not.'

'I'm so sorry!' I handed him another dry towel for his hair.

His blue eyes flashed at me. Understandably, he looked furious. 'When you told me you were fostering dogs, Judith, I thought you'd just be having a second dog to live with you,' he said, in a controlled voice. 'But Millie seems to have taken over your whole life. Unless your life is always like this?'

'No!'

His expression softened. 'I'm sorry. I don't mean to get angry. And I don't want to interfere. But, well, you can't leave Millie here, and you can't take her out anywhere, so you're stuck at home and . . . I can't even have you to myself for five minutes. Not even in the bedroom!' He looked around at the glittering plastic floor, overlaid with scattered, unused training pads. 'It's all rather . . . rather . . .'

As he searched for the right word, I decided to help him out: 'Unbearable?'

He smiled. 'You've got it in one. George is no trouble at all . . .'

'Well, you're the first man to say that!'

'But Millie . . .' He shook his head. 'Look, I've always regarded myself as a pretty tolerant person. And I certainly don't want to put any pressure on you. After all, what you do is none of my business. Except, of course, that I rather like you,' he added.

I looked into those blue eyes. 'Even after this?'

'Amazingly, yes. The last few years have been so grim,' he went on, 'trying to pick up the threads of my life and carry on after my wife died . . . I don't have to tell *you* what it's like because you've been through it, too. But since we met . . . Well, let's just say that I'm beginning to feel alive again. And I'd very much like to keep on seeing you.'

There was a pregnant pause. 'But . . .?' I prompted.

He sighed. 'Honestly? I really don't think I can take much more of this.'

And who could blame him? I was reluctant to give up on Millie before a permanent home was found for her but I spent a sleepless night thinking about what Matthew had said. Then, the following morning, my madcap Labrador-able had made my mind up for me. I'd popped out to the shops for half an hour, leaving the two dogs with the run of the flat. By the time I'd come back, the place was in turmoil. There were puddles in both bathrooms, a broken vase in the living room and a trashed pot of hyacinths on the stairs. While I was clearing up, Millie picked up her full water bowl and ran through the living room with it. Then, desperate for a game, she'd leaped playfully off the sofa and right onto George's back. He'd squealed – this time in real pain – and I'd had to rush him to the vet.

'You're in luck,' Howard pronounced, after examining him. 'There's no permanent damage, just a little bruis-ing. But he's an old boy, dear, and you'd better not risk it happening again.'

The staff at Many Tears had been very understanding when I'd phoned them. I wasn't to feel bad about it: foster placements didn't always work out, they told me. And when a mismatch like this happened, the best thing was either to bring the dog back to the centre or to move it to a different foster home.

Penny, who lived in Southend, was one of their most experienced fosterers. Once upon a time she'd run a rescue centre of her own, but for the last ten years she'd been taking in dogs for Sylvia. Scores and scores of them, three or four at a time. At the moment she had Molly, a Jack Russell-Chihuahua cross, and Buffy, an unwanted Jack Russell pup. Toby, yet another Jack Russell, was the bossy top dog of her canine household, and Cheddar was a Jack Russell-miniature-Dachshund cross, who'd already been returned from two 'for-ever' homes for biting both her owners. So far Penny had had no trouble at all with her, so much so that she'd decided to adopt her and had taken Cheddar off the website. Cassie, a three-year-old black Labrador, was another dog that she'd taken in as a foster case but couldn't bear to part with: 'She was very nervous when I got her, but now she's absolutely superb,' Penny told me, when I arrived, giving the Lab a pat. 'She makes up for all the little horrors!'

The only sad face among this large, happy pack belonged to Nell. A smooth-haired black-and-white collie, when she'd first arrived she'd been utterly terrified of every-thing – hers was the worst case of trauma Penny had ever seen. Five weeks on she was still too scared to look her fosterer in the eye, or take a treat from her hand. She simply sat in a dog-basket by the open door in Penny's spotlessly clean kitchen (how *did* she manage it, with so many dogs in the house?) and she quaked if anyone went near her.

'I don't know what to do with her,' Penny confessed. 'She needs a life. I keep wondering what on earth must have happened to her to make her like this.'

Poor Nell. She didn't realize what she was missing in Penny's back garden. It was like Muttlins or Center Barcs out there: a long, wide lawn complete with a whole pack of cheerful dogs to play with, a pond, a pet tortoise and enough dog bean bags, dog mattresses, dog balls and toys lying around to please a whole battalion of them.

As if all these dogs weren't enough to deal with, Penny had now volunteered to take on Millie as well.

When I first led her out into the garden, Millie seemed uncharacteristically nervous. She stuck to my side and, when I sat down at the table opposite Penny, she rested her nose on my knees – a trusting gesture that, under the circumstances, brought me close to tears. But while we humans talked about why I could no longer cope with her ('I must be crazy, offering to have her!' Penny laughed, when I explained about the non-stop peeing and the water-bowl carrying) Millie wandered off and began to explore her new surroundings. One by one, the other dogs came over and sniffed her, and she sniffed them back, and within fifteen minutes she was engaged in a playful wrestling match on the lawn with her fellow Lab, Cassie.

It was clear that Penny's was a much more suitable environment for Millie than my home had been. There were so many young dogs for her to play with, and more space for her to run around in. That didn't stop me feeling as if I was betraying her, particularly when I got up to leave and she trotted obediently after me, wagging her tail; she took it for granted that she was coming home with me.

Following Penny's advice I didn't linger over the good-byes in the hall, I just planted a quick kiss on the top of Millie's head and left. Back in the car I burst into tears. I'd done exactly the same after I'd dropped Joshua off at his university hall of residence six months previously. Fostering dogs was supposed to help me get over my empty-nest syndrome. But I hadn't moved on: I was grieving again.

Back in London, I picked George up from the pooch parlour, where I'd left him earlier that morning. A cut-and-blow-dry had transformed him from the overblown sheep he'd lately become into a trim showstopper again. As always, the haircut also seemed to have taken years off his age. He skipped into the flat like a puppy and, without even looking round to see if Millie was there or not, settled happily on the sofa to eat a dog chew while I got out the Marigolds and J-cloths. It was time to make a clean sweep of things. Literally.

I flung open the windows to let in some fresh air, then lit some scented candles. I dunked the mop head in disinfectant, then swabbed the bathroom and kitchen floors, in particular the hearthstone where Millie had peed a hundred times, and the place behind the kitchen table where she'd pooped that very morning. The unused puppy training pads were folded up and consigned to the recycling bin, and Millie's big muddy paw-prints were polished off the glass panels of the balcony doors. That done, I Flashed the kitchen cabinets she'd scratched in an attempt to open them, and even Dettoxed the fiddly knobs on the stove – although Millie hadn't got her tongue into those particular crevices, they might have been cleaner if she had.

Watched by a curious George, I went from room to room downstairs, ripping up the sticky carpet protector in a frenzy, then took great armfuls of it outside and dumped it in the dustbins. Millie's urine had penetrated the film in several places so I got down on my hands and knees and shampooed those spots. After that, I tidied away the bottles of anti-bacterial spray, the pet deodorizer and the stain remover that had accumulated on the side of the bath, threw all the dog blankets into the washing-machine, then went on a lavender-scented Airwick-fest, spraying the rooms as liberally as a sales assistant in a perfumery department misting her customers with Christian Dior's Poison.

That done, I donned more rubber gloves and went out into the garden, where I removed every scrap of dog shit from what remained of the lawn. If Matthew ever turned

up with that Flymo again, I didn't want a repeat performance of what had happened the first time.

Empty of its usual air traffic, Millie's landing strip at the
bottom of the steps gaped at me. While I was crouching
near it, bag and trowel in hand, I found three well-chewed
tennis balls nestling under some dead leaves – and a tooth-
marked squeaky pink plastic bone. They were all Millie's.
With tears pricking my eyes, I picked them up and put them
on the garden table, arranging them as carefully as if they
were relics in a shrine.

When I went back inside, the house sparkled. It was so
clean that it looked sterile. As I walked around it, not
knowing what to do with myself, I kept glancing behind
me in search of that grinning face, but it was no longer
there. Millie, that big, soppy, solid lump of boisterous *joie
de vivre*, was gone from my life for ever, and it was I who'd
banished her.

I'd got what I'd wanted: my home and my life back. So
why did I feel so bereft? Millie was much better off with
Penny and her pack of six assorted dogs than she'd been
with me. Besides, she'd only ever been my foster dog, she
would have gone to a permanent home sooner or later.
Still, I couldn't help feeling I'd failed her and, at the same
time, failed myself. My career as a fosterer had ended in
humiliation.

But at least I now had the freedom to leave the house
occasionally, not to mention time to get down to work. I
also had the opportunity to find out whether or not my
relationship with Matthew was going to lead anywhere. I'd
met a man who was kind, funny, attractive and incredibly
tolerant. How lucky was that? Although I'd decided to give

up men for good, I'd be mad not to see what developed. Matthew certainly deserved it.

Just then the doorbell rang.

'Here's the food, here's the tank, and here's Jimmy.'

Sue, Philip and Jessica were on the doorstep. Or, rather, Sue and Philip were already halfway down the garden path, and Sue was saying, 'Got to go or we'll be late for our flight. Thanks, darling!'

'Yes, thanks so much, Judith!' My seventeen-year-old niece threw her arms around me and hugged me. A moment later she and her parents were back in their car, heading for Luton airport and a few days in France. No sooner had Sue driven off than the car screeched to a halt. She reversed along the road and wound down her window. 'Whatever you do, don't put him in *cold* water or you'll kill him,' she called. 'It's got to be room temperature. Got that? Remember, if he dies Jessica will never speak to you again.'

She drove off. I stared down at the stuff they'd deposited on the doorstep: one large glass tank, empty but for some multicoloured gravel and a plastic tree; a tiny tub of fish food; and Jimmy, Jessica's goldfish, who was currently imprisoned in a small rectangular plastic travelling box. As I picked this up, carried it into the kitchen and put it on the counter, he and I glared at each other through the walls of his tiny prison. I reminded myself that fish-sitting for a few days could hardly be as complicated as dog fostering. Besides, it was the least I could do to make up for all the times when Sue and Philip had had George to stay with them, never mind the times they'd looked after Joshua when he was younger or taken him on holiday with them.

Jessica had won Jimmy at a house party a few months

before. Oddly, given the limited, one-way nature of their relationship – she could lavish as much affection on him as she liked, but all he'd ever do was gawp at her – she was more attached to him than she'd been to her guinea pig, a short-lived pet ten years before. While he swam back and forth in his small box, eyeing me suspiciously through his protruding black eyes, I put the large fish tank on the draining-board, filled it with cold water, then added a splash from the hot kettle. I dabbled my hand in the water, then in Jimmy's travelling box, then added some more cold water. More hot and more cold followed. I didn't want to freeze Jimmy's rocks off, but neither did I want to turn him into fish chowder. My past record with goldfish was far from perfect. Won by my father at vast cost at Hampstead Heath funfair during my early childhood, and brought back to our Cricklewood semi in small, dripping plastic bags, they'd invariably survived for just a few days in the fish bowl before floating to the top. There, they had lain on their sides, gasping for breath and gradually turning from a pretty sparkling gold to a deathly blue.

At last the water temperature felt right. Now all I had to do was transfer Jimmy from the box in the sink into the tank on the draining-board. 'Please don't pour him in because you might injure him. Use a cup,' read the instructions that Jessica had left with him. I duly lowered my best china teacup into the water, and tried to scoop the goldfish up. He wasn't having it: small as the box was, he kept managing to evade my improvised scoop. Since there wasn't much room to manoeuvre it, I decided to try a soup ladle, with which, after several failed attempts, I eventually succeeded in lifting him out.

As I very carefully and slowly moved the ladle towards the tank, Jimmy thrashed about in it hysterically; maybe he thought he was heading for a pot of bouillabaisse. Then, just as I was about to lower him into the water, he thrashed so hard that he flipped out of the ladle, landed on the draining-board and slid down the stainless-steel channels into the sink. I looked on in horror as he swirled round, as if in a whirlpool, then slipped into the dark well of the waste disposal. Fired on by the thought of having to call my sister up even before she'd got to the airport to inform her that Jessica's precious pet had already met a grisly end, I plunged my hand down the opening, scooped up his writhing, slimy body with my bare fingers, pulled him out and dropped him into the tank. Disaster averted, but only just.

No sooner had he settled down – no visible ill effects, thank goodness – than the doorbell rang again. To my surprise, it was Hannah, who was carrying two outsize fully laden blue Ikea bags in one hand, and a cardboard box under her other arm. Billy was standing next to her, wagging his tail and straining at the leash.

'Hannah!'

She frowned at me. 'You did remember? About having Billy this week?'

'Well, actually . . .' My stepdaughter looked crestfallen. 'Of course I remembered,' I agreed. 'I just hadn't realized he was coming today. But that's fine. Lovely. Just what I need.'

'Really? His food and treats are in here,' she said, plonking one of the groaning bags on the kitchen table. 'And his toys are in this box. I've also brought two beds for him –

one for upstairs, the other for downstairs, so you don't have to keep moving them around. By the way, will you let him sleep in your bedroom at night?'

'Of course not!' I knew her feelings on the subject: she'd been determined from the start to learn from my past mistakes. 'He'll sleep in the study with George.'

'Well, that *should* be all right. He *might* just settle there. Only . . .' She looked embarrassed. 'The thing is, he's sort of ended up sleeping in my bedroom at night. Some of the time.' I raised a quizzical eyebrow – far more tactful than saying *I told you so*. 'And I think he's, um, rather got used to it.'

'Well, I'll see how it goes.'

'Thank you! I can't tell you how grateful I am. It's so wonderful to go away and not to have worry about him. He's been so accident-prone lately.'

'What do you mean?'

'He dived into a canal a couple of weeks ago when we were walking along the tow-path and caught some kind of virus. And the other day, a cyclist ran right over him in Richmond Park! It's a miracle he wasn't injured, let alone killed.'

'Don't worry – I'll look after him.'

'Thanks. I know he'll be safe with you.'

She gave me instructions about Billy's eating and ex-creting schedule (it boiled down to in one end and out the other), then hugged Billy goodbye and headed off to Gatwick and Spain.

The moment she left, Billy's tail stopped wagging and he ran to and fro by the front door, whining inconsolably. Nothing I did, including offering a smorgasbord of treats, would tempt him away or placate him. Having grabbed a few treats for himself while they were on offer, George watched our new lodger from a distance, head to one side, as if he couldn't understand what all the fuss was about.

Jessica's Jimmy *and* Hannah's Billy? The responsibility felt awesome – like looking after other people's children for a week.

2 2

Two dogs in the house again. No, make that three. Because the following morning I had a telephone call from James, the kennel manager at Many Tears, asking if I could help them out.

'We've just got a little Westie in, Judith. She's a three-year-old ex-breeding bitch who's come from a remote farm in Wales, and she's been given to us to be rehomed. I'm sure she'll be adopted very quickly, because she's an absolute beauty, but in the short term she's, well, finding being in kennels rather upsetting. It's all a bit confusing for her. We think she'd be much better off in foster care until she goes to her permanent home. So, if possible, we'd like to get her on to tomorrow's van and into a home straight away.'

The upshot was that he and Sylvia thought that living with me and a gentle dog like George would be ideal for Sophie. Even though I'd failed so miserably with Millie?

'I don't think you'll have any trouble with this one,' James reassured me. 'She's an absolute honey.'

Naturally I said yes. What else could I do? And, as soon as I'd hung up, I ran outside and rescued the puppy training pads from the bin before they were condemned to recycling oblivion. An ex-breeding dog was bound not to be house-trained. Like Millie.

My heart felt light again. I was back in business as a dog

fosterer. What was one more pet when I already had two – three, including Jimmy? The more the merrier, as far as I was concerned.

Though perhaps Matthew wouldn't feel quite the same.

I soon understood the attraction of keeping a goldfish. His food smelt like *bottarga*, that rare Italian delicacy of cured grey mullet roe, and he must have appreciated it because one pinch of it three times a day and he couldn't have been more contented. That was it. There was no nagging for extras, no crying himself to sleep on my bed, and no dirt other than the occasional sausage string of faeces, which he trailed around after him, as if reluctant to let go of it and mess up the bottom of his tank. If there was a downside to looking after him, it was that communication between us was minimal. The most we could do was to exchange the odd flirtatious glance through the thick glass walls of his prison. Just like having a relationship with a lifer in a maximum-security gaol.

Billy was almost as easy to look after. Playful, curious and affectionate, he fitted into the household as if he'd lived with us all his life. Now nine months old, he was still a tiny sprite, slighter-built than most Jack Russells. His black-and-white coat was sleek and smooth, rather than wiry like Elizabeth's Molly's, and there were two tan smudges above his black beady eyes, like the painted-on eyebrows of a Japanese geisha, which gave him a permanently surprised expression. I'd rarely seen a terrier quite as petite and pretty as he was, and it wasn't just me who thought so: when Hannah had entered him for the Most Handsome Dog contest in a local festival a few weeks before, the judges had awarded him one of the top prizes.

Those who presume that dogs are creatures of loyalty should revise their ideas. Less than a day after he'd arrived at my house, Billy, who couldn't bear to be separated from Hannah, had transferred his affection to the hand that now fed him – mine – just as George did every time he went to stay with Sue. In fact, it took Billy just half an hour to give up his lonely vigil on the doormat. After that, he followed me around the flat on his teeny paws, wagging his tail and looking blissfully happy.

Ever since she'd adopted him, Hannah had been taking him to training classes. The results were impressive: Billy came when called, sat when asked, and stopped whatever it was he was doing the moment I so much as raised a warning finger. At mealtimes he sat on the floor, fixed me with his beady eyes and waited patiently for me to put down his bowl, which he then not only cleared but licked sparkling clean afterwards, thus sparing me the bother of having to wash it up. What good manners.

Rather than needing to be entertained, Billy amused himself for hours on end by nosing a tennis ball around the living room, daintily chewing a rawhide stick or sorting through the contents of his cardboard toy box with all the concentration of a curio collector at a car-boot sale (as well as stuffed toys, some well-chewed balls and a Frisbee, these included a couple of big stones, a cuttlefish bone and half an empty coconut shell). Showing a healthy deference towards the older generation, he kept a respectful distance from George, didn't try to steal his food, however slow he was to eat it, and never hassled him except to chance the occasional quick kiss on the cheek. The King of the Canines responded by graciously allowing his young admirer to worship him. He even let him share his favourite basket. This was progress indeed.

With George and Billy getting on so well together, where did that leave my new foster dog? The answer was simple: either clasped in my arms or sitting on my knees.

West Highland White Terriers have an impeccable Scottish pedigree. They were first bred in Argyllshire in the late nineteenth century by two local aristocrats: Colonel Edward Donald Malcolm, the 16th Laird of Poltalloch and a member of the ancient Malcolm clan, and his neighbour at Rosneath Castle, George John Douglas, the 8th Duke of Argyll, Master of the Household of Scotland, Chieftain of the Campbells and Sheriff of Argyllshire. Working dogs, used for hunting foxes, badgers and otters, the terriers were compact, doughty creatures with large eyes, big ears and short legs suitable for scrambling over rough terrain. Their special feature was not one but two white coats – a short, thick, soft layer beneath a long, hard, wiry one. This double insulation not only helped them to withstand the cold Highland winters, it also made them more visible in the field. To be honest, Westies, as they're known, had never really appealed to me. I'd always found their faces rather inexpressive, and their characters hard to gauge. And, just like white cars, they always looked grubby unless they'd recently been washed. However, three-year-old Sophie melted away my prejudices.

With her round black eyes, black button nose, thick fluffy coat, surprisingly long legs and the gigantic ears that stood out on top of her head like twin mountain peaks frosted with snow, she was one of the prettiest little dogs imaginable. Compared to the bedraggled Westies I'd seen on the van when I'd gone down to visit Many Tears, she looked in peak condition, too, which made me think she must have come from a reputable breeder who'd cared for her well.

And yet, aside from Nell, the collie who was being looked after by Penny in Southend-on-Sea, Sophie was the most terrified dog I'd encountered so far. What was she scared of? Certainly not George or Billy. Neither of them was remotely aggressive. Overjoyed to have another friend to play with, Billy danced a little jig around her, and even presented her with one of his chews, while the King himself went up to her and, in an unprecedented friendly gesture, honoured her with a royal sniff. He was quite put out when she cut him dead.

'The best way to make a dog feel confident is to take her for a walk the moment you get her home,' Joshua advised me, when I phoned him to say that I was going to foster a Westie. Deeply upset that I'd given up on Millie, he was nevertheless slightly mollified that we were to have a new arrival. 'Keep her on a short rein, Mum, just behind you, to show her that you're the pack leader.'

I duly leashed Sophie up and, leaving the other two dogs at home so that I could concentrate on walking her, took her for a short stroll around the block. Though it appeared that she was leash-trained, everything she encountered seemed to freak her out. Belly close to the ground, ears flat to her head, tail between her legs, she scuttled along beside me without resisting. However, every noise, from a child's voice to the slam of a car door, made her flinch as if she'd been struck by lightning.

Back home, she refused a drink of water and a dog biscuit. After negotiating the stairs slowly and with some difficulty, she let me lead her out into the back garden. The moment I unclipped her leash to let her run around, however, she crawled over to the back wall, and sidled along it as if searching for an escape route. When she failed to find one, she sat down behind a hydrangea, and peered out at me fearfully through its leaves.

No amount of coaxing on my part, or nudging by George and Billy, would make her move from there so I left her to settle in for a while and, knowing that no harm could come to her, went back into the house. When I came back out, I found her hiding underneath a rose bush. Since she didn't respond to being called or coaxed, I had no choice but to fight my way through the thorns and pick her up.

Back in the kitchen, covered with long red scratches, and feeling like the mother of fussy triplets, I put down three bowls containing three different dog foods: there was George's special diet rubble and chicken, Billy's special puppy rubble and Cesar, and the special moist mush that I'd been instructed to feed Sophie (Many Tears always provided food for their foster dogs, in case a sudden change of diet upset their stomachs). Though the other two tucked into their bowls immediately, Sophie refused to touch hers or, again, to drink any water. Worried that she must be hungry, I tried hand-feeding her a morsel of chicken: she gobbled it from my fingers, and before long had eaten a whole handful.

When she realized that no more was forthcoming, she took refuge behind the sofa. And there she stayed for the next couple of hours. 'I don't know what to do to help her,' I told Matthew, when he dropped by that evening 'to visit the new menagerie', as he commented somewhat ironically. Instead of the chaos he'd expected to find, my living room was a picture of domestic harmony. Billy and George were both stretched out asleep in front of the open fire – a real live pair of fire dogs – Jimmy was exploring his plastic tree for the millionth time that day, while I was reading a book.

'Give Sophie some time. I'm sure she'll settle down,' Matthew said, in a soothing manner, taking my hand.

'I'm sure you're right. I feel so sorry for her, though. What can have happened to her in her former life to have made the poor little thing so afraid?'

'Maybe it's just that everything here is so new to her. Don't worry, she'll probably settle down and be causing havoc in a few days' time, just like Millie did. Then you'll be happy again.' He smiled at me. 'In the meantime . . . while we have a five-minute window of opportunity . . . shall we forget about dogs and concentrate on other things?'

Just as he pulled me towards him, I felt something brush my ankle. I looked down to see Sophie's face peeping at me around the side of the sofa.

'Look!' I breathed. 'She's come out of hiding!'

We both froze as, belly close to the floor, the little Westie sidled around the front of the sofa.

'She's beautiful!' Matthew whispered. 'Just like one of those dogs in the old Black and White whisky ads.'

Head to one side and with one front paw raised, Sophie glanced up at us quizzically. I held my breath as she reached up and rested a paw on one of my knees. A moment later, she leaped onto my lap, crawled over my legs like a caterpillar, and wedged herself into the small space between me and Matthew.

And there she stayed, with her head resting touchingly on my lap, for the rest of the evening. George and Billy came over to say hello, but neither Matthew nor I dared move in case we frightened the newcomer.

That night, all three dogs slept in the study, which I'd scattered with enough of the rescued puppy training pads to cover the entire stretch of freshly laid carpet protector. I woke at five and crept in there, dreading what I might find. George and Billy were both curled up asleep together in one of the baskets, while Sophie was lying on the day-bed, wide awake and trembling. To my astonishment there was no mess – just one puddle on a training pad. Hurrah! She was a genius!

Letting the sleeping dogs lie, I picked her up, unlocked the french windows in Joshua's room and took her into the garden on a leash. After fifteen minutes of standing on the lawn in the grey dawn light, both of us shivering, she finally squatted on the grass and peed. I slipped her a dog treat. Once you took charge of it, housetraining a dog really wasn't that difficult. Just rather cold.

Back inside, belly still low on the floor, Sophie shadowed me into my bedroom. To my surprise, the moment I got into bed, she leaped straight onto the end of it.

I got out, gently lifted her trembling body off, and put her on the floor, with a gentle 'No, darling!'. She immediately jumped back up, which I felt was remarkably brave of her, considering how terrified she was. 'No,' I said again. We repeated the process three more times before guess who gave up. Knees bent in a submissive fashion, Sophie slowly crawled up the duvet towards the head of the bed, pressed herself against my ribcage and looked pleadingly into my eyes, as if begging to be allowed to stay there.

What was it with me and dogs, I wondered, as I drifted off to sleep with my hand on her head. Sophie had only been with me for a matter of hours, but she was already sleeping on my bed – something even George wasn't officially allowed to do any more. As well as that, she'd got me to ditch her diet of mush in favour of human food. Timid as she was, she'd already got me eating out of her hand. Or, rather, got herself eating roast chicken out of mine.

By the time I woke up again, her head was beside mine on the pillow, and George and Billy were standing on their hind legs next to the bed, with their paws up on it. George looked scandalized. Like an unfaithful wife who'd been caught *in flagrante* with a lover, I felt like crying out, 'It's not what you think!'

The next moment, he sat back on his haunches, jumped up and sat down heavily on my chest. Billy followed a few seconds later.

Four in the bed. And that was how it stayed for the rest of the week.

What was it about Sophie that got to me so quickly? Why did I feel such empathy towards her? Vulnerable, needy and scared of everything – though not, surprisingly, of people – she endeared herself to everyone. She only seemed to be happy when sitting on someone's lap or being carried around the flat, tucked under my arm – which was where she ended up most of the time. Looking after her was like caring for a traumatized baby, one who never showed any emotion other than fear, and clung to you without making a sound.

Later I was to learn that she had been brought up in a remote rural area of Wales, where the only person she ever saw, other than her breeder, was the postman who delivered mail once or twice a week. But at the time I could only speculate at what made her so scared all the time. Like many ex-breeding dogs, Sophie hadn't been properly socialized, and she didn't behave like a normal dog.

Not even when it came to housetraining. Here, she was at the opposite end of the scale to Millie. My Labradorable had never stopped going. Sophie, on the other hand, never went at all. Maybe she was an anally retentive type: she certainly seemed to be retaining everything she'd eaten.

After a few days I called up the Many Tears office to ask their advice. Liza consulted Sylvia, who advised giving Sophie a little liquid paraffin mixed with the chicken and rice that, try as I might to include dog food with it, was still all she'd eat.

Liquid paraffin? It sounded very Dickensian – the sort of medicine that might have been meted out as a punishment to Nicholas Nickleby in Dotheboys Hall.

'The kind you buy from a pharmacy,' Liza stressed. 'Definitely *not* the sort you cook with when you go camping.'

I rushed out to the pharmacy and bought some. Since the directions on the bottle advised giving six teaspoons to an adult human, I compromised by giving Sophie a half teaspoonful. I dreaded to think what the consequences would be, but twenty-four hours later, there was still no sign of them.

In the hope that a brisk run might get things moving, I leashed up all three of my charges and, feeling like a professional dog-walker, took them out to the Heath. It wasn't easy to get there, because as we walked down the road Billy forged ahead, Sophie trotted alongside me obediently, and George lagged behind, pulling to go home.

Once let off it, however, he cantered in great circles across the big meadow as if to demonstrate to his juniors that he was still a match for them. He made a half-hearted stab at chasing a rabbit into the undergrowth, then took an enthusiastic roll and back-scratch in a patch of mud. Meanwhile, Billy ran back and forth in pursuit of his ball, and Sophie trotted fearfully beside me.

After heading down through the muddy East Heath woods, we emerged at the large, deep Viaduct Pond beneath a high, red-brick Victorian bridge. I wound Sophie's leash more tightly around my hand. Though a mass of water-lilies in midsummer, at other times of the year the pond often became clogged with duckweed and algae, and so it was that day. Instead of the dark but clear water, a smooth lime-green carpet appeared to stretch ahead of us to the viaduct. Long ago, George had once mistaken the algae for a lawn, and tried to walk across it. Having learned his lesson, he now stopped on the bank and peered down at it suspiciously.

Billy, on the other hand, ran towards it. I called to him, but for once he took no notice. Before I could grab him, he launched himself onto the flat expanse of what he presumed was grass.

As his tiny frame plunged beneath the surface, I suddenly remembered what Hannah had told me about him falling into the canal the other week. Afterwards he'd gone down with a high fever, and he'd been ill for days. Her other words came back to me, too: 'I know he'll be safe with you.'

A second later his delicate head bobbed above the surface, nose pointing away from the bank. Slime dripped from his forehead, and his tiny paws were paddling frantically as he tried to keep himself afloat.

'Billy!' I called. 'Billy, over here!' He turned his head, and I caught a glimpse of the terrified whites of his eyes before he sank again.

I knew that most dogs could swim by instinct – but not all of them. When he'd fallen into the canal, Hannah had had to jump in and rescue him. If he were to drown now, she'd never forgive me. And I'd never forgive myself.

I dropped to my knees and, as he bobbed up again, I stretched out to grab his collar. But he was still out of reach. 'Billy!'

He paddled hard, but in the wrong direction, out towards the middle of the pond. Then he disappeared beneath the green slime again.

There was nothing for it but to jump in after him.

Back home, I stripped off my squelching boots and my streaked, sodden jeans, then carried the shivering Billy downstairs and put him into the bath. A nice warm shower, shampoo and towel-dry completely revived him, and he ran around the hall and up and down the stairs, before settling to steam dry in front of the fire.

I scrubbed out the bath, showered, then threw the dirty clothes and towels into the washing-machine. Disaster averted, mess cleaned up. It was now time for a well-earned cup of tea – and a whole packet of biscuits. I was just about to go upstairs and make one when I saw Sophie. The consequences of the liquid paraffin had suddenly appeared on the hall floor. And some were stuck to her nether regions.

I put her into the bath while I cleaned the carpet. Then I shampooed her, too. She spent the entire time trying to clamber out of the tub, with the result that the bathrobe I'd put on ended up as wet as she was.

After I'd towelled her dry she ran around my bedroom wagging her tail for a full five seconds. Then she must have remembered that she was suffering from post-traumatic stress disorder because her tail drooped and she scuttled under the bed. I fished her out, kissed the top of her head and, tucking her under my arm, went upstairs to make myself that tea. Though the tail-wag hadn't lasted long, it was the first time I'd seen it, and it felt like a real achievement.

Later, I lay down on the sofa and she crawled onto my lap. George jumped up on one side of her, and Billy on the other. I laid my hand on Sophie's warm damp head, and stroked her flattened ears.

I'd grown terribly fond of her in the last few days. In fact, I'd grown to love her. Now it occurred to me that if I was to adopt any dog as a companion for George she would be the one.

Then I noticed that the answering-machine on the desk was flashing.

I went over and pressed the play button.

'Hi, Judith,' said a familiar voice. 'This is Liza from Many Tears. Great news: we've found a permanent home for your Westie.'

23

Five days later, I stood on the front doorstep with a grim smile pasted on my face, while a woman called Jean carried Sophie down the garden path and out of my life for ever.

I was determined not to cry. Still, I felt a terrible sense of loss. Looking after foster dogs could be hard, but saying goodbye to them was much, much harder, and the vulnerable little Westie had touched me in a way that even Millie and Inch hadn't. Out of the three of them, I had a feeling I'd miss her the most.

Billy had survived his dip in the pond without any ill effects, thank goodness, and the day before Hannah had come over to collect him. I was now down to two pets – and Jimmy was due to go back to Sue's in a few days' time. The flat felt horribly quiet with only George and me walking around in it and, rather than being pleased to see the back of his canine companions, as he'd been with the other two, George was wandering around looking lost. He seemed to miss Billy and Sophie as much as I did.

The following day found me back on the Many Tears website, with George sitting on my lap staring at the screen as I scrolled down it. I even called up the kennel manager, James, and asked him to recommend a dog I could foster next.

'How about another Westie?' he suggested. 'I've got a really nice one in at the moment.'

'No, it wouldn't be fair to the poor thing.' I sniffed. 'I'd just be wishing it was Sophie all the time. If possible, I'd like a different kind of dog this time, James. Bigger, perhaps. Maybe a bit livelier.'

'Really?' He sounded doubtful. 'You ran into a spot of trouble with Millie, didn't you?'

'True. But, you know, I think I've really got the hang of fostering now. I'm more experienced. And much more confident. I'm ready for a challenge.'

'Sure?'

'Absolutely!'

'Okay!' he said cheerfully. 'In that case I know exactly who I'm going to send you.'

Matthew and I spotted him the moment we drove into the lorry park. Not just because he was the only dog there but because Murphy was impossible to miss in his own right.

'You never told me you were fostering a horse,' Matthew remarked, as he stared at the creature standing beside the blue car, which was the only other vehicle in the otherwise empty car park. 'He's very big, Judith.'

'Maybe *they*'re very small,' I suggested, pointing at the two glamorous blondes standing next to him holding his reins – correction, leash. 'Vertically challenged, I mean.'

'Sadly not, I fear.'

'On the website, it said that he was a little under grey-hound height.'

'They must have meant a Greyhound bus.'

Since there weren't enough dogs going to foster homes that week to make a van trip worthwhile, my new foster dog, a smooth-haired Lurcher called Murphy, had been taxied up to Reading by Naomi and Carol, two of Many Tears's dedicated volunteers. Both of them lived near Brighton, but they had driven all the way to South Wales for the weekend to help muck out the kennels, play with the dogs and bath the new arrivals; this was the kind of loyalty and dedication that Sylvia and her team inspired in their supporters. Now they were on their way home.

Brimming with energy, and managing to look band-box smart after what must have been an exhausting and very grubby two days, if my own experience was anything to go by, the two women gave me a lively account of Murphy's even livelier behaviour during the journey from Llanelli. Apparently, he was quite a character, and had spent the entire three and a half hours trying to clamber over the backs of the front seats onto their laps. Only the fact that they'd tethered his leash to one of the seatbelt points had stopped him. They suggested that I use the same technique. Heaven only knew what the consequences would be if I didn't.

It was now seven o'clock in the evening, and I expected my new foster dog to be tired and tense after travelling for hours in a strange car with people he didn't really know. Instead, Murphy seemed as elated and up for madness as a twenty-year-old out clubbing on a Friday night. He opened his long, pointed muzzle and grinned at me as I approached him, and as soon as I was within touching range he reared up on his hindquarters like a stallion, threw his front paws around my shoulders as if he'd known me all his life, and gave me slobbery face-to-face kisses. Standing on his back legs, he was as tall as I was.

In preparation for his arrival I'd spent the previous

evening lying on the sofa watching DVDs of dog trainers Cesar Millan and Victoria Stilwell (George had watched them with me, curled up on my chest). So, rather than let my new charge dominate me now, I turned my back on him until he jumped down, then took a good look at him as he strained to get to me again. He was magnificent.

As his name suggested, Murphy came from Ireland. He was between eighteen months and three years old. He might well have been an ex-racer or hare-courser that had outlived his usefulness and been turfed out by his owners (a not-uncommon occurrence in rural areas), or he might once have been someone's pet. Because he was a stray, all that was definitely known about him was that he'd been found a few weeks before roaming the countryside of County Wexford, emaciated, wet, and with two scars on his back that might have been caused by scrabbling through a barbed wire fence or, alternatively, were the result of a dog fight. We would never know.

Murphy's rescuer had taken him to a local pound, but since no one had come forward to claim him, and the pound had failed to find him a new owner, he was put on Death Row. Young, beautiful, sweet-tempered and full of life, he was only hours from being euthanized when Sylvia had arrived, scooped him into her van, along with a load of other condemned dogs and puppies, and taken him on the ferry to Wales, where he'd been bathed, inoculated and castrated (a fate that an alpha dog such as he was might have considered worse than an untimely demise).

'Since he's only just been neutered he might mark at first,' James had warned me.

Marking? Didn't that mean spraying every surface he

could reach with urine in order to stake out his territory?

'That's right. But it should stop in a couple of weeks or so.'

Rather than take George with us to collect Murphy, I'd parked him at Sue's for the afternoon. And before Matthew and I had set off, we'd Googled 'Lurcher'. It turned out that it was a cross between a sighthound and any other dog, usually a terrier or a pastoral breed. Since this had left us little the wiser, we'd Googled on, and discovered that a pastoral dog was any dog with a herding or droving instinct (the collie was a prime example) and a sighthound was the same as a gazehound and *that* was a hound that primarily hunted by speed and sight, instead of by scent and endurance.

Gazehounds – among other breeds, the group included Greyhounds, Whippets, Irish Wolfhounds, Salukis and Scottish Deerhounds – were originally bred to bring down game in full flight; hence their bodies were honed for speed like those of Olympic athletes. They were all muscle, no fat, and so aerodynamically built that they had no need even for Lycra shorts. Because they were such good hunters, in times past only the aristocracy had been allowed to own them. Any commoner or Traveller caught with a gazehound was deemed to be a poacher and subject to severe punishment, such as transportation to the colonies or death by hanging – or perhaps a year of having to look after Tinkerbell, Paris Hilton's Chihuahua.

Some Lurchers were relatively small and smooth-haired, like Whippets. Others were as tall as Greyhounds, with thick, wiry coats that looked like cheap fake fur; it depended on what gazehound it was descended from, and what pastoral dog this had been crossed with.

My ex-boyfriend Alex's Lurcher, Rocket Ron, had been a black Greyhound cross and a gentle giant. Despite the comic difference in their shapes and sizes – he was the canine equivalent of a racehorse, while my Cavalier resembled a well-stuffed teddy bear – he and George had become firm allies in the days when Alex and I were going out. Sitting side by side in the back of Alex's convertible, the wind blowing in their faces and their tongues lolling out, they'd accompany us to cafés and restaurants (Alex always insisted on taking them with us, even though it meant we had to sit outside, whatever the weather). When the food was served George had distracted us by jumping up and down and barking, while Rocket Ron, whose head was at table height, had snatched scraps from our plates. Some of these he'd eaten, others he'd dropped on the ground for George to hoover up. This Laurel and Hardy double-act had continued in Alex's back garden during the barbecue season. Needless to say, my Cavalier had been heartbroken when Alex and I had eventually split up; in fact he still stopped at Rocket Ron's garden gate whenever we walked past it, in the hope that he'd be invited in for another meal.

Like Rocket Ron, Murphy was Greyhound-sized; he must have measured about twenty-eight inches tall at the withers. His coat was smooth and the colour of rich golden syrup marbled with cream. His ribs jutted through his skin, as if he'd been starved for weeks. His head was surprisingly small for such a big dog, and his face was identical in shape to a bicycle saddle: a pair of comically outsize pointed ears stuck out from the back of the imaginary seat, and his black nostrils formed the tip. His neck was as thick and muscular as a wrestler's, and it sloped into a big, curved ribcage. His elongated, S-shaped back ended in an elegant tail, which, when hanging down between his hind legs, almost touched the ground.

His legs were Murphy's most impressive feature. While they don't necessarily have the stamina to keep the pace up for long, Greyhounds, and Greyhound-type Lurchers, are among the fastest sprinters on earth: with their large hearts and their double-suspension rotary gallop, in which all four paws are lifted off the ground at the same time, they can travel at speeds of up to eighteen metres per second, which translates into about forty miles an hour. Accordingly, their hind legs are made of long bones and solid muscle, with quadriceps and biceps that would leave a body-builder or professional cyclist drooling with envy.

So, when you looked at him from the side, Murphy appeared to be Mr Universe. On the other hand, if you looked at him head on you could easily miss him. For, like most gazehounds, his body was as narrow as an arrow. You could almost have threaded him through the eye of a needle.

While Naomi, Carol and I discussed him, Murphy's small but keen almond-shaped eyes moved from face to face as if he was following the conversation and understood every word we were saying about him. He was clearly an intelligent animal. And a supremely self-confident one, too: on the short walk over to my car he sauntered alongside me with the air of a young Jack-the-lad who knew exactly where he was going in life *and* how he was going to get there. After a few steps I began to wonder who was leading whom. When we reached the car, he clambered into the open hatchback without even being asked, sprawled full length on the duvet I'd thrown over the lowered back seats (he was far too big to fit in the crate) and, without a 'Please, may I?' or 'Thanks', he started gnawing at the large rawhide bone I'd brought along for him. As if he'd expected nothing less.

Unlike my previous foster dogs, this handsome fellow obviously wasn't overawed by anything or anyone. Least of all me.

Just as Naomi and Carol had warned, once he'd demolished the rawhide bone Murphy spent the rest of the trip to London trying to climb over the back of our seats so that he could sit with us in the front. But since Matthew had tethered him to the seatbelt point, as advised, the best he could do was to tap our shoulders with his huge, elegant front paws, or poke the back of our necks with his cold wet nose. Eventually he gave up trying to vault the head-rests, and took up a position right behind me. Like a back-seat driver, he stared intently over my left shoulder and out through the windscreen, his muzzle grazing my ears every time I turned a corner, and his tongue occasionally washing them with short, wet flicks.

Back home, he leaped out of the car and, eager to inspect his new quarters, cantered down the front path and into the kitchen so quickly that his long legs almost skidded away underneath him. Sue had returned George half an hour before, so he was waiting there for us. The moment Murphy saw him his eyes lit up and he ran to him, bent down, poked his nose underneath him and attempted to give him oral sex. Poor George froze in horror at being molested by the new intruder, who towered over him.

'Well, you can't say that he's unfriendly,' was Matthew's comment, as I shooed him away. 'I thought he'd been *done*? I mean, unmanned.' He shuddered as he said the word. 'Or does one say undogged, in this case?'

'The dastardly deed was done a few days ago, so there's probably lots of testosterone still washing around in his body. When that dries up, his urges will too, and with any luck he'll stop doing disgusting male things. Like that,' I said, as the Lurcher marked the edge of the door.

Matthew shuddered again. 'Time I went home now,' he said, as I reached for my Marigolds. And he left.

Marking and oral sex aside, I was half in love with Murphy by the end of the evening. How could I not be when he was so handsome, so genial, so funny, so enchanting? To cap it all, he seemed genuinely interested in my company and what I had to say – and what could be more seductive than that?

Having vacuumed up his own food, he stood beside me and watched closely while I cooked something for myself. He was so tall that his nose was at counter height; if he'd had hands, not paws, at the end of his front legs he'd have been able to take things down from the top shelves without the aid of a ladder. Head to one side, big ears flopping over, he followed my every move with his beady eyes and, before I knew it, I found myself explaining to him the rules of making salad dressing. I even demonstrated how to whip up an omelette. Every now and then he nodded, as if he'd never heard anything so fascinating. How could I not be besotted?

When I sat down to eat, he stretched out at my feet, his long tail drumming the floor. Not until George had vacated the furry dog-bed where he'd been sleeping in favour of the sofa did Murphy go over to it, give it a sniff, then throw himself down on it, squashing it flat as he did so.

And there he went to sleep, with his head, legs and hindquarters radiating over the edge like the spokes of a bicycle wheel.

I gazed at him for a while with a foolish grin on my face, then sifted through the paperwork that had come with him to find out what, if anything, was known about his history. I was just putting it away when I noticed a few phrases scrawled in biro on the top of the envelope: 'Castrated two days ago. Stitches to be removed in one week's time. Stitch cutter enclosed.'

They had to be joking.

24

Later that evening, Murphy presented me with one of the only two gifts available to him – a Vesuvius-like pile, from which a sulphurous cloud rose into the air. After I'd cleared it up, I put him and George to bed for the evening. Separately. Once over their initial blip, the two dogs had co-existed quite happily together upstairs. But the Lurcher was so large, and had such big teeth, and was such an unknown quantity that, until I got to know him better and was sure I could trust him, I decided not to leave him alone with George.

Happy to sleep solo (and, after the oral-sex attempt, I couldn't blame him) George plodded into the study and settled down for the night on the day-bed. As for Murphy, I put Millie's doubled-up duvet on the hall floor outside my bedroom. Even the largest dog-bed in the house was far too small for him; he needed a queen-sized double at the least.

What he wanted, however, was a super-king-size model. What's more, as I now discovered, he'd already found one – mine – and had made himself comfortable in it by kicking back the duvet, moving the pillows, and creating a nice big nest for himself in the middle. Now cosily curled up in it, he raised his head from between his paws and leered at me.

'Get off!' I said firmly. His mouth fell open in bewilderment. This was not the reaction that the great seducer had expected: since I'd brought him back to my place, he'd presumed he'd be sleeping with me. 'Off, Murphy!' Unfolding his long legs, he stood up on the mattress hesitantly, as if he couldn't quite believe he was being rejected. I stood my ground and pointed at the floor – this was one battle I had no intention of losing – until, tail wagging again, he jumped down. 'Good boy. Now, out! Out!' I pointed to the door, shooed him through it, then indicated the duvet. He lay down on it hurriedly. When he started to get up again I made a sharp barking noise, like Joshua had taught me to do with Millie. The method certainly worked, because Murphy sat down again pretty sharpish.

'Good boy. Now, stay! Stay, Murphy! Do you understand me?'

He must have, because he immediately lay down and went to sleep.

At six o'clock the following morning, I awoke to the sound of chomping. I opened my bedroom door to find the new arrival still lying on the duvet, happily gnawing at a rawhide bone I'd left out for him. Delighted that my pack-leader act was working, I let him out into the garden for a few minutes. Then, leaving the still-sleeping George in the study, I took my new foster dog out for a walk. Since he was so big and muscular, I didn't quite trust that a collar alone would hold him, so before I left the house, I fetched George's expandable seatbelt, strapped Murphy into it and clipped a leash on that, too.

With a leash in either hand, and looking like one of the stunt-kite flyers who congregated on the summit of Parliament Hill on Sundays, I set off for the Heath, keeping Murphy firmly at my side. Head raised, big ears pricked, and with the tip of the left one flopping over at a comical angle, he drank in the new environment he found himself in, his eyes alert to every leaf or bird that moved. Happy as he'd seemed in the flat, I had a feeling that the great outdoors was his natural habitat.

Once in Pryors Field, he strained to be free, and it took all my strength to hold him. I just about managed, until he spotted a grey squirrel at the edge of a clump of trees. A split second later, he was off after it, towing me behind him through a blackberry thicket. Luckily for all concerned, his potential prey took refuge up an oak tree. Murphy stopped beneath it, crying with frustration, and leaping at the lowest branches in an attempt to clamber up them.

'Come on, Murphy, time to move on,' I said. 'Come! Good boy! Murphy, come!'

To my astonishment he completely blanked me. As if I hadn't spoken, his eyes remained fixed on the furry-tailed rodent now gloating at him from its safe haven in the uppermost boughs, and neither my powers of persuasion nor my frequent tugs on the two leashes would make him move away. Come hail or thunder, hurricane or earthquake, his body stance indicated, Murphy wasn't going to leave until *he* was ready to, so I might as well give up trying to make him.

What, I wondered, had I taken on?

My life with George had been funny, eventful, poignant, and sometimes even infuriating. My life with Murphy over the next six weeks would turn out to be a thrilling adventure. I never knew what was going to happen next. Neither did George. The two of us were often left open-mouthed by Murphy's antics and his larger-than-life personality. Always amusing and good-tempered, never boring or predictable, Murphy kept both of us on our toes. If we expected him to be bad, he'd behave like an angel. And when we trusted him to be good? Always a mistake.

Fearless, handsome and über-friendly, Murphy managed to seduce everyone he came in contact with. He arrived in Hampstead a stranger and a vagabond. Within a week, he had his own fan club on the Heath – and it was even bigger than George's. Dog walkers and strangers would stop and ask about him. What was his name, and where had I got him from? What breed was he? Could they pet him? Murphy responded by jumping up and slobbering over them, in the same way he'd greeted me when we'd first met in the car park. If he'd been able to talk, I swear he'd have invited everyone down to the local pub and bought them a round (or, more likely, let them buy *him* one).

This was a party animal who knew how to enjoy himself. It left me thinking that, as a dog's life went, there were worse things than to be a country stray. Not for him the cowering fearfulness of the ex-breeding dogs I'd come across. On the contrary, Murphy was happy-go-lucky, self-reliant, a streetwise survivor who, by sheer force of personality, would have thrived anywhere in the world.

To my delight it turned out that, give or take the occasional accident, he was clean in the house. He was also a dab hand when it came to home improvements, particularly when it came to improving things for himself. Soon after he'd taken over George's fake-fur dog-bed, he adapted it by pulling out half of the stuffing with his teeth, so that the sides lay flat on the floor. Next, he selected several small cushions from the sofa, carried them over to the flattened bed and placed them strategically around the edge, so that it was even more comfortable. Nest-building was obviously his forte.

Greyhounds are sometimes called 'Forty-five m.p.h. couch potatoes' because, although they can sprint incredibly fast for short periods, they spend much of their lives lying around sleeping. I can only think that Murphy must have had a lot of Greyhound blood in him, because his adapted bed was soon loaded with so much food, and so many useful items, that he never needed to leave it unless he had to. On one occasion the contents included an unopened packet of HobNobs he'd removed from the biscuit tin after knocking it on to the floor; a toast crust; a well-gnawed beef bone, and a rotting banana he'd stolen from the fruit bowl. Alongside them were half a chewed-up tennis ball, the screw top from a plastic milk carton, a hyacinth, a telephone, a book and, inexplicably, an old rubber torch that had been missing for years.

I found this hoard strangely touching, as well as a little puzzling. That Murphy should stash food and treasure trove in his bed seemed to indicate that he was determined to establish a permanent base there. But why had he chosen those particular items? What, for instance, had attracted him to the milk-carton top? And why, of the hundreds of books within his reach, had he selected the *Rough Guide to Berlin*? Perhaps he'd overheard me and Matthew one night, discussing – in a theoretical way – the possibility of us spending a long weekend there at some time in the distant future, and had wanted to stop us going. Perhaps that was why he'd buried the car keys as well.

As for that torch – what nook or cranny had Murphy unearthed it from? And why did he want it? Was he planning a midnight flit or did he use it for reading the book when I turned out the lights at night? I extracted the car keys from under his cushion when he wasn't looking, then covered up the other items so that he wouldn't know they'd been discovered. I didn't want him to think I'd been spying on him.

On another occasion, while I was downstairs working, Murphy managed to get into the fridge, the door of which hadn't shut properly for years. When I came upstairs, a carton of orange juice was lying on the floor next to half a pound of butter and a bottle of white wine. Meanwhile, in the furry depths of his basket, the Lurcher was curled up asleep amid a branch of vine tomatoes, a lettuce, half a cucumber and a slab of feta cheese, still in its wrapper. His head was resting on four red onions, and the bag that had once contained them was lying nearby – he'd taken it out of the crisper compartment, and removed the onions one by one.

As I took all this in George, who'd followed me up from the study, joined me in the doorway. He looked as impressed as I was.

'Murphy! What have you *done*?'

He woke up, raised his head to peer at me, then looked down at his creation with an expression of supreme pride. As well he should have: he'd turned his basket into a perfect Greek salad. Jamie Oliver would have been proud of the lad. I should have told him off, but I couldn't keep a straight face. Since every item was punctured with toothmarks, I threw the lot away, Sellotaped the fridge door shut and went back downstairs.

That evening, I found a bar of white soap on the corner of my desk. It, too, was punctured with toothmarks. Murphy must have stolen it from the bathroom washbasin and placed it there as a peace offering. I picked it up, took it to the kitchen and binned it, pausing by Murphy's flattened basket to stroke his head.

Another day, after I'd taken the dogs for a long walk in the rain, I shut Murphy in Joshua's room and went out to buy groceries. While I was gone, he pulled down the white towelling robe that was hanging on the back of the door, breaking the brass hook as he did so. By the time I came back, the robe, which I'd given Joshua for Christmas, was lying in a mangled heap on the floor, with Murphy tangled up in its shredded remains, fast asleep and looking very cosy.

I blamed myself for his destructive behaviour. Obviously what the Lurcher needed were more dog chews and things to play with. So I clipped on his leash and walked him and George down the hill to our local pet shop.

Owned by Nora, who used to be a nuclear physicist before she discovered the pleasures of selling bird seed and Bonios, Animal Crackers is a veritable pets' sweet shop overflowing with food and treats. Ever since Nora had taken the shop over three years before, it had been George's favourite place in the world and, as she did with all the dogs that came in, she spoiled him terribly.

Nora, who owned two rescue dogs herself, both Golden Retrievers, and she immediately fell under Murphy's spell. While she was hand-feeding him and George a delicious meaty treat, I rushed around choosing yet more squeaky toys for Murphy, a multi-pack of dog chews, an expensive three-pronged knobbly yellow plastic 'ever-lasting' chicken-flavoured bone that resembled one of those Rabbit vibrators that had suddenly become so popular, and various other bits and bobs, including a new collar and a leash. For good measure I added some 'long-lasting' dog biscuits to the hoard, a pack of mint-flavoured dental chews soft enough for George's almost toothless gums, and a bone-shaped cow-hide chew almost the length of Murphy's legs.

The bill came to forty-three pounds, and as I handed over my credit card I realized it would have been cheaper to buy Murphy a towelling robe of his own. I could just imagine him lounging on the sofa in it, sipping a Guinness and throwing peanuts into his mouth while he watched *Ballykissangel* on television.

To my shame, when it was time to leave the shop, George refused to come with me. Instead, he dug his heels in before the treat counter, alternating his gaze between Nora and a jar of sausages, and licked his lips repeatedly in case she hadn't got the message. I decided to call his bluff: I dropped his leash and left the shop, thinking that he'd follow me to the door, since he loathed being separated from me. But when I glanced backed through the glass panel he was running in the opposite direction, and when I went back inside he hid behind the counter, where Nora rewarded him for his perfidy with another sausage. And after I'd been his slave for so many years!

Matthew had bought tickets for a play that night. So, with some trepidation, I left Murphy in Joshua's room, with a selection of the toys and treats I'd bought, and a radio set to LBC so that he had company. I tried to put him out of my mind, but the play, *Life Is a Dream*, was about a seventeenth-century prince who'd spent his whole life chained up in a tower and all I could think of was Murphy locked up by himself in the flat.

'God knows what the mess will be like when I get in,' I told Matthew on the way home.

But the room was clean, and Murphy was curled up in his basket, fast asleep. He woke up the moment I opened the door and flung himself at me, almost knocking me down.

While I got ready for bed, he lay on the hall floor with his head and front paws in his basket and all his new toys – balls, chews, rubber bone – lined up in a row in front of him. As his nose darted from one to another, he looked as thrilled as a child on Christmas Day who'd just opened his presents and couldn't believe his luck.

25

The following day Murphy took the furry cushion out of his basket, shook it violently, then attempted to hump it. When he got no satisfaction, he beat it up in frustration, pulled out some of the stuffing, then tried to hump it again.

I felt this showed a hitherto hidden, and rather unpleasant, side to his character.

'The poor sod,' Matthew commented, when I called him and told him about it. 'Even though the wherewithal has gone, the urge is obviously still there.'

So were his castration stitches. I pointed out that it was now twenty-four hours past their sell-by date and, since Murphy hadn't been rehomed yet, removing them was down to me.

Matthew guffawed. 'You're not going to take the stitches out yourself?'

'Well, Many Tears sent me a stitch cutter, so I guess other dog fosterers must do this sort of thing. And if they can do it, why shouldn't I be able to?'

He didn't give a direct answer. Instead he said diplomatically, 'If it goes wrong and Murphy bites you, you might end up losing some fingers.'

'In that case, I'll save on manicures. They can't charge you full price if you've only got one hand.' Despite my flippancy, I could see he had a point.

'Look, if you're determined to do this I'd better come over and help you,' Matthew said.

'No, I simply can't let you. Okay, I can. What if I cook you dinner first? And maybe you might like to stay the night afterwards?' I suggested. 'As an added incentive, I mean.'

So there we were at ten p.m., replete with food and with the prospect of our first night of passion in front of us. We were sitting on the kitchen floor with two dogs, a towel, a bag of dried liver and the stitch cutter, which, when I tore its sterile packaging open, turned out to be a tiny but lethal-looking surgical razor blade with a curved hook on the end. Presuming it was some sort of chocolate – after all, it had been wrapped in silver foil – George darted forward, and tried to snatch it from me, but I took it away just in time.

'Okay,' I said, looking at the huge dog galloping in dizzying circles around us, trying to get at the treats. More specifically, I was looking at the alpine range of his gleaming white teeth. 'How are we going to get the stitches out from you know where? Either you hold Murphy down and I'll do the cutting, or vice versa, I suppose.'

'I'm not sure which job is more unenviable.'

'Come on, Matthew! Vets must do things like this all the time!'

'I'm not a vet. Neither are you.'

'True, but my grandmother was a dress designer, and I was practically brought up in the business. I must know how to unpick a few stitches.'

He raised an eyebrow. 'This animal is far more slippery than a length of satin. And it might help if you could get him to stand still for a second.'

I eventually succeeded in getting hold of Murphy's collar.

Then, while Matthew stroked his ears, I lay down on my back on the floor with my head underneath him, in the style of a car mechanic looking for a leak, the razor blade clasped in my hand. As I gazed up at Murphy's unmanned manhood, which, half shaved at the base for his castration op, resembled a pink palm tree with white foliage sprouting from the top, I began to have doubts about the whole procedure. 'I can't even see the stitches from here,' I said, as I squinted up at the site of the operation. 'Perhaps we should get him to lie down instead.'

Unaware of what was about to happen, and bribed with a lump of dried liver, Murphy let himself be gently pushed to the ground. He rolled over helpfully into a submissive posture, bending his front leg up and stretching out to reveal his long pale belly, complete with palm tree, and the slack, black empty testicles sack beyond it. For some reason the sight of it made Matthew blanch.

'Are you okay?'

'Look, can you just get on with it? And do be careful with that blade!'

'Okay, okay. Don't rush me. I'm doing it now.'

He stroked Murphy's muzzle. 'The important thing is not to hurt him. Take your time. Take as long as you like.'

But as my hand approached the blanket stitches that were its target, my fingers began to tremble and I dropped the blade onto the floor. 'I can't do it!'

'Then I will. Give that thing to me!'

We swapped places. However, by now Murphy was getting bored with lying down and had started to wriggle and writhe around on his back. Blade flashing, Matthew's hand hovered over the Lurcher's exposed nether regions and his face took on a strange look with pursed lips and twitching nose – I can only describe it as a sort of cocktail of concentration and revulsion. 'OK, I can see them. I'm going in.' He bent closer over the palm tree. 'How hard can it be?'

At which point I started to giggle.

Seizing his chance, Murphy sprang up, snatched the entire bag of liver treats and hot-pawed it onto the sofa to join George, who'd just settled down there.

'Oh, bugger it! I don't care what it costs, I'm taking him to the vet tomorrow,' I said. 'Let Howard have the pleasure! Why don't we relax and forget all about it? Have a drink. A kiss and a cuddle. Maybe even . . . if we felt like it . . .? You know?'

But, for some odd reason, Matthew wasn't in the mood. He wrapped the stitch cutter up in newspaper and threw it in the dustbin. 'Actually, I think I'll go home now,' he said, as he scrubbed his hands thoroughly with washing-up liquid. 'I can't say this is the most romantic evening I've ever spent.'

The following morning I drove Murphy to the vet's, where a nurse picked him up single-handedly and stood him on the examination table. While I held his head, and the receptionist steadied his flanks, the nurse put her head underneath him and removed the stitches, a process that took her all of two seconds. It must have been completely painless, because Murphy didn't even flinch.

Clutching my worn-out credit card, I asked for the bill. For once, they didn't charge me a penny.

26

It was Sunday, and Billy's first birthday. Hannah was throwing a party for him and, naturally, she'd invited George and Murphy along. She'd also asked if I'd like to bring Matthew.

'There are going to be other dogs there, too,' I warned him over the telephone. 'Believe me, you don't want to come.'

'Are you kidding?' he said. 'Miss the Mad Ratter's Tea Party? Not for the world.'

With Murphy and George both strapped into seatbelts on the back seat of his car, we drove over to Hannah's. Since adopting Billy, she'd made friends with loads of other dog-owners, most of whom she'd met in the park, and quite a few were there with their pooches. They included another terrier called Benji, a Boxer named Spud, who lived across the road, and Esmé, a white terrier who lived around the corner and was Billy's special girlfriend. What with my two and Billy himself, that made six dogs charging around Hannah's once pristine kitchen. Actually, since Murphy was at least twice as big as the others, it felt more like seven.

There were balloons and streamers everywhere, dog biscuits galore for the canines, and home-made birthday cake, tea and wine for the grown-ups. We certainly needed a few alcoholic hits to cope with the noise and chaos, which put me in mind of the birthday parties Udi and I used to have for Joshua when he was very young. Then, between ten and fifteen boys and girls would converge on the house mid-afternoon. While polite and well behaved when they came over one at a time, in a pack they turned distinctly feral. I'd be standing by with gritted teeth, waiting for the moment when things turned nasty, as they inevitably did. I always used to say that the worst moment in the year was just before his birthday party began, and the best was when the last hyped-up guest was finally collected.

On one memorable birthday we took a group of boys swimming. Two of them started fighting, and one ended up breaking his nose. It bled into the pool, which then had to be vacated on health and safety grounds. On another occasion, we held the party in a baby gym. Within five minutes, a little girl tripped and knocked out a front tooth. While her mother rushed her off to a dentist to have it pushed back into its socket, we retired to a room upstairs for the birthday tea. Since, like most parents, I swallowed the line that sugar and e-numbers were responsible for children's wild behaviour, that year I'd swapped the usual chocolates, sweets and biscuits for wholemeal egg sandwiches and carrot sticks. The blighters wouldn't touch them; they only ate the crisps. By the time it came to the birthday cake they were ravenous.

I loved making birthday cakes, and that year I'd excelled myself by creating a dinosaur-themed sponge crowned by a mini-volcano with chocolate lava flowing down its sides and a tiny sparkler hidden inside the crater. But, for some unknown reason, Joshua threw a fit just before he blew the candles out, jumped up from the table and rushed into the adjoining kitchen in hysterical tears. While his friends waited impatiently for him to come back out (they wanted to get their mitts on my marzipan mini-T. Rex even if he didn't), I ordered him in no uncertain terms to resume his place at the head of the trestle table. He refused.

'Oh, for God's sake, leave this to me!' Udi snapped. 'You've no idea how to talk to him!'

Wreathed in smiles, the great psychotherapist ambled into the kitchen, picked Joshua up and sat him on the top of the catering-sized gas stove (the jets were off at the time). Then, in his best couch-side manner, he attempted to reason his son out of his strop. Ten minutes later he stormed out of the kitchen in a rage, and slammed the door behind him, shouting, 'You deal with him! He's your son – and he's impossible!'

I would have gone back in, but the catch had sprung on the kitchen door when Udi had slammed it, and it was now firmly locked – with Joshua alone on the other side of it, still perched on the gas stove. As I peered at him through the door's glass porthole, he screamed and reached out his arms to me. None of the staff seemed to know where the key was, so it was half an hour before we got him out.

Things at Billy's birthday party were almost as chaotic, as the dogs chased each other under the table and around our legs, all in pursuit of the same squeaky plastic bone. One moment Billy was worrying it, then Esmé snatched it from him and disappeared with it into the living room. The others bounded after her, and soon Murphy reappeared proudly toting it, pursued by the others.

Back and forth they went, time and again. It was all very good natured until Spud suddenly had a go at Murphy. A lot of snarling and barking ensued, and all the dogs, bar George, joined in. Spud was taken home in disgrace.

Despite his size and those razor-like teeth, Murphy, like most Lurchers, was a sweet soul without an ounce of aggression in him. Having behaved like a real gentleman during this mini-scrap, he ran up to me for a reassuring pat, then carried on playing with the little ones. He was in his element, the life and soul of the party. Everyone admired him, all the other dogs looked up to him – literally – and he blossomed in the general adoration.

Needless to say, George didn't take part in any of the festivities. Like the old boy he was, he sheltered behind my legs to avoid the mayhem, then, later on, leaped onto someone's lap. There he stayed for the rest of the after-noon, metaphorically and literally looking down on the proceedings as if he couldn't understand what all the fuss was about and couldn't wait for it to end. Victor Meldrew again. And no wonder: in the equivalent human years, the other dogs were all between six and twelve. He, of course, was in his seventies.

Matthew and I were almost home when my mother called me on my mobile. She sounded distressed. 'Judith, I'm in big trouble!' she wailed, over the roar of traffic I could hear coming from her end of the line.

The last time she'd called and said the same thing down the phone had been almost exactly two years before, when a week before her eighty-first birthday, she'd tripped on a kerbstone and badly shattered her right leg and hip. It had taken a DIY store's worth of nuts, metal plates and bolts, plus six weeks in hospital, to get her back on her feet, not to mention a good year of physiotherapy afterwards for her to be able to walk normally again. Understandably, ever since then she'd been terrified of falling.

'What's happened?' I don't know why I bothered to ask. I already knew what was coming.

'I've just been knocked over,' my mother said.'

'*What?*' That sounded much worse than a fall. My head filled with terrible visions of her talking to me while lying in a busy road, half underneath a lorry. But at least she was talking. 'Where are you?'

'In St John's Wood.'

'Are you bleeding?'

'I don't think so.'

'Can you walk?'

'Well, someone helped me up and brought a chair over. But I can't seem to move my legs. They've called an ambulance . . .'

'I'm on my way.'

Feeling sick, I explained to Matthew what had happened. He immediately swung the car in the direction of St John's Wood, and said, 'What can I do to help?' Those six short words meant more to me than any Shakespearean love sonnet. He was, I realized, a man whose support I could rely in the bad times as well as the good. Unable to stop myself, I burst into tears.

By the time we reached her, my mother was being stretchered into an ambulance. To my relief, there were no pools of blood on the road. Leaving the dogs with Matthew ('Don't worry about a thing. I'll take them home for you,' he said), I climbed into the ambulance with her and squeezed her hand – she was shaking with shock – while the male and female paramedics, jovial angels both of them, gave her a brief examination. 'What happened, Mum? Did a car knock you down?'

'No . . .'

'A lorry?'

'No . . .'

'Can you push my hand with your heel, love?'

'Was it a cyclist, Mum?'

'Ow, that hurts. No, no, Judith.'

'Then what?'

She shook her head as if she herself couldn't believe it. 'It was a dog, darling!' I was dumbstruck. 'Nothing like dear George, of course. This was a monstrous thing. It looked like a wild animal – like a bear,' she went on. 'Ow. The police think it was a . . . Excuse me, dear, what did they call it?'

'I think they said it was some kind of mastiff, love,' said the male paramedic.

'Yes, that was it. They took the owner's address and phone number because it was completely out of control.'

'Wasn't it on a lead?'

'I don't know. It might have been on one of those extendable things like George has. All I know is that it just barged into me, grabbed my hand between its teeth and then bowled me over. Oh, I do hope I haven't broken my hip again.'

So did I. Since it had been badly smashed by her previous fall, this would have been disastrous for her. But from the expression on the female paramedic's face, I suspected that she had.

What with my mother's previous accident, various emergencies concerning my late grandmother, several squashed fingers during Joshua's childhood and, lastly, Udi's cancer, I seemed to have spent an inordinate amount of time in our local A and E department, so I felt dismally at home among the blood-pressure monitors, stretchered-in heart-attack victims and loud-mouth drunks with black eyes and bleeding foreheads, not to mention the dedicated staff who flitted back and forth through the blue-paper curtains like extras from *Scrubs* or *Nurse Jackie*. From the smiles they gave me, I had the feeling that some of them presumed I must work there. If I'd had a stethoscope around my neck they'd probably have got me to triage the patients.

When I eventually got home late that evening, George and Murphy both flung themselves at me. I sank down on the sofa and let them curl up on top of me – even Murphy, who took up most of the space. I needed their comfort.

It turned out that, while her leg and hips weren't broken, my mother had fractured her pelvis. Though this was the lesser of three evils, it was going to take a week in hospital and at least three months, and a great deal of pain, physio-therapy and help, for her to get back on her feet.

And all because of an out-of-control dog! As I said to Elizabeth, when we spoke on the telephone the following day, how unfair was that?

'Big dogs are a real handful.' 'Take Murphy, for instance. He's a wonderful character, but incredibly strong, not to mention self-willed.'

'You mean disobedient,' Elizabeth said.

'Honestly, at times I can hardly hold him, even with two leads.'

'Two?'

'One on his collar, the other on George's seatbelt – I strap Murphy into it, and use it as a halter. He could easily run off and knock someone over without meaning to. The trouble is, he's got all this pent-up energy, and he can't get rid of it because he's either being held back on the leash or else cooped up at home with George and me. I play endless games of fetch with him in the garden in the hope of tiring him out but, given that my lawn's about ten metres long and Murphy can run at eighteen metres a second, he manages to get the ball back to me before I've even thrown it.'

'Hmm. What you need is a large, secure space where he can really let off steam,' she mused.

'Exactly. But where? It'd have to be some kind of walled-in space.'

'Pentonville Prison?'

'Romford Greyhound Stadium?'

'You should take him to puppy training classes,' Liz observed.

'Can you imagine him, with all the tiny three-month-old balls of fluff? He'd look ridiculous, and cause complete havoc. Anyway, where am I going to find the time to take him to classes, now that my mother's hurt herself and needs looking after?'

'Well, I found time to take *our* dogs, and it was certainly worth the effort,' she went on, somewhat sanctimoniously, I thought, before shouting off-telephone, 'Molly, leave the cat alone! Flynn, get off that armchair! I know what you need, Judith – a visit from Juan-Carlos.'

'Who?'

'Juan-Carlos MacDonald. Don't tell me you've never heard of him? He'll sort Murphy out.'

27

As I now discovered – ten years too late for training George, alas – thirty-year-old Juan-Carlos MacDonald was to the dog-owners of north London what Cesar Millan was to the celebrity pooch owners of LA. Some even called him the Brazilian Barbara Woodhouse, but since he was half Scottish, didn't wear tweed skirts or pearls and was one hundred per cent male, the moniker didn't necessarily please him.

He strode into my kitchen one morning later that week, an imposingly tall figure dressed in jeans, hiking boots and a flak jacket, his mane of thick dark curls pushed under what looked like a knitted red tea-cosy, and about a dozen assorted leads hanging around his neck. He looked the epitome of an alternative, tree-hugging eco-warrior. But there the New Age resemblance ended. As he assured me, in his rich, sexy accent, there was nothing remotely hippieish or faddish about his approach to dog training, which was based on the one method that apparently never failed to work: bribery.

Doling out treats galore from a small nylon pouch he wore around his waist, Juan-Carlos soon had Murphy on his knees and eating out of his hand. Literally. The happy drifter who, so far, had ignored almost every command in favour of doing exactly what he liked whenever he wanted (the exception was to respond to 'Come!' when I put down his food bowl) was suddenly transformed into a circus-standard performer who sat to attention, lay down, stayed, rolled over, bowed, shook hands and even barked to order. And all in the hope of getting a few nuggets of dried liver – the same stuff that he gobbled out of my hand without doing a bloody thing in return.

Next, Juan-Carlos clipped on Murphy's leash and took him to the Heath for some outdoor training, while George and I watched the proceedings from a respectful distance, and gave each other the odd, conspiratorial glance. My Cavalier knew from past experience that I was the worst, most inconsistent dog trainer in the world. This wasn't my fault – no, of course it wasn't: it had to do with the way I'd been brought up. The pooch of my youth, a Yorkie called Freddy, had been as indulged as George was, and the sole training method my parents knew about then was a rolled-up copy of *The Times*, a weapon that was only used to threaten, never to hit. As far as Mum and Dad were concerned, dogs either behaved or they didn't. So Freddy didn't.

No doubt Juan-Carlos would have had his character defects licked in twenty seconds with the aid of a few chicken scraps. However, when I was growing up dog training wasn't as big a thing as it is nowadays, and no other dog in my circle behaved any better than mine did. Not Sheba, my best friend Barbara's hairy Battersea Dogs Home mutt, who'd sobbed frantically whenever she'd been separated from Barbara's mother, and certainly not Higgins, another schoolfriend Toni's Beagle, who'd been one of the most disobedient animals ever to lift his leg in London's West End, where his owners had lived.

Taking Higgins for a walk had been a nightmare for me and Toni. The moment he was let off the lead in Hyde Park, he would run towards the cafeteria, where he'd jump the queue and leap straight on to the counter, the better to get at the ham salads set out on the self-service display. Toni's parents' dining room had offered similarly rich pickings; on one occasion, her mother had ushered in some special guests only to find Higgins standing in a pile of broken crockery on what had been a carefully laid table, polishing off the last of eight hors d'oeuvres. It wasn't that Higgins had been underfed, he'd just liked eating. If there wasn't any food around, like Millie, he'd scoffed whatever was available: shoes, hats, carpets, sofa corners and even, on one memorable occasion, an heirloom wedding veil due to be worn by Toni's sister two days later. A pack animal, with neither a pack nor a pack leader to guide him, Higgins had been wild, untrainable and aggressive to humans as well as other dogs: he'd bitten Toni's father if he'd dared to go near her mother and had often attacked my Freddy who, although he was only a quarter Higgins's size, had fought back like a little fiend. Both dogs had really enjoyed hating one another.

Out on the Heath, Juan-Carlos clipped a ten-metre training lead onto Murphy's collar. In the space of ten seconds, he had him running around in a ring like a performing horse, and taught him to come when his name was called. Perhaps there was a dog-training gene, I pondered. You were either born with the right DNA, or you weren't. Needless to say, I hadn't been.

Watching Juan-Carlos at work made me realize that in the right hands – hands like his – my happy-go-lucky wanderer could become the perfect pet. However, in the wrong hands – mine, for instance – he'd remain undisciplined, untrained and, ultimately unhomeable. He might even become a menace to people, like the mastiff who'd sent my mother flying.

Meanwhile, as George stood beside me, watching Murphy in a virtuoso performance that was beginning to resemble *Strictly Heelwork to Music*, his face wrinkled in horror. Frightened, perhaps, that he, too, would be forced to participate, he did a one-hundred-and-eighty-degree turn and pulled for home. Instead of going with him, I reeled him in on his extendable leash, at the end of which he was flapping like a hooked salmon.

'Look and learn, Georgie-Porgie,' I told him sternly. 'And watch this space. I'm through with being a hopeless dog trainer. From now on, I'm turning over a new leaf.'

That evening, Murphy was unusually subdued, and even more affectionate than usual. As I sat at the kitchen table, he walked slowly over to me, put his nose on my knee and gazed up into my face.

I stroked his ears tenderly. 'You know, Murphy, I've never been that interested in Lurchers,' I found myself telling him, 'so before you came here, I didn't think I'd grow that fond of you. But of all the foster dogs I've had I think you're the cleverest. And the most characterful. And the most adorable. I haven't admitted this to a soul, but I'm even tempted to keep you for ever – that is, if I can only train you properly. Now, will you co-operate with me?'

As if to say that he'd like nothing better, Murphy gazed up at me with his gentle, adoring eyes.

Then he opened his mouth and emitted a foul-smelling belch.

By the following morning, Murphy was throwing his weight around as never before.

After I'd let him out into the back garden at five thirty, I allowed him into my bedroom where, at first, he settled down quietly on the floor by my bed. I must have dozed off, because the next thing I knew I was dreaming of being kissed on the lips by a tall, thin, interesting-looking man with an elongated face; he might have been Rhys Ifans.

I opened my eyes to find a long, thin, elongated face inches from my own, grinning at me inanely, with its tongue hanging out. 'Get off me!'

Instead, Murphy lunged forward and started nuzzling my neck. I pushed him away, but he lunged again, and this time put his left paw on the bed. His right paw followed, and before I knew it he'd manoeuvred his entire long torso on top of mine, followed by one back leg. This was a bloke who wasn't used to taking no for an answer.

I pushed him off with a gargantuan effort, then quickly got dressed and took him straight out onto the Heath to cool off, remembering at the last minute to grab a bag of treats and George so that I could continue Juan-Carlos's training. I psyched myself into being pack leader in the style of Cesar Millan, and attempted to emulate the bribery techniques, but it was no good: my mind soon became a blur of commands and rewards, and as for the pack-leader-psyching business, the Lurcher soon sensed that I'd lost it. After that, any air of natural authority was his.

On the other hand, once George cottoned on to the fact that food was involved in the training process, he became putty in my hands.

28

'I don't believe it!'

'What?'

'It's snowing!'

'*What?*'

Matthew followed me into the living room. He immediately froze – an appropriate response, considering the wintry scene in front of us.

It was eight o'clock at night, he'd just picked me up from the hospital, where I'd been visiting my mother, and I'd invited him in for a bite to eat. Outside, the evening couldn't have been milder. Inside, the weather appeared to have gone mad. Soft white snowflakes were swirling in the air and settling on the back of the sofa. They already lay an inch thick on the seat cushions, the coffee-table and the bookshelves, and there were knee-deep drifts covering the floorboards and the black slate hearth. As I waded through them, they lifted up and floated around me in a great white cloud.

'Amazing!' I gasped.

'Yes.' Matthew struggled to keep a straight face. 'Very unusual weather for May. I blame it on global warming.'

I looked at the ransacked sofas, then bent down and picked up one of the two ripped cushion covers that were lying on the floor, as shrivelled and empty of their former stuffing of feathers as a castrated dog's scrotum was of *cojones.* 'I know what *I* blame,' I said, through gritted teeth. 'Or, rather, *whom*. MURPHY!'

There was the thunderous sound of a horse running upstairs. Two seconds later, the Lurcher skidded into the middle of the living room, sending the white spume flying skywards again. A grinning George toddled in after him: his long hair was all over the place, there were feathers stuck in his collar, and his spaniel eyes, which were twice their usual size, glittered darkly and gazed at Murphy in awe. It was clear that my Cavalier had a brand new hero and that this was the most exciting day of his life.

'No, Murphy! Stop. I said, STOP!'

Ignoring me completely, the Lurcher sprang into the largest snowdrift, sending another wave of feathers flying through the archway into the kitchen where they gently floated down onto the table, the worktop, the gas-stove . . . everywhere. Murphy grinned. He looked incredibly pleased with himself. As well he might: this was the most enchanting new game, and he'd invented it all by himself.

At nine the following morning, I set off for the Heath, intent on exercising the hell out of him in the hope of tiring him out and curbing his destructive energy. Matthew and I had spent a good hour clearing up the feathers the night before, but there had been no way we could get rid of them all. A layer of down, fine as frost, now coated everything from the cornices to the floorboards, and odd feathers drifted under the tables, and collected in the glasses on the kitchen dresser and in the sink. And when the sun shone into the living room it illuminated a multitude of fronds floating in the air like super-sized dust motes. Murphy had had a great time trying to catch them.

Now he was raring to get out of the house. However, despite the treats spilling out of my pockets, his new acolyte, George, was refusing to come with us, and as he dug in his heels and walked backwards I found myself being pulled in two directions at once. I felt like Stretch Armstrong, a gel-filled action figure that Joshua had once owned (like a medieval torturer operating the rack, you pulled his hands in opposite directions and, instead of breaking, his arms grew longer and thinner). Innocently suspecting that yet another grass seed was to blame for George's reluctance to walk, I crouched on the pavement and examined his paws for swellings. There were none.

After tugging him halfway down the street, I eventually gave up and took him home. If the old boy didn't want a long tramp through the woods, what Puritan ethic should make me force him to have one? I asked myself, as he charged back to our house at top speed, champing at the bit to resume his career as a couch potato. If you couldn't give exercise a miss when you were in your seventies, was there any advantage at all in ageing?

After I'd shut him into the flat, I immediately headed off again with Murphy. But by the time we'd walked the four metres to the garden gate, George was already perched on the back of the sofa in angry-parrot mode, glaring me through the window, as if I'd done the dirty on him and left him behind against his will. I couldn't win.

Once out on the Heath, I clipped on the new ten-metre leash that, inspired by Juan-Carlos and his training methods, I'd bought from Animal Crackers a few days before. Swaggering confidently and holding my head high in the manner of a bona-fide pack leader, I marched down the tree-lined path known as Elm Walk, gradually allowing Murphy more slack as I went along. Since I couldn't let him off the leash completely until such time as he learned to come back when I called his name, I thought this would allow him a little leeway to exercise, while at the same time teach him to stay within close range of me.

But although he'd behaved like a performing horse in a circus ring when Juan-Carlos had had hold of the training leash, with me in charge it was a different story. Even bribery didn't work. The lumps of dried liver and slivers of sausage I offered Murphy were nothing compared to the temptation of a live juicy squirrel, and there happened to be scores of the critters around. At the first glimpse of one, Murphy was off after it. Trying to stand my ground when he reached the end of the ten-metre slack was like trying to hold back an accelerating McLaren on the Grand Prix starting line by hanging on to a tow-rope tied to its bumper. I was practically yanked off my feet.

By the time I'd staggered up to the football pitch, with Murphy alternately wrenching my arms out of joint and binding my legs together by running in circles around me, I was more at the end of my tether than he was at the end of his. It was the perfect moment to run into a dog walker and his pack – or, rather, to lurch into one with the aid of my Lurcher (perhaps that was how the breed had got their name).

'Hey, you want me to take him while you do that?' he asked, in an American accent, as I juggled to control Murphy, keep my balance and, at the same time, pick up the giant-size rosette he'd just deposited slap-bang in the middle of the path.

'No, no, I can manage. But thanks.'

'You sure? Let me hold him.' He held out a long hand, the fingers heavily decorated with silver Navajo rings. I gave the leash to him while I scooped. As if he knew he was now in the hands of a proper master, Murphy immediately stopped trying to get away and sat down beside the man to be stroked. 'Hey, this is some beautiful guy!'

With my foster dog as our focal point, we soon got talking. Born in Oregon, Ched was a visual artist who'd fallen into dog walking by accident after a friend had asked him to look after his Labrador one day. With his long silver ponytail, fringed suede jacket and Native American jewellery, Ched emanated an aura of calm and harmony, which the dogs obviously picked up from him. Although the pack he was walking included a number of large and supposedly aggressive breeds (they included a Rhodesian Ridgeback, an English Mastiff and a Dogue de Bordeaux, built like a rugby prop), they were all playing together as co-operatively as a group of spaniels, and kept coming up to Ched for treats, wagging their tails.

After watching them play for a few minutes, Murphy was fed up of being on the sidelines and pulled to be allowed to join in.

'Can you let him off?' Ched suggested, as the ten-metre leash got twisted around his legs, lassoed an unfortunate Wheaten Terrier who'd strayed near us, then got tangled up around me.

'I'm not sure I dare.'

He bent down and untangled Murphy, who by now was going mad with frustration at being unable to play. 'I'm sure he'll be all right, won't you, boy?' he said, as he slipped

Murphy a treat, and the Lurcher looked up at him sub-missively. 'Dogs seem to like me. They never run away.'

But would Murphy? As he was my foster dog, I felt almost more responsible for his safety than I would have for a dog I actually owned. But it seemed cruel not to let him play with the pack for a while, and we were right in the middle of the Heath, a long way from any road. Had I been alone I would never have risked it, but Ched exuded such confidence that I took a deep breath and let Murphy go.

For a moment he stood still, looking at me. Then he took a few steps away, then a few more. A toss of his head told him he was free of all restraint, and he gambolled round in a small circle, grinning delightedly. A moment later he cantered away across the pitch, with the other dogs following hard on his heels, barking and wagging their tails.

In a matter of seconds Murphy was way ahead of them, and accelerating faster all the time. I caught my breath as he reached the trees on the far edge of the football pitch, but instead of disappearing between them he swung round at ninety degrees and, barely touching the ground with his feet, galloped along the perimeter, then back towards us. I breathed again.

Around and around the pitch he went, as graceful as a racehorse in full flight, leaving the other dogs so far behind him that they eventually gave up the chase. Faster and faster he went, flying over the turf with joy, relishing his freedom, as if he'd been waiting for this moment all his life. It was simply beautiful to witness – like seeing a cheetah running in the wild – and quite dizzy-making, too, as Ched and I spun round on our heels to follow his progress.

I watched him with wonder, and a new understanding of his nature. Was it any surprise that he was sometimes destructive in the house when he'd been suppressing so much energy?

After about five minutes of galloping at top speed, Murphy slowed down to a canter, headed back towards us, then collapsed at my feet and grinned up at me. I praised him, kissed the top of his head and offered him a dog treat. For once, he wasn't interested. He'd completely exhausted himself.

'Greyhound-type dogs are sprinters rather than marathon runners,' Ched explained, as he took out a battered plastic water bottle from his shoulder bag and offered Murphy something to drink; unlike the treat, it was gratefully received. 'Better let him rest up for a while.'

As he and his pack were about to move off, I clipped on Murphy's leash again. I needn't have bothered: far from running away, he'd tired himself out so much that he now refused to walk at all. Instead, he lay panting on his side with his head on the ground and his tongue hanging out. Nothing I could do would make him move until he'd got his breath back ten minutes later.

Then, he walked calmly to heel as I headed back down Elm Walk. He even ignored a squirrel.

Once he'd got rid of his phenomenal pent-up energy, Murphy became less destructive at home. And since I'd seen him come back when let off the leash, I decided to risk doing it again. So, a few days later, armed with a tennis ball and bags of treats, Matthew and I walked both dogs over to Kenwood House and let Murphy loose in the huge open field known as the West Meadow.

Enclosed by trees, hidden behind which were a wire fence and the iron railings that surrounded the whole Kenwood estate, this seemed the safest place to experiment with letting him have his freedom. Murphy fetched the ball when we threw it and, once again, raced in huge, manic circles before cantering back to us and collapsing. My footloose stray was obviously learning that I was his master or, rather, mistress and, as I was still playing with the idea of adopting him, I couldn't have been more pleased.

The following day I woke up at six thirty and headed out alone to the Heath with both dogs. At first George was most put out by having to go for a walk before he'd had his breakfast and ritual post-prandial nap but, on the way to Kenwood, he soon got into the swing of things, especially since Murphy, who'd remained his hero ever since the indoor snowstorm, was obviously raring to go.

The Heath was almost deserted at that hour. An early-morning mist rose from the grass, and there was a damp chill in the air. The only people around were a handful of individual dog walkers like myself, and the odd runner who jogged past us, invariably clutching a water bottle in one hand and an iPod in the other. Murphy watched enviously as they passed us, and shot jealous glances at George, who was flaunting his leash-free status by rooting under piles of soggy leaves and stopping for an ostentatious roll in the mud every hundred yards or so.

By the time we walked through the open gates of the Kenwood Estate and entered the deserted West Meadow, my foster Lurcher was straining to be off. So, after feeding him a handful of treats, I unclipped the leash from his collar.

I whistled loudly, then hurled the ball towards him. Instead of running to fetch it, Murphy glanced at it scornfully, then cantered off in the opposite direction. Unconcerned, I picked up the ball and threw it again. 'Murphy! Fetch, Murphy!'

The ball zoomed past him, but Murphy ignored it. 'Come, Murphy!' He carried on running. 'Come here!' I shouted. He took absolutely no notice of me.

By now he'd reached the eastern edge of the meadow. I waited for him to swing round and follow the line of the trees that bordered it. But he didn't. Instead, he stopped beside a huge rhododendron shrub at the edge of the woods, sniffed the ground at its base, then disappeared into the foliage.

'Mur-phy!'

I wasn't particularly worried because I was sure he'd come out in a minute. Besides, what was there to worry about when the entire Kenwood estate was fenced in – all 132 acres of it? Murphy couldn't escape – unless, that was, he found one of the handful of gates back on to the Heath, and that seemed a remote possibility.

I waited. One long minute turned into two, then three, and there was still no sign of him. I called his name again, only to be answered by birdsong and the distant roar of a jet. '*Mur*-phy?' I walked slowly towards the rhododendron and called again. Still nothing.

I looked at George. He looked back questioningly, as if to ask why the hell we were hanging around in a field at this unearthly hour in the morning when he hadn't even had his breakfast. I suddenly remembered the awful day a few years before when Zach and I had been going through one of our 'difficult' periods and we'd taken George on a picnic to Kenwood on a Sunday afternoon. It was George who'd run off into the woods then, and no sooner had I realized that he was missing than it had started to pour with rain. Zach had insisted that I take refuge with him inside Kenwood House, but I'd wanted to find my Cavalier, and the situation had immediately escalated into a bitter it's-me-or-the-dog row. In the end, I'd stomped off alone to search for George, while Zach had stomped off and sheltered in the mansion. It was months before we'd spoken to each other again. Meanwhile the cause of our split had got lost in the woods. He'd eventually been rescued by a lovely stranger who'd called me when she'd read his dog tag, and driven him home in her Porsche.

'Murphy! Where are you?'

I hesitated at the edge of the trees, torn between going to look for him and staying where I was in case he re-appeared and didn't know where I'd gone. But Murphy didn't reappear. I began to worry. With George trailing after me, I fought my way through the rhododendron foliage in case he was hiding in it. He wasn't. But behind it was a narrow path, which, when I followed it, crossed a muddy stream and led to a waist-height wire fence. Since there was no sign anywhere of Murphy, I realized that he must have leapt over it.

A good quarter of an hour had now passed since I'd last clapped eyes on him, and I was berating myself for having let him off the leash. How could I have been so stupid as to presume he'd come back to me? Murphy had a wild streak in him, and since he ran faster than any dog I'd ever known, he could be anywhere by now – not just on the other side of Hampstead Heath but halfway across London. I imagined him galloping fearlessly down Oxford Street, knocking over pedestrians like skittles, just as the mastiff in St John's Wood had knocked over my mother. Even worse, I pictured him dodging precariously in and out of the rush-hour traffic, causing not only havoc but fatal accidents. Fatal to himself, maybe fatal to others.

With this worst-case scenario playing in my head, like a fusion of *Jurassic Park* and the car chase in *The Bourne Ultimatum*, I shouted his name again. This time there was an answering bark! But where exactly had it come from? If Murphy could hear me, why didn't he make his way back to me? Was he trapped somewhere beyond the wire or deliberately avoiding me?

Either way, I had to find him. I picked George up – all those treats he'd been scoffing since I'd got my first foster dog had piled the pounds on – and clambered over the wire fence with him, ripping my jacket in the process. I now found myself in an overgrown mini-rainforest of fallen, mossy tree trunks, knee-high thickets and piles of rotting leaves. With George following, I struggled slowly through the tangled, thorny undergrowth, calling Murphy's name as I went. He barked again – but this time from behind me, so I turned around and struggled back the way I'd come.

Suddenly I caught a glimpse of a golden-syrup coat, flashing through some distant tree trunks. 'Murphy!' Relieved that he was still in the area, I climbed over a broken wooden fence, having first helped George to scramble underneath it, and found myself on one of the narrow paths that criss-crossed a maze of small, similarly fenced-off areas of woodland at the southern edge of the Kenwood Estate, on the border with the Heath.

I set off down the path, which then forked in two directions. I looked up and down it, trying to work out which way Murphy had run, then set off to the left, only to hear him bark behind me again.

At last I saw him! And he was charging down the path towards me, tail out behind him like a baton, nose down, sniffing the ground . . .

'Murphy, darling! You're okay!' I exclaimed, throwing my arms wide to welcome him into them.

To my horror, he swerved past me without even acknow-ledging my existence. And in a flash he'd disappeared down the path, intent on catching the fox or squirrel or whatever trail he was following. I ran after him. But to no avail. I'd lost him again.

Our game of hide-and-seek continued for the next three-quarters of an hour. Murphy was winning hands down. One moment he'd appear inside an enclosure in front of me, so I'd climb over the fence, and pick my way carefully over the fallen trunks, twisting my ankle in the many treacherous rabbit warrens and fox holes. Then, just when I thought I was cornering him at last, I'd lose sight of him, only to see him run down the path *outside* the enclosure a moment later. By the time I'd climbed back over the fence, he'd have disappeared.

Throughout all this, George followed me with loyal determination. He hadn't a clue what all the fence-leaping, gate-vaulting and swearing was about.

There came a point when I didn't, either. I was furious,

frustrated, exhausted, utterly fed up. If Murphy was determined not to be caught, there was nothing I could do about it. Unlike me, he was in his element in the great outdoors, and he was far faster and nimbler at negotiating the terrain than I was.

'Come on, let's go home,' I told George, somewhat tearfully. 'Either he'll find his way back or he won't. I can't do this any more! I'm starving and tired, and I want a cup of coffee and some breakfast.'

Maybe it was the B-word that did it: just then Murphy appeared at the next turn in the path, and instead of running away, he walked towards us with a smile on his face, looking as calm and matter-of-fact as if he'd just popped out to the corner shop to buy a packet of biscuits. Then he sat down in front of me and licked my hand.

To tell him off at this point would have been counterproductive. So I merely clipped on his leash and, keeping him on a very tight rein, walked him home.

We were almost there when I spotted his doppelganger.

He was the same height as Murphy, and the same golden-syrup colour. He had the same big flopping ears atop the same-shaped head, the same thick neck, and the same endless legs. In fact, the only visible difference between them was that, unlike Murphy, this Lurcher was wearing a thick leather collar.

Naturally his owner and I got talking.

'How amazing!' she said.

'Yes! They could be twins!'

'Absolutely! Lurchers are great dogs, aren't they?'

'Mmm,' I enthused. 'Mine's so sweet-natured.'

As I said this, the doppelganger sniffed at Murphy's

nether regions and Murphy turned on him with an uncharacteristic mini-snarl.

'Absolutely!' the woman said. 'My darling Morgan wouldn't hurt a fly.' As the words came out of her mouth, her darling saw off a dear little Staffie puppy that happened to be walking by.

'How long have you had him?'

'Four years. And you?'

'About as many weeks.' I explained that I was just fostering Murphy for a rescue centre, and that he was looking for a permanent home. 'I don't suppose you'd want another?' I said, half joking.

To my surprise, she immediately said, 'You never know, I might.'

We arranged to meet early the following morning so that the dogs could get to know one another. Then I went home, feeling slightly lighter at heart. Much as I loved Murphy, he was getting too much for me to deal with. But a 'for-ever' home was in sight.

29

When she turned up on the Heath the following morning Jennifer, as she was called, had thoughtfully brought along a spare Lurcher collar for Murphy. Apparently Lurchers were bred to hunt and, as I now knew from bitter experience, their instinct was to charge off after any possible prey as fast as possible. When they did so, they could reach speeds of 40 m.p.h. in under ten seconds, and if they happened to be on a leash at the time, they could jerk their necks with considerable force. Designed to span two vertebrae, a proper Lurcher collar, like the one Morgan was wearing, spread the force over a larger area of the dog's neck, and helped prevent it being hurt or even broken. I offered to pay Jennifer for it, but she insisted that it was an old one of Morgan's and a gift: 'I just don't want to see Murphy getting injured,' she said kindly.

With the dogs looking like twins in their matching collars, we set off through the woods towards Parliament Hill, with Murphy on his training leash, Morgan running around free, and George, who was also off the lead, sticking to the safest place he could find: sandwiched between my legs and Jennifer's. And while we walked, we had a long Lurcher-themed conversation. It turned out that Jennifer had kept the dogs for years, read every book about them ever written, and spoken personally to countless experts in the Lurcher field. Even so, it had taken her ages to train Morgan. All this made me feel a lot better. And even more so when she told me she was serious about adopting Murphy, if the two dogs got on well.

Desperate to play by now, Murphy pulled on his long leash and kept getting his legs tangled up in it. By the time we reached the wide open space of Parliament Hill, I felt so sorry for him that I decided to let him off for one short run. There seemed less risk of him running away when he was with a well-trained dog like Morgan.

I was right. While George sat down on the grass and watched them, the two dogs shot across the fields like twin rockets, then came bounding back towards us joyfully. Murphy threw himself down at our feet to catch his breath. I was just about to clip on his leash when a young Japanese woman appeared over the crest of the hill, accompanied by the tiniest miniature Yorkshire terrier I'd ever seen.

I'm not prone to premonitions, but as the Yorkie scuttled along, half hidden in the long grass, I had one: the Lurchers would think it was a rat, and attack it. I immediately tried to grab Murphy, but he'd already spotted the diminutive dog and had run over to sniff it. I hurried after him. So did Morgan. And before I could do anything about it, Morgan grabbed the Yorkie in his mouth picked it up and shook it, as if it were a stuffed toy.

The little thing squealed in terror. Its owner screamed. When she realized what was happening, Jennifer yelled at Morgan, and, in a commanding voice that must have come from my deepest recesses, I yelled at Murphy to stay back.

Since I was nearest, I ran forward and tried to grab Morgan's collar. But he evaded me. The next moment he dropped the squealing dog on the ground, and he and

Murphy prodded it with their noses. Now Morgan grabbed its belly between his teeth and picked it up again. I could just imagine him and Murphy tossing it from one to the other, and tearing it limb from limb.

'Drop it!' I shrieked. As he let go of the Yorkie, its near-hysterical owner snatched it up. But the drama was far from over: a large pack of assorted dogs suddenly appeared out of nowhere. Among them were an English Bulldog, a Rottweiler and a Staffie. Attracted by the commotion, they came running over and surrounded the woman, who was now kneeling on the grass, bent over her squealing, squirming pet, and trying to protect him with her hands. 'Get them away!' she screamed repeatedly as they, too, tried to get at the object wriggling in her arms. 'Make them go away!

The ugly situation could easily have escalated into something even more nightmarish. But just then the dog walker in charge of the pack called them off, and both Jennifer and I succeeded in getting our Lurchers on their leashes. We were both devastated by what had just happened, and the Yorkie's owner was, understandably, in a state of shock.

As was her little dog. Although he didn't appear to have been injured, he began running around in small circles, squealing, and there were toothmarks indented on his tiny pink belly. Jennifer and I volunteered to ferry him and his owner to a vet's, and since my home was nearest to where we were, we hurried back there.

Having left George and Murphy safely in the flat, and grabbed my car keys, I drove the Yorkie's owner there as fast as I could. My hands trembled on the wheel as badly as hers did as she clutched her dog. For someone whose adored pet had just been molested by mine, she was remarkably understanding. 'These things happen,' she said. Still, I felt dreadful as I waited for her to come out of the surgery.

'By some miracle, he's absolutely fine,' the vet pronounced, after she'd examined the little dog. 'Just a bit shocked. But that's it.'

I could have cried with relief. The Yorkie's owner did.

'I'm extremely sorry about the whole thing,' Jennifer said apologetically, when I phoned her to pass on the good news. 'Morgan's never attacked anything before. I think he must really have mistaken the little thing for a rodent. The trouble is that the breed has such a strong hunting instinct.'

Didn't I know it by now? I'd certainly learned my lesson. Never again would I risk letting Murphy off the leash in a public place. Though he hadn't been the one to pick the Yorkie up, it could just as easily have been him as Morgan, not through viciousness, simply because he'd been bred to hunt.

This incident, and my mother's accident, had made me realize that looking after a large dog like a Lurcher was a far cry from looking after a soppy little pooch like George. If they weren't properly trained and under control, large dogs were potential lethal weapons – accidents waiting to happen. This wasn't their fault: it was solely the responsibility of the humans who looked after them. In Murphy's case, that was me.

But not for ever. Rehoming Lurchers could be a slow business. Sweet-natured as they were, not everyone could deal with one, for reasons that were becoming obvious to me, and so far Many Tears hadn't yet succeeded in finding anyone who wanted to adopt Murphy. But had I? In a tentative manner, I now raised the subject with Jennifer, but I think I already knew what her answer would be.

'He's a glorious dog, and in many ways I'd love to have him,' she said, 'not least because he and Morgan are so alike. But, you know, Judith, after what happened today, I'm not sure I can. The two of them make such a formidable hunting pack when they're together that I really can't risk it.'

30

A week later, while I was out doing my mother's shopping for her, Murphy trashed the flat so badly that, when I came home, I thought I'd been burgled.

Earning himself yet another saintly halo, Matthew came round to help me clear up the mess.

'Do you think this dog might be trying to tell you something?' he said, in a measured voice, as he scooped up a ripped yogurt carton from the kitchen floor and dropped it into a bin bag.

'You mean, apart from the fact that he didn't like my book?' I quipped, as I shoved my hands into my trusty Marigolds, the better to dispose of my pissed-upon first novel, *Dear Sister*, which was lying on the sodden living-room rug.

'Very funny.' He stopped what he was doing, straightened up, and turned to look at me. 'However, I'm being serious.'

'Perhaps it's *you* who's trying to tell me something,' I said, rather defensively.

His mouth twisted into a wry smile. 'Would that be so terrible? Look, Murphy's obviously frustrated as hell living here. And no wonder. He needs room to run around, and other big dogs to play with so that he can let off steam. Isn't it time he moved on? And before you jump down my throat,' he added hurriedly, 'I'm not telling you what to do.

It's just a suggestion. He's only your foster dog. You never meant to keep him for ever. Did you?'

'Of course not, but . . .' I looked over at the sofa, across which Murphy was currently stretched out fast asleep. There was a blissful, self-satisfied smile on his handsome face, three of his legs stuck out like ski poles over the edge of the seat cushions, and the fourth, a front one, was thrown familiarly over George, who was curled up asleep next to him. 'No one's come forward to adopt him yet. And, besides . . .'

'What?'

'He's such a character. I never thought I'd like him so much.'

'It must be true love, then.' Matthew smiled at me. 'If you're prepared to put up with all of this.'

I looked at the man standing in the middle of my wrecked room, holding a bin bag in one hand and a chewed-up plastic ketchup bottle in the other, and it suddenly occurred to me that I could say exactly the same to him. Due mostly to the dogs, and my difficulty in integrating them into my life, our relationship had stalled halfway along the line between friendship and a full-blown love affair. But why else would Matthew still be around, and still be so supportive, if it wasn't because he really cared for me?

I swallowed, and said, 'Look, I failed with Millie, and I don't want to do the same with Murphy.'

He looked amused. 'So, it's a matter of your pride rather than Murphy's welfare?'

'No!' I protested, rather too strongly. 'I just don't want to give up on him.'

'Ah. I know the feeling well. However,' he went on, and

I blushed, 'as things are, I'm not sure you're doing him any favours by keeping him. Or doing George any favours, for that matter.'

'What do you mean? George seems perfectly happy. He's grown to like Murphy. They've become pals.'

'Haven't you noticed how Murphy's started to nip George's neck a lot recently? I think he's jealous of him. And what about you? Look at the amount of work he causes you. No wonder you're not getting on with writing your novel. Adorable as he is, that dog is chaos personified.'

'But it's not his fault! He just doesn't understand. I'm trying to make him learn but . . .'

'Perhaps he'd be better off with someone who was a little more . . . well . . . experienced at dog training,' Matthew suggested.

I shook my head. 'I'm not going to fail this time, Matthew. I'm keeping Murphy until Many Tears finds him a proper home.'

A day later, the physiotherapist from my mother's local surgery was on the phone wanting to rearrange Mum's appointments. I went into the study to talk to her, and as I did so I caught sight of Murphy running upstairs. Two minutes later, while we were deep in a discussion about the effects of regular exercise on osteoporosis, there came a series of crashes so loud that the physio heard them in St John's Wood.

'What was that?' she said.

'Oh, nothing. Do go on, please.'

During her next sentence there came another crash, followed by the rattle of a bottle or tin as it rolled across the wooden floor above my head. Her voice faltered. 'It sounds like you're in the middle of something . . . important. Would you like to call me back another time?'

'No, no. It's absolutely fine.'

She hesitated. 'Tell me if this is none of my business, but . . . are you in some kind of difficulty?'

There was another crash. 'Sort of,' I admitted.

'Only, we do have a list of refuges at the surgery. You know, for women wanting to escape from violent situations.'

I burst out laughing. 'It's just my dog. I'm afraid he's a bit frustrated at the moment.'

'Oh, right! How stupid of me! This must be the one that knocked your mother over?'

I got off the phone as soon as possible and ran upstairs to survey the damage. It wasn't too bad. A J-cloth had been reduced to a pile of blue-and-white tagliatelle, and the contents of the recycling bag were strewn across the kitchen floor. The creator of this mess was standing in the middle of the newspapers and empty cans, lapping up the dregs that had leaked from a discarded wine bottle.

I shooed him away, and at the same time saw off George, who'd ventured into the pile of newspapers and was currently reducing a three-day-old *Guardian* sports section to shreds. Not one to hold a grudge, he plodded over to lick me, and I bent down and gave him a stroke.

Quick as a shot, Murphy was there, sticking his nose between us and levering my Cavalier aside. Then, to my astonishment, he bent down and fastened his big pointed jaws around George's neck. While he didn't actually bite him, he gave him a substantial nip, more warning than playful, and sharp enough to make George back off, looking distinctly upset.

The next moment Murphy rubbed his head against my legs. If there was any attention going, he obviously wanted it for himself. I stood up and walked away from him. I certainly wasn't going to make a fuss of him under those circumstances.

I thought of what Matthew had said about him nipping George, and then I suddenly remembered what I'd promised Joshua before I'd started fostering: that if it made George at all unhappy I would stop. Up till now he hadn't seemed unhappy. Quite the contrary. Despite the difference in their sizes and ages, he and Murphy had got along fine. Now, though, I began to have my doubts.

I pushed them to the back of my mind, and went downstairs to work. My novel had moved on during the past few weeks, but my progress was terribly slow. No sooner did I sit down at my desk, it seemed, than Murphy was demanding my attention. And so it was now. Out in the garden, he dug up the mouldy remains of a rope toy that Millie had played with. He worried it for a while, then, leaving a set of muddy paw-prints behind him, took it upstairs and buried it in the sofa. A moment later he was foraging outside again and found a snail, which he delicately deposited on my desk, as if it were a precious gift. Next he rampaged around the flat on a seek-and-destroy mission, pulling down everything within reach, including the fruit bowl from the kitchen table, a pair of shoes from the hall console (don't ask me what they were doing there) and a crazy gold-lamé shower hat I'd been given years ago, which was hanging on the back of the bathroom door.

'Put that down!' I said, jumping up as he toted it past my study door, his nose held high. 'Drop it, Murphy! I said, drop it!' He glanced at me in a sly manner, dropped it, than ran back into the house and upstairs, pausing only to knock down a half-empty mug of cold coffee, which was perched on a ledge near the bottom of the stairs, and then to lap up its spilled contents.

I gave up trying to work, and decided to take him and George for their second walk of the day. I hadn't dared let Murphy off the leash since the Yorkshire terrier incident, which was probably why he was becoming so destructive again. In order to try to get him to walk at my side, I'd also bought him a head-collar, known as a Halti, which fitted over his ears and muzzle, and stopped him pulling away. What with this, the Lurcher collar Jennifer had lent me, and the canine seatbelt I still used as a harness, Murphy was beginning to resemble Bondage Dog. No wonder he was frustrated.

Strapped into the Halti, and with an extra leash attached to the seatbelt, he walked by my side like a perfect gentleman until we got to the Heath. As I let George loose, Murphy twitched impatiently at his bonds. It wasn't just competition with a Cavalier that was making him itch to be free, it was the ducks on the Vale of Health pond, the squirrels running up the trees and the scent of fox and rabbit that assailed him at every step. It was almost too much for a hunting dog to bear.

I felt so sorry for him that I took off the Halti, undid the seatbelt, and fastened the training leash to his wide Lurcher collar. Freed of bondage, Murphy rolled on the grass with pleasure, and skipped along so happily beside George that the feeling was infectious. My heart lifted. I was managing him at long last.

Then he spotted a rabbit leaping through the grass.

His ears pricked up and, before I could stop him, he took off.

A split second later, so did I.

Suddenly I was lying on the ground, winded, with a sharp pain running down my right leg, and another in my head. I opened my eyes and caught a glimpse of him disappearing into a nearby copse. This view was soon blocked by a fluffy chestnut-and-white monster. Its enormous round black eyes stared down at me. It looked worried. Then it tried to lick my face.

'It's okay, George,' I said. 'I'm fine.'

But was I?

As I lay there, too scared to try and move my legs in case I discovered that I couldn't, I thought of my mother being knocked over by the mastiff just weeks before. If I'd broken a bone, I'd no longer be able to help her. In fact, I'd need someone to help me.

That was how accidents happened: without warning, and on the turn of a sixpence. One false step and that was it.

I suddenly pictured Mum and me shuffling along Hampstead High Street side by side, each of us on our own Zimmer frame. People we limped past would stop and ask us whether we'd been in a car crash together. Instead, we'd have to explain that we'd been both been knocked over. By dogs. In separate incidents.

No one would believe us.

31

Minutes passed, but no knight on a white charger or damsel dog-walker came by to rescue me. I had to deal with this one all on my own.

Except I had George at my side, staring down at my face with what appeared to be growing concern (it might well have been impatience to get home for his afternoon snack, of course, but I decided to give him the benefit of the doubt). Having reassured him again that I was all right, I took my courage into my hands or, rather, my feet, and attempted to wiggle my toes, then stretch them. So far so good. Slowly, I moved my head, then my shoulders, then my arms, and pulled myself up into a sitting position, from where I took stock. There was a small stone just behind me, on which I might have bashed the back of my head when I fell, but otherwise, apart from a pain in my lower back and some grazes on the palms of my hands, my upper half was okay.

Still winded, I looked around for Murphy, but there was no sign of him. At that moment I felt so angry with him that I felt like going home without him, but I couldn't. I had to find him somehow. I bent one knee, then the other, and struggled to my feet. My right hip, upon which I'd fallen, was hurting, but to my profound relief my legs were still in working order, though a sharp pain shot through my right ankle when I put weight on it.

Pleased to see me upright again, George trotted obediently after me as, feeling sick and more than a little dizzy, I limped slowly towards the copse where I'd last glimpsed Murphy. He wasn't there, of course: given the speed with which he'd shot off, and the head-start he'd had, by now he was probably halfway to Hertfordshire – or, at the least, standing on the other side of Hampstead Heath, three-quarters of the way through a fresh rabbit fricassée. How was I ever going to find him? And, if I did, how would I ever catch him? I shook my head in despair. It was Kenwood all over again.

I called his name. There was no answer. I called again, this time in fury, and thought I heard a distant yelp. Clambering painfully over fallen branches slippery with moss, George and I worked our way down a small forested hill, across a muddy stream that left his paws and my boots looking as if they'd been dipped in liquid chocolate, then up a steep embankment overgrown with thorny brambles that tore at my jeans.

'Murphy!'

This time, his answering yelp seemed nearer, and it was followed by a heartfelt cry. Guided by the noise, I limped on through the woods. Eventually, I emerged into a grassy clearing. And there he was, looking like a golden fawn in a shaft of sunlight, twisting and writhing with frustration on the end of his training leash, which had become entangled in the branches of a fallen tree.

Before I unknotted it, I clipped him back into his seatbelt and Halti bondage, muttering, 'That's it, kiddo, you're not getting away from me ever again!'

Back home at last, I washed the mud off George's paws,

disinfected my grazed hands, made myself some tea and put my throbbing foot up on the sofa. Feeling as helpless as an invalid, I lay back on the cushions with George stretched across my lap, and watched the magnificent Murphy maraud around the flat in search of mischief to make. Pulling cushions off the sofa and tossing them into the fireplace. Putting his paws up on the kitchen counter, the better to see if there was any available food. Pausing to give George a rather bossy prod with his nose, and me a loving nuzzle, then raiding the fruit bowl of its last banana, which he carried over to his basket, ripped open, chewed into a mushy pulp, then proceeded to bury under his blanket.

As George and I watched him go about his business in his happily self-absorbed manner, ignoring my cries of 'Stop that!' and 'No!' as if I'd never spoken, I suddenly realized that Murphy was the nearest thing to a wild animal I'd ever had the privilege to meet. Nature, coupled with a life on the road, had made him a law unto himself. Bred to be a hunter, and thrown into the big wide world to survive on his own, he could do no less than act on his instincts. What had ever made me think that *I*'d be able to counteract *those* with a handful of treats?

It was finally time to accept my limitations. Just as I was never going to compete in a triathlon, win the Nobel Prize for Literature or make the front cover of *Vogue*, so I was never going to manage to take this wonderful dog in hand. He was simply too hot for me to handle.

Before I'd started fostering rescue dogs, I'd presumed it would be non-stop cuddles and ball games. Instead, it had turned out to be the hardest work I'd ever done, and looking after Murphy had been hardest of all. By now I had nothing but admiration and respect for the men and women who fostered dogs repeatedly, as most of Many Tears's 192 registered volunteers seemed to. To be really good at it took a huge amount of dedication and patience – not to mention an endless supply of J-cloths and rubber gloves.

There was something else you needed, too: an indefinable quality called natural authority. I could act it out for all I was worth, but I simply didn't possess it, and the dogs knew it. All I could offer them was a roof over their heads, an endless supply of chicken titbits and unconditional love. And while that might be perfect for an Inch or a Sophie – and certainly for a George – for a Murphy, it wasn't nearly enough.

If fostering dogs had taught me anything, it was that dogs weren't fashion accessories. You shouldn't choose them because you liked the look of them, but because they fitted in with your lifestyle and, just as important, you fitted in with their needs. A Chihuahua wasn't any good if you were looking for a helpmate to round up sheep on your farm, and if you needed a guard dog for a factory, you'd be foolish to choose a soppy Cavalier. Likewise, keeping a Lurcher if you didn't have the skill to handle it was like buying a Lamborghini when you didn't know how to drive.

What Murphy desperately needed, if he wasn't to remain unhomeable, was a Lurcher-savvy person who knew how to deal with him.

And what I needed was a break.

I had a feeling that my relationship with Matthew could do with one, too, if it wasn't to reach a breaking point of its own. Ever since Udi had died eleven years before, I'd effectively had to cope with the everyday nitty-gritty of life on my own. But now there was someone around who actually seemed to want to share it, the prospect filled me with terror, with the result that I – that we – were still teetering on the brink, six months after we'd first met. Being so preoccupied with Murphy was providing me with the perfect cover not to take that leap over the edge. But was I being fair to Matthew? Or even to myself? Maybe not.

And so, after having my house well and truly trashed, and my arms wrenched, and my fridge raided, and my favourite dress chewed up, and my sofa cushions turned into snow, and my legs nearly broken, I got on the phone to Many Tears that afternoon and, shedding many tears myself, asked for Murphy to be moved to a more experienced foster home.

When I called Matthew that evening and told him what had happened, he came straight round, bringing with him a packet of Maltesers and a chilled bottle of Champagne. 'To cheer you up,' he told me, when I opened the door to him in my dressing-gown, looking a wreck and feeling extremely sorry for myself. After examining my swollen ankle and the bump on my head, he ordered me to bed, where I was now lying under the duvet, propped up on a pile of pillows, with a tray of boiled eggs and toast soldiers in front of me and a glass of fizz in my hand.

'I've failed!' I sobbed into it.

'Judith, what are you talking about?'

'I've failed poor Murphy!'

'Murphy?' He glanced at the Lurcher, who was sitting

on the floor beside the bed, with George next to him. Both dogs were wagging their tails and staring fixedly at the soldiers as if they were expecting them to leap off the plate and right into their mouths. 'He doesn't exactly look like he's having a bad time here. Of course you haven't failed him.'

Instead of being mollified, I snapped, 'I'm sending him away, aren't I? See? I'm a failure as a dog fosterer! So don't try and humour me!'

'Okay. I'll 'fess up: you've completely ballsed up the whole business.' And when I gave an outraged gasp, Matthew raised an ironic eyebrow and said, 'Far be it for me to contradict you. Actually, I'm not sure why succeeding at this is so important to you,' he went on, when I'd stopped laughing. 'Surely you're doing this because you enjoy it?'

I nodded. 'And to do some good in the canine world.'

He suppressed a smile. 'Well, maybe you're not really the do-gooder type. Which is one of the reasons I like you,' he added hurriedly, when he saw I was about to explode. 'Besides, what with one thing and another, you must have done an awful lot of do-gooding and caring and looking after others over the last decade. Perhaps . . .' His voice faded away.

'What?' I prompted.

'Well, just perhaps it's time you let someone look after *you* for a change.' I bristled. I was about to retort that I could look after myself perfectly well, thank you very much, when his bright blue eyes looked straight into mine and he took my hand. 'When you first told me you were fostering dogs, I presumed it was because you were lonely after Joshua had left home. I understood perfectly, because I've been there too. Recently, though, I've begun to suspect there's another reason why you're still doing it.'

'Like what?' I mumbled defensively.

'To stop me getting too close.'

I winced. Damn it, as well as being perfect, Matthew was also wise.

And witty, too: 'A relationship isn't a puppy crate, you know.'

'What on earth are you talking about?'

'No one's trying to lock you into it. You're free to come and go. If you want to go, that is.'

Now Matthew did get close – he moved the tray away, then lay down on the bed beside me and put his arms around me. 'As you've probably worked out by now, I don't give up easily,' he whispered. 'I guess neither of us does. But, sometimes, darling, there's no shame in admitting defeat. Who knows? It might even turn out to be a positive experience.'

I soon understood exactly what he meant.

The sound of gentle snoring woke me up in the early hours. I opened my eyes. Yes, there was George, not in his special place between the chest and the wardrobe, but actually on the end of the bed, curled up by my feet.

Oddly, though, the snores weren't coming from him. No, they were coming from the person just behind me. I could feel his heartbeat against my back, and his warm breath tickling my neck. A surprisingly muscular leg was slung across one of mine, and an elbow was jutting sharply into my ribs.

Recalling what had happened last night, I rolled over to

embrace him. Instead, I found myself eye to eye with a pair of enormous pointed ears and a bicycle-seat-shaped face, which was resting on the pillow.

Sensitive to my every move, Murphy woke up, opened his beady eyes and blinked at me victoriously. A moment later he too rolled over, and, with a delicious yawn that seemed to take over his entire body, stretched out his racehorse legs in front of him, pushing the sleeping Matthew to the extreme far edge of the bed.

Epilogue

A week after Inch was adopted, I received the following email from her new owner, Heather:

Dear Judith

Just a short note with some pictures of Petal (as we now call Inch) and our old Bichon, Casper. As you can see, Petal went to the poodle parlour on Friday and loved it. The dogs are so alike now that at first glance it's hard to tell them apart!

Petal has slotted into our lives so well. We have only had one accident! She loves my son so much that he has a new shadow. We take her out daily and she walks well on and off the lead. Today for the first time she had a spring in her step and gave Casper a little chase.

Many thanks once again. It was lovely to meet you and we can't thank you enough for our new addition.

Attached to Heather's email were some photographs of the ex-breeding Bichon I'd picked up at Reading. She was almost unrecognizable as the sad, neglected creature she'd been then. Here she now was, showing off her very own bright pink furry dog-bed; and stretched out on a comfy sofa with Heather's sons; and playing ball with her new mate, Casper, out in the park. My favourite photograph of all was of both dogs sitting proudly on a delighted Heather's lap: Casper was wearing a blue-and-white striped T-shirt, and Inch was in a matching pink one. Primped by the beauty parlour, and basking in love, Petal, as she was now known, looked relaxed, happy and every 'inch' the pampered pooch.

Heather and I have kept in touch over the past year, and recently she sent me another update:

Petal is just fantastic. She's my ray of sunshine. She has an amazing personality and is now firmly a mummy's girl! She has found her place in our home and hearts. She has claimed the bed . . . the sofa . . . the car . . . the list is endless. Petal can snore louder than my husband Pat, stretch from one end of the sofa to the other, and sits like a queen in the car with her doggie seatbelt on. She rarely leaves my side.

Do you remember how, when we first had her, Petal froze when you picked her up? I think she was unsure of how to accept love, but now she melts and wrestles Casper for space next to me. Also, we made her a little step to get on the sofa when we first got her home as she couldn't jump. The vet said she had wasted muscles as she had never used them. Big mistake in teaching her to jump!!!! Now she jumps everywhere. I feel she may have been a rabbit in a former life.

When she first came to us, she couldn't get up and down the stairs very well, so Pat carried her. But she learned very quickly and now follows me like a sheep . . . except at bedtime when Pat is home from work and she suddenly loses the use of her legs . . . so Pat carries her to bed every night!

She is just a happy, waggy dog who has many new doggy friends and is totally accepted by each of them, and I think she

now loves her life. She was five in June, so we gave her a tea
party and she had a cake of chicken and rice with her friends . . .
Yes, I know we are totally mad!!!

Given all this doggy madness, you'd presume that Heather's
life was one big party. Not a bit of it. On a personal level,
things were not easy for her, she explained without a shred
of self-pity. Among other problems, she had some serious
health issues to face.

So, you see, we don't get out much. But Petal has brought so
much happiness into our lives that we would be lost without her.
So thank you once more for fostering her and allowing us to
become her new owners.

What an inspiring woman! There she was, battling on in
the midst of the maelstrom, and yet every day she managed
to get so much pleasure from her dogs. She gave them her
love, and in return they gave her a sense of joy and fun that
made life worth living, no matter what.

Which I guess just about sums it up. That's what dogs
do for us.

But what did Heather have to thank me for? What had I
done except to take Inch in for a couple of weeks, for reasons
of my own? No, it was thanks to Many Tears that the little
Bichon had been snatched from the jaws of canine hell, and
dropped into canine clover – platinum-plated, at that.

In Britain, each year, around a hundred thousand abandoned dogs are taken in by rescue centres. In 2009 alone
fifteen hundred of those were rehomed through the efforts
of Sylvia, Bill and their dedicated band of staff and
volunteers. That's fifteen hundred dogs and puppies who,
instead of having their lives cut short, were given a second

bite of the cherry by the equal number of kindly souls who welcomed them into their homes.

Times may be tough out there, but Sylvia's dedication to saving animals is even tougher. So are the dogs she rescues. No matter what life may have thrown at them before they arrive at Many Tears, they find the courage to trust again.

As soon as Sophie went to live with her new owners, the little Westie began the slow process of becoming properly socialized. At first she was so terrified that she refused to eat anything but, given time and patience – and plenty of roast chicken dinners – she soon settled down well.

Six months down the line, she was as devoted to Jean and John as they were to her. She liked nothing better than sitting on Jean's lap, showering her in doggie kisses, or snuggling up with her for a nap. Though she loved her food now, when it came to her evening meal she refused to touch a morsel of it before her owners sat down to eat theirs. 'She comes running as soon as I call out, 'Dinner!' to my husband,' Jean told me, 'and she has to have her own bowl placed in the doorway between the kitchen and the dining room. I think you've probably got the picture, Judith – she's completely spoiled!'

Though still frightened of strangers, and children in particular, Sophie thoroughly enjoyed the puppy training classes Jean was taking her to. She was even doing agility training, and loving every minute of it. Quick to get to grips with each new skill she was taught, she'd turned out to be a natural performer. Quite a change from the terrified little creature who'd huddled behind my rose bushes and refused to come out.

Madcap Millie had lived with me for six weeks without anyone taking an interest in her but – wouldn't you know? – within three days of moving to Southend-on-Sea, someone came forward to adopt her. When they came to visit her, she casually tossed a full water bowl across the room and, as her new fosterer, Penny, tried to laugh it off, she chewed a hole in a beanbag, sending a million polystyrene beads rolling across the already wet floor. Needless to say, they didn't take her.

But a few days after that another couple did. Though Malcolm and Jean are the first to admit that Millie doesn't come close to the breed standard and will never win any prizes for her looks (and there I beg to differ), that doesn't matter a hoot to them. Far more important is that Callie, as they've renamed her, has grown up to be fit, healthy and full of life and vitality. She's now an adored, reliable pet who, when their grandchildren come to visit, looks after them as gently and enthusiastically as Nana, the dog employed as a nanny by the Darling family in J. M. Barrie's *Peter Pan*.

That's not to say that Callie has completely calmed down. She can open any door in their house (that's one skill she picked up at my home) and at night she monopolizes her owners' double bed. Playful as ever, she gives high fives, swims and relishes the company of other canines, and, like most Labs, she'll still eat anything she can get her teeth into, including dried flowers and olives. Her favourite pastime is pursuing rabbits along the banks of the nearby estuary. To date, she hasn't caught one, or even got close to it, but that doesn't seem to bother her: as far as she's concerned, the fun is all in the chase.

As for Murphy ... I loved him so much that I hated to part with him, but I wasn't doing him, or myself, any favours by keeping him when I could neither let him off the leash nor control him when he was on it, unless he was in his seatbelt and his Halti. It simply wasn't fair to strap the lad into bondage gear every time I wanted to walk him when he was built to run like the clappers. Besides, even though he'd taken an interest in cooking from day one, he needed a fosterer who could teach him more than how to make an omelette.

The night before I drove him over to his new fosterer's, Murphy stole the frayed green silk bolster from the day-bed in my study and carried it carefully to his basket. After giving me a somewhat defiant look, he lay down and went to sleep with his head resting on it. I didn't know whether to laugh or cry. He was so funny and lovable that I dreaded the thought of being without him. But here was one street-wise dog that knew exactly how to look after himself, and I was sure he'd make himself at home anywhere.

It turned out that his new fosterer used to train German Shepherds for the show ring at Crufts. Naturally, Murphy didn't dare play her up. However, like a big baby who was missing his mother, he cried every evening for the first five nights, or so she later told me.

Hearing that just about broke my heart.

Like Millie, he was rehomed within a fortnight of moving foster homes but, sadly, I haven't been able to find out where he now lives. No doubt he's got his new owners licked into shape by now – how could such a strong character not? One day I'm sure I'll run into him. I have a feeling I'll walk into a country pub, and there he'll be in a natty check jacket, propping up the bar and regaling his rapt audience with colourful, and exaggerated, stories about his past.

It's springtime out in the back garden. After a cold winter spent hibernating underground, the bindweed is sending up strong pea-green shoots and bursting into life, the better to plague me. Odd blades of grass push their way through Millie's muddy landing strip, the felled dandelion forest is regenerating itself, and the robins have returned to their empty nest. I watch the little hen darting in and out of the ivy all day long, carrying bits of leaves and moss to line the cup where she'll lay this year's eggs. Among the stuff she's picked up in the garden is a small clump of dog hair, which will make a soft, warm bed for them. Does she remember the day last year when the fox killed her fledglings? If so, she's carrying on regardless. No matter what tragedies have befallen her in the past, life must go on.

And what of my own empty nest? Fostering dogs, and that evening at the Freud Museum, seem to have cured me of acute isolophobia. I no longer find the silence of the house eerie, or pine for the days when Joshua was at home all the time. When he turns up, I'm thrilled to see him. After he leaves, I miss him, but that's okay. As long as I know he's happy, I feel the same way.

As I've discovered, there are advantages to having an empty nest, and they don't *all* have to do with filling it as quickly as possible. There's peace and quiet, and time to read, and think, and work. Time to make more of friendships that have been shoved to one side during the busy child-rearing years, and the opportunity to develop new ones. And there are liberating freedoms, such as being able to walk around starkers, or eat sweets instead of salad for supper just because I feel like it, or not do the washing-up for three days.

Over at my step-daughter's house, the baby gate has gone the same way as the crate did. Not only is Billy allowed upstairs nowadays, he even sleeps in Hannah's bedroom. Occasionally he's banished to his basket but, more often than not, he's on her bed.

'Last Sunday morning I woke up to find him actually under the covers with me,' she admitted the other day.

We both giggled. I wonder, is it just in my family that hearts are softer than brains?

Maybe not. Jane, who lives down the road from me, recently inherited a Cavalier from an aunt who'd died. Jazz is a Tricolour male who, at the grand age of thirteen and three-quarters, makes George seem like a mere stripling. Since she'd never been a doggy person, Jane tried to find a home for him. But no one wanted him. So she kept him. And, eventually, fell under his spell.

Jazz is by no means perfect. He barks at strange dogs, and he barks when people come to the house, and he barks when they leave. The only time he doesn't bark, apparently, is when he needs to go outside at night to pee. Jane tried spreading newspapers across the floor, so that he wouldn't ruin her carpet, but somehow Jazz, like Millie, always managed to find the one square foot of flooring that wasn't covered. So now Jane's taken to sleeping on the sofa in the living room, so that she can wake up and let Jazz out the moment he starts scrabbling at the back door.

I have to say that my heart lifted when she told me

this. Call it *Schadenfreude*, if you like, but to my mind it's more like recognizing that the breed has a talent for getting its own way. In other words, it's not that I'm a failure as a dog owner, it's rather that George is a success as a Cavalier.

Sylvia was right: having foster dogs in the house did give him a new lease of life. He's seen how the other half lives now, and learned that, sometimes at least, the demands of others are equal to his own. That he is but a prince among princes, not the only ruler in the world. From King George the Bad, he's metamorphosed into King George the Good. True, his crown slips occasionally. But, then, he's an old boy, so I guess he's entitled to that.

Just as it's hard to believe that the eight-year-old who had to deal with his father's death is now an independent young adult, it's hard to accept that the puppy I brought home from Mrs Coleman's has become a gentleman in his canine dotage. Where have all the years gone? And how many more does George have left? On average Cavaliers are said to live to between ten and twelve, although a report into their lifespan found one that survived to the age of eighteen.

At the moment George is approaching his twelfth birthday, and still looks like a puppy, so I guess he's doing well. Out in Highgate Woods, where I've just been walking with Elizabeth and her dogs, he put on a pretty good show of keeping up. Obviously, the secret of getting him to go for a decent walk nowadays is to fool him that he isn't walking by driving him somewhere first.

Alas, he's going grey. But, then, aren't we all? He's also losing his short-term memory: five minutes after I've given him his dinner, George is back at the top of the stairs again, barking as if he'd never been fed. His hearing is not what it used to be, either. In fact, it's almost gone. When we're out on the Heath and he's marching ahead of me, I can call or whistle till I'm blue in the face, but George doesn't even look round. Being locked in his own, silent world has made him rather thoughtful. The other night he sat in front of the fire for half an hour, simply staring into the flames . . .

Lately I've found myself resorting to hand signals to get his attention. There I stand, in the middle of the kitchen, trying desperately to communicate with the fluff-ball lying on the sofa at the other end of the room, as if I'm a bookie's assistant signing in tic-tac. Two exaggerated waves in front of my face mean 'Come'. A flat palm facing him is 'Stay!' A pointed finger and dog bowl held up high in the air indicate 'Grub's up!' Two claw-like hands held above my head, coupled with a screwed-up face, translate as 'Don't you bloody well dare!' Like the passers-by who occasionally catch a glimpse of my efforts through the window, George stares at me as if I'm completely off my head. Either he doesn't understand what I'm trying to communicate, or he's playing dumb so that he doesn't have to comply. After a lifetime of taking no notice of what I say, what makes me think he has any intention of changing now?

'Stone deaf,' Howard said cheerfully, when I took George to the surgery to be examined, in case his hearing problems were the result of ear wax. 'Perfectly normal for an old boy like him, dear. Just like those trembling legs of his. These things come to us all with age.'

'Well, there's something to look forward to,' Matthew commented, when I reported back.

Miraculously, given everything I've put him through, this perfect man is still around. When he invited me round to dinner at his house the other night, he even told me to bring a dog-bed for George. Later, we put it in the bedroom next to his, and I tried staying over. But George wouldn't have it: he barked and barked and barked until, in the end, Matthew slept in the spare room and my Cav slept with me. Shades of old times.

'I'm sure he'll soon get used to staying here,' Matthew said innocently.

'Of course he will,' I lied.

'And at least you only have one dog nowadays.'

What he doesn't know yet is that someone phoned from the Many Tears office today. They urgently need a foster home for Mimi and You-Two, two adorable four-year-old Tricolour Cavaliers whose owner has had to go into hospital . . .

I'll deal with that tomorrow. Because who knows what might happen tonight? That is, if King George allows it.

As I write this he's lying in his basket in the kitchen, looking the picture of sweetness as he dozes in and out of sleep. His greying head is tilted upwards and his ski-jump of a nose is resting on the basket's side, the better to smell the aroma of the chicken that's roasting in the oven. His body stance tells me that George *will not* leave the room until that bird is cooked, carved and eaten. Preferably by himself. He may have to wait until his royal taster and her trusted assistant have sampled it first, but he knows that he'll get it in the end.

As my father used to say, it's a tough life, but someone's got to live it.

And as George would no doubt add if he could, 'Why not me?'

Acknowledgements

Although this is a true story, some names have been changed to protect the privacy of individuals. The dogs, however, appear as themselves. I hope they don't sue.

Many Tears Animal Rescue does an incredible job on a shoestring budget. It would not have been possible for me to write this book without the support and co-operation of owners Sylvia and Bill VanAtta, and the dedicated team who work at the Llanelli centre, among them Liza McLean, Yvonne Watts and James Muir. I'm sure I wasn't the most capable dog fosterer they'd ever had on their books, but they proved as patient with me as they are with their canine charges. Anyone wanting to find out more about the centre's work can find it online at http://www.freewebs.com/manytearsrescue/. And those wishing to support their sterling work should contact the very active Friends organization at http://manytearsrescue.webs.com/friendsofmanytears.htm/

Many thanks to Penny Varney, Malcolm Lunn, Jean Cooper, Pawel Krzus and Ania Dzioba; and very special thanks to Heather Brown.

My brother-in-law Philip Norman came up trumps with the title, for which I am very grateful. Hazel Orme has yet again been a terrific copyeditor. Clare Alexander, the best of literary agents, was, as always, a fantastic support throughout the writing of this book, and so was Katy

Follain at Penguin UK. Many thanks to all of them.

Thanks to my friends and family for letting me write about them again, in particular Elizabeth Meakins; my sister Sue; my mother Honey; Barbara Lambert for her picture of Murphy; and my step-daughter Hannah, who generously shared her exploits with Billy.

Showing great stoicism and remarkable good humour, George has put up with having his beds taken over, his food stolen from under his nose, his beauty sleep ruined and his various thrones usurped. I'd like him to know that, though there have been some serious contenders along the way, in my eyes he's still the best dog in the world.

Huge thanks to my son Joshua for throwing himself into the spirit of dog fostering so wholeheartedly, and for keeping me focused, and laughing, as always. And very special thanks to Paul for rolling up his sleeves and sharing this unforgettable experience with me – and for still being here at the end of it.

JUDITH SUMMERS

MY LIFE WITH GEORGE

In the summer of 1998, Judith Summers lost her husband and father to cancer. Life for Judith and her eight-year-old son Joshua looked bleak.

But then George bounced into their lives. A Cavalier King Charles Spaniel with a loving character and a penchant for chewing up paper, George re-awoke their joie de vivre and gave them back their sense of humour. Yet George has his drawbacks. He's as time-consuming as a full-time job and as expensive to run as a Ferrari. Wilful, stubborn and badly-behaved, he refuses to eat anything other than roast chicken, preferrs cars to walks, and won't let any man show an interest in Judith.

My Life with George is the hilarious and moving account of the impossible but adorable George, of his adventures and misdemeanours, and of the wonderful way in which he helped to fill the void in Judith and Joshua's lives – whilst driving them barking along the way.

'The sentiment is keen, the journey captivating and the pain heightened by the charming honesty of the writing' *Good Housekeeping*